"Pithy, pointed, perceptively biblical. Dan Phillips unpacks the Gospel's practical implications in this wonderfully readable and supremely helpful handbook."

—**John MacArthur**, Best-selling author and
Bible teacher for Grace to You Ministries

"I've been reading and learning from Dan Phillips ever since I discovered his blog in 2005. His insights never fail to amaze and instruct me. This book reveals why he is such a careful, critical thinker: because his worldview is shaped by Scripture and centered on the timeless truth of the Gospel. This book is a great tonic for the postmodern tendencies that poison so many young minds today."

—**Phil Johnson**, Executive Director of Grace to You Ministries
and cofounder of the *Pyromaniacs* blog

"Dan Phillips is both easy and edifying to read, and I have been doing so for many years, so I am delighted to commend this book to you. *The World-Tilting Gospel* is a sound introduction to what it means and what we need to understand to be followers of Jesus Christ. Dan knows that for the Christian life to be lived, personally and congregationally, the way Jesus intends us to live it, we need to know: 'who we really are, what kind of world we are really living in, how the world really operates and where it is really going, who God really is, what His eternal plan really was, why we really needed Him and His plan so desperately, what His terms—the Gospel—really were, and what difference the Gospel will really make on every day of our lives.' Furthermore, I agree with his diagnosis of our present need (see the introduction!), and the meaty biblical prescription of truth and grace that he offers as remedy. This book hits on all cylinders. I will use it in discipleship in my own congregation and recommend it widely."

—**Ligon Duncan**, PhD, President of the Alliance of Confessing Evangelicals
and Senior Minister at First Presbyterian Church, Jackson, Mississippi

"Who would have thought that tilting the world would set it right? With humor, creativity, and insightful surprises, Dan Phillips captures all the beauty and freshness of the Gospel. The Gospel turns us rightside up, and this book uses sound teaching to cure worldly vertigo."

—**James M. Hamilton Jr**, PhD, Associate Professor of Biblical Theology at
Southern Baptist Theological Seminary, Louisville, Kentucky

"Pick this book up, flip to any page, and start reading. You won't want to put it down."

> —**Robert L. Plummer**, PhD, Associate Professor of New Testament Interpretation at Southern Baptist Theological Seminary and author of *40 Questions About Interpreting the Bible*

"*The World-Tilting Gospel* is the sort of foundational resource that will serve everyone—from those considering the Christian faith to church leaders. With meticulous attention to the biblical text, Dan Phillips unfolds how the cross-centered Gospel polishes a crystal clear lens through which the distorted reality of a fallen world can be seen upside down . . . revealing the Good News that we can be rightside up with God."

> —**Chris Brauns**, pastor of The Red Brick Church, Stillman Valley, Illinois, and author of *Unpacking Forgiveness: Biblical Answers for Complex Questions and Deep Wounds*

"Dan Phillips begins his book with the crucial assertion that a person's worldview is not what they say it is, but how they live. Furthermore, as explained by Phillips, many professing evangelicals are fundamentally confused about the Gospel. The result is that people live lives and preachers proclaim messages that are anything but 'world-tilting.' *The World-Tilting Gospel* unfolds the biblical framework needed for the Gospel to make sense while simultaneously responding to the slick Gospel-avoiding marketing gimmicks of modern evangelicalism. Phillips faithfully explains the Gospel using a whole-Bible approach and does so in vivid, highly colorful language suitable to the most contemporary reader. In creative and highly illustrative style, echoing his *Pyromaniacs* blog site, Dan Phillips has produced a work that is part Gospel tract, part systematic theology, and part blog post . . . very helpful for those in need of the Gospel's bigger picture and who prefer a twenty-first-century mode of presentation."

> —**Brian and Janet Rickett**, The Bible Church of Beebe and The Baptist Missionary Association Theological Seminary

The WORLD–TILTING GOSPEL

Dan Phillips

Embracing a Biblical Worldview & Hanging on Tight

Kregel
Publications

Published by Kregel Publications, a division of Kregel, Inc., P.O. Box 2607, Grand Rapids, MI 49501.

Library of Congress Cataloging-in-Publication Data
Phillips, Dan.
 The world-tilting Gospel : embracing a biblical worldview and hanging on tight / Dan Phillips.
  p. cm.
 Includes bibliographical references.
 1. Christianity—Philosophy. 2. Christian philosophy. 3. Ideology—Religious aspects—Christianity. 4. Christianity—Essence, genius, nature. I. Title.
 BR100.P475   2011   230.01—dc22   2011009629

ISBN 978-0-8254-3908-7

Printed in the United States of America
11 12 13 14 15 / 5 4 3 2 1

To God the Father Almighty, Maker of heaven and earth,
Creator of the plan of the ages;
And to Jesus Christ His only Son, the Focus and Executor of that plan;
And to the Holy Spirit, Revealer of that plan,
and Life-giver for its beneficiaries—
All glory, honor, and praise!

Contents

Contents

Preface

The idea behind the core of this book was born in something I heard David Wells say at the Founder's Conference in Oklahoma, on June 27, 2007.

Wells delivered a message titled "Preaching the Truth of the Cross for the Modern Age." In it, Wells let loose an arresting thought that he later expressed in *The Courage to Be Protestant*:

> Christianity is not just an experience, we need to remember, but it is about truth. The experience of being reconciled to the Father, through the Son, by the work of the Holy Spirit all happens within a *worldview*. This worldview is the way God has taught us in his Word to view the world. *That is why the Bible begins with Genesis 1:1 and not with John 3:16.*[1]

---

1. Wells, *Courage to Be Protestant*, 45 (emphasis added). For all source notes, full bibliographic information is available in the bibliography proper.

I love compressed truth. Wells's observation was as brilliant as it was pithy. It went off in my imagination like a thrilling cascade of fireworks, effectively illuminating and framing so much that had been troubling me about today's church scene.

People leap for an experience, fall short of truth, and wander off lost and aimless. A truncated "half-spell" has been substituted for the biblical Gospel. The "nice bits" have been snipped out, isolated, and dolled up as more marketable. Folks have signed on without any real grasp of the Gospel in all its fullness and power.

Many professed Christians regard the Gospel as our ticket "in," and then we're done with it. It's like a contract: We ignore the lawyer-talk, sign it, and then forget about it. We think that the Gospel was *beginner's* material. Pray a prayer, pen your name, you're "in"; now move on to something else.

But what too many of us have not grasped is:

- who we really are
- what kind of world we are really living in
- how the world really operates and where it is really going
- who God really is
- what His eternal plan really was
- why we really needed Him and His plan so desperately
- what His terms—the Gospel—really were
- what difference the Gospel will really make on every day of our lives

To discover the reality of these issues, to begin to understand that reality in its fullness, we simply must start with Genesis 1:1.

This is precisely where I am wading in, as I will explain in the introduction.

Acknowledgments

My fear has a name (which I made up): *acharistojerkopho-bia*. It is the completely rational fear of failing to thank someone to whom heartfelt thanks are owed. So, trying hard to avoid that . . .

Thanks to Brian Thomasson, who was the catalyst for getting this book written, and whose editing work helped focus and streamline the manuscript.

Thanks to Ed Komoszewski of Kregel, for reaching out to me, and for his passion for the message of this book. Thanks also to Sarah De Mey of Kregel, for her excellent "detailing" work.

Thanks to Dr. Matthew S. Harmon, Associate Professor of NT Studies at Grace College & Theological Seminary, for bringing his expertise to bear in checking my Greek translations and comments.

Thanks beyond the power of intelligible speech to Chris Anderson, pastor of Tri-County Bible Church in Madison, Ohio. A busy pastor and devoted husband and father, Chris gave generously of his time to go over this manuscript with a fine-tooth comb, utterly brutalized me and my purple prose . . . and I cannot possibly thank him enough (Prov. 27:6). Chris's comments were on target, wise, penetrating, well considered, and enormously helpful. I owe him big time.

To these two brothers' credit lie many of this book's strengths, and none of its weaknesses.

Thanks to Phil Johnson for his friendship; for graciously inviting me to share a larger platform to broadcast the Word via his team blog *Pyromaniacs* (http://teampyro.blogspot.com), and for his enthusiasm for this project—in that order. Thanks to Frank Turk for his infectious and instructive love for the Gospel, and for being an iron-sharpening friend. And hearty thanks to our readers for their loyalty, for their gracious encouragement and prayers, for their sight-unseen eagerness to read this book, and above all for their love for Christ and His Gospel.

Thanks to my dear and only daughter and her husband, Rachael and Kermit (parents of adorable grandson Timothe), for their prayers.

Finally and above all other mortals, thanks to my dear, omni-competent, pretty wife Valerie, and to my youngest sons, Jonathan and Josiah. Valerie's encouragement, her sharing the excitement of this opportunity, and her sacrifice in seeing to it that I had time to work on the manuscript, were a dear gift. Jonathan and Josiah prayed for me, and cheerfully accepted that the project meant I usually had to be visited in my office.

Honey, let's go out!

Boys, let's go fishing!

Introduction

Flash back with me nineteen-hundred-plus-change years ago. We're in the Macedonian city of Thessalonica in Asia Minor. Local citizens (religious and sacrilegious, upstanding and gutter-wallowing) have just dragged a few of their fellow townsmen before the city officials. Here is their outraged complaint: "These men who have turned the world upside down have come here also, and Jason has received them, and they are all acting against the decrees of Caesar, saying that there is another king, Jesus" (Acts 17:6–7).

That was quite a charge! Perhaps it reflects a combination of mob-hysteria and hyperbole. Perhaps it was a cynical "massaging" of the facts, calculated to alarm the authorities and win their powerful support. Regardless, this was the effect these Christians had on the mob.

13

The accused (Jason and friends) represent the first generation of Christians, and they are fairly typical of the believers of those days. These Christians, whose activities are recorded carefully by Luke in Acts, seem eventually to cause some sort of disturbance or riot everywhere they go.

How did they do it?

The first Christians didn't have any power base whatsoever. They didn't control the local media. They had no big name celebrities giving concerts with two-minute "testimonies" at the end. They didn't have massive popular numbers. They didn't have PR firms shining their image.

They didn't have lines of clothing, entertainment, or holy hardware. They didn't even own buildings. Their assemblies could mostly be contained in people's houses. They didn't control any institutions—religious, educational, or political. They didn't have money, equipment, or rapid-transport vehicles. They couldn't even Twitter!

Yet they created something like blind panic virtually everywhere they went.

How did they do it?

Fast-forward to our day and glance around at evangelicalism. All the things that Group A (first-century church) lacked, Group B (modern evangelicalism) has: institutions, sway, numbers, technology, money, equipment, connections, glitz, and glamour.

Everything except world-tilting! Whatever you can say they are doing, you can't say evangelicals are turning the world upside down. In fact, you could make a better case that the *world* has turned the *church* upside down.

Why is that? Verse 7 provides a very strong hint as to what our forebears in the faith did: "They are all acting against the decrees of Caesar, saying that there is another king, Jesus." Allowing for ignorant misrepresentation, surely this means that the offenders are not fitting in—that they had a different allegiance which in turn produced a different way of looking at everything. In modern parlance, we would say they held to a different worldview that showed in the way they lived.

How does it show? Had they advocated the overthrow of government? Had they campaigned against civil institutions? Had they taken out ads complaining when the world acted like . . . well, like the world? Did they hold concerts, dances, "forty days of sex" campaigns (as one pastor promoted)? No, no, no, and you've-*got*-to-be-kidding-me, respectively.

What they did can be seen a few verses earlier:

> Now when they had passed through Amphipolis and Apollonia, they came to Thessalonica, where there was a synagogue of the Jews. And Paul went in, as was his custom, and on three Sabbath days he reasoned with them from the Scriptures, explaining and proving that it was necessary for the Christ to suffer and to rise from the dead, and saying, "This Jesus, whom I proclaim to you, is the Christ." And some of them were persuaded and joined Paul and Silas, as did a great many of the devout Greeks and not a few of the leading women. (Acts 17:1–4)

After he was run out of Thessalonica, Paul followed the same procedure in the next town, Berea (v. 10). The results were initially happier, but ultimately the same: He was once again run out of town (vv. 13–14). And then, when he landed in Athens, Paul opened the Word in the synagogues; then he took it to the marketplaces, telling passersby about Christ (v. 17).

In all these towns and elsewhere, Paul went where the people were, and preached Christ to them, from Scripture. He preached the Gospel. The apostle defined this as his very mission, in varying language:

He was set apart for the Gospel (Rom. 1:1).

He served God in the Gospel (Rom. 1:9).

He was sent to preach the Gospel (1 Cor. 1:17).

His lot would be abject misery if he could not preach the Gospel (1 Cor. 9:16).

He was dedicated to giving full expression to the Gospel (Col. 1:23–25).

So it is unsurprising that Paul did in Thessalonica what he did everywhere. It was his standard operating procedure. Paul did two things:

1. He found people, and
2. He preached Christ to them.

Paul preached scripturally, thoroughly, fully, pointedly, effectively— and upsettingly. Paul showed not only the *fact*, but also the *necessity and purpose* of Christ's death on the cross.

The rest of what happened in Thessalonica can be pieced together from Paul's letters to the church there, written not long afterward. We read there that the Thessalonians received the Gospel as what it was, the Word of God (1 Thess. 1:5). This resulted in a paradigm shift. They abandoned their false gods to serve the true and living God (1:9). Their faith prompted work, and their love produced hard and persistent efforts (1:3). And all of this centered on the Thessalonians' very real hope in Jesus (1:3b, 10).

The Thessalonian believers themselves became conduits of the Gospel. The same Gospel that had gripped and transformed Paul also captivated them. Even after Paul left, wholly independently of him, the Gospel sounded out from Thessalonica far and broad, to such a degree that Paul found that their testimony often had actually preceded him (1 Thess. 1:8–10).

The apostle's delight leaps off the pages. These poor, persecuted

Thessalonian Christians had a vital grasp of the Gospel. They were turning the world upside down, too! World-tilting is not confined to the apostles. It is for every Christian.

What happened? What divides most Christians then from too many Christians now? Simple:

1. The leaders preached Jesus from the Word of God, and continued to preach the Word. Modern evangelical pastors, too often, don't.
2. People became Christians for one reason only: They believed Jesus because they received the Word of God *as* the Word of God. Modern evangelicals, too often, don't.
3. Converts to Christ knew what they had been, what they had needed, and what God had done to rescue and transform them. They had a biblical worldview that explained the need for and nature of the Gospel. Modern evangelicals, too often, don't.
4. Christians in church fellowships made the instant and necessary connection between believing and obeying. They got on with it so effectively that it threatened the world and made Jesus *the* issue. Modern evangelicals, too often, don't.

Excellent books have been written and passionate voices raised about the first and second points—including John Stott, David Wells, John MacArthur, and a host of others.

This book deals at length with the third point, to demolish modern, muddle-headed *barriers* to the fourth point.

Barrier Busting

As I see it—and as poll after poll proves—too many people who regard themselves as Christians are utterly clueless about the most fundamental truths. They don't understand what God says about the human condition. They don't know what God meant to do when He made man, what happened to us to wreck us up, or what we really need. Cherished traditional notions they have in abundance; biblical truth in all its raw, intrusive, and transforming power, they lack.

Consequently, they aren't at all prepared to grasp the grandeur of what God has done for people in Christ. With that wobbly and incomplete foundation, they may claim to have "received" Jesus, may really believe they have done so—but nothing comes of it. They think and live just like the world.

As I said: They don't tilt the world. The world tilts them because of various barriers erected in their minds through exposure to *bad teaching*. A variety of false doctrines hold them back from enjoying the life to which God calls them in Jesus Christ. They bank on bad teaching, they're burdened by bad teaching, and they're bound by bad teaching.

Banking on Bad Teaching

Some professing Christians are naturally indolent, lazy, retiring, introspective, self-involved, perhaps even selfish—and the rotten teaching they get magnifies and calcifies those tendencies. They refuse to trust and obey; they feel no need to try and to dare and to engage. Worse, they do all this *nothingness* in the name of the Lord.

God's Word has good news for just such folks: The cross of Christ means far more than you've been told, and Jesus wants to have much more to do with your life than you have thought!

Burdened by Bad Teaching

Other Christians dearly want to soar, but they keep crashing. These poor souls fell into teaching that promised quick fixes and jump starts to their spiritual lives. "Just follow our instructions" (they were told), "and you will soar to victory! Pray ____! Bind ____! Unleash ____! Receive ____! Claim ____!"

So they followed the instructions. They prayed, bound, unleashed, received, claimed . . . and maybe they danced a little jig, to boot. Yet they kept crashing, and crashing, and crashing.

Now they feel like giving up. Maybe they have given up. There is great, glorious news in the Word for them as well: The cross of Christ means *far more* than you've been told, and Jesus has yet more grace and wisdom for your path.

Bound by Bad Teaching

Still others are reluctant captives who would love to break out and live boldly for God's glory. But they have been fed a line of bad teaching that has convinced them that they dare do no such thing. It has them stalled on the roadside in a holy haze. They cannot risk making a move for fear of doing it wrong and ruining all.

The Bible has wonderfully good news for them as well! The cross of Christ means *far more* than you've been told, and it brings a freedom for you that you've only dreamt of thus far! Once the good news grips you (as one of my blog readers gladly reported), "some major chains" will shatter, and you'll be free to blast off.

The world needs tilting, and bad doctrinal barriers need busting. I say we do it.

A Whole-Bible Gospel

The greatest need of the church today is a strategic, full-orbed, robust, biblical grasp of the Gospel of Jesus Christ and its transformative implications. We don't need more glitz or glamour, better marketing or programs, snazzier décor or entertainment. We do need a *whole-Bible* grasp of the Gospel.

What I am going to do for you is lay out, in plain language, that biblically framed Gospel. I'll spell it out so that any willing reader can grasp it. You will see, from the Bible:

- who we are
- who God is
- how we got where we are
- what we need
- what God has done
- what difference it makes

Engage yourself in this study with me, with an open mind and an open Bible, and you will be in a position to understand, grasp, and explain the Gospel *biblically*. You will see how God Himself framed and laid out His eternal plan. You will see the difference it makes in how we view and relate to the world.

As we launch out on this venture together, we will encounter those core, essential biblical truths in four movements and a crescendo.

Part One

In the first three chapters I lay out the Bible's portrait of you, me, all human beings everywhere. We will see that sin did not merely damage or cripple us. It ruined us; it killed us. Accordingly, we will see that none of us needs just a little help or a leg up from God. No, we need a massive rescue operation that only God could undertake, and only without our "help."

Part Two

In chapters 4 through 6, we will learn more of God's nature. We'll see how the plan of redemption springs from His great heart and His vast, immeasurable wisdom, in line with His devastating purity.

We will see the very first primeval glimmer of His plan, and then trace its unfolding through the ages. Scripture will teach us how the whole symphony of revelation points to Christ. Then we will come to understand how Christ came to execute and consummate this plan, gaining a vital grasp both of Jesus Christ's person and His work.

Part Three

The great nineteenth-century British preacher Charles H. Spurgeon told pastors, "Know where Adam left you; know where the Spirit of God has placed you."[1] This is good advice for us all, and I seek to keep to it in chapters 7 and 8, where we learn how God's "out there" work of salvation comes to have a revolutionary and transforming impact "in here," in our own individual lives.

Part Four

Then, in chapters 9 through 13 we will apply the Gospel to directly confront and lay waste to some of the forces reducing Christians to a miserable state of vapor lock today, and keeping them from having an impact for His kingdom. Some of these are dragonlike dogmas that intimidate and frighten Christians into paralysis. Others are seductive sirens that lull them into a trance-like sleep. Either way, what passes for modern Christian living bears little resemblance to the biblical Gospel model. I mean to strike a resounding blow to upend the status quo.

Crescendo

Then it all comes together and pays off in the last chapter, titled "Culmination: Putting It All Together." You will see what everything

---

1. Spurgeon, *All-Round Ministry*, 51.

has led to, how all the truths fit, and what worldview impact those verities have. We will synthesize everything we've learned in the preceding thirteen chapters, and express in crystallized form how these truths make us world-tilters and barrier-busters.

Ready? Keep a Bible at hand, and pray for a discerning, but teachable spirit. I commend to you (and frequently pray) the prayer of the psalmist:

> Open my eyes, that I may behold
> wondrous things out of your law. (Ps. 119:18)

Part One

Who Are We?

Getting at the Truth of Our Identities

Chapter 1

Knowing God and Man

Which Comes First?
What Difference Does It Make?

We want a relationship with God that is real, dynamic, and *going somewhere*. To do that, we must know who this God is. What is He like? What does He love? What does He hate? What does He give? What does He want? And how do we even go about answering any of those questions?

Further, if we are to know and serve God, must we not also have *some* sort of clue about ourselves? Who are we? What do *we* bring to the show? Are we basically good people who need to simply listen to our hearts and everything will be peachy, as Hollywood keeps assuring us? Do we bring God good hearts and good agendas? Is He mainly there to sign off on our itineraries, so we can have our best lives—and our whitest smiles!—right now?

The answers to those questions make all the difference.

But where do we start? With knowledge of God, or of ourselves? Which has priority? Must we know God in order to know ourselves? Or do we need to know ourselves in order to know God?

Calvin was here, way back in 1536. John Calvin grappled with these very questions, though you might not have guessed he would. He wasn't in Geneva to cut the cake (nor sample the chocolates that Swiss chocolatier Blaise Poyet produced in his honor), but the great Reformer/theologian/expositor's five hundredth birthday fell in July of 2009. Calvin is perhaps best known for his *Institutes of the Christian Religion*, which he wrote[1] as devotional reading for Christians, not as brain-jerky for theologians. The *Institutes* was structured along the familiar lines of the Apostles' Creed, for easy consumption.

Nonetheless, Calvin has gotten a reputation as being the ultimate button-down theologian, the man with the answer to anything and everything.

Yet even Calvin admitted that this was a hard call.

After asserting that all wisdom starts with knowledge of God and of ourselves, Calvin confesses that "which one precedes and brings forth the other is not easy to discern." He continues:

> In the first place, no one can look upon himself without immediately turning his thoughts to the contemplation of God, in whom he "lives and moves" [Acts 17:28]. . . . Again, it is certain that man never achieves a clear knowledge of himself unless he has first looked upon God's face, and then descends from contemplating him to scrutinize himself. For we always seem to ourselves righteous and upright and wise and holy—this pride is innate in all of us—unless

---

1. Finishing his first draft at age 25!

by clear proofs we stand convinced of our own unrigh-teousness, foulness, folly, and impurity. Moreover, we are not thus convinced if we look merely to ourselves and not also to the Lord, who is the sole standard by which this judgment must be measured.[2]

It's impossible to measure without a standard. It's impossible to apply a standard if we don't know what we're measuring. But which comes first?

Chronologically, self-awareness comes first, and indeed fills our whole conscious life. No healthy baby has to be persuaded to be self-concerned. Nor have I ever met an infant who would say, "You know, some nice, warm milk would be great . . . but it would glorify God more if I let Mom get some sleep." Babies don't even rise to "I am fearfully and wonderfully *made*," but rather, "I am fearfully and wonderfully *wet*."

Yet while self-awareness comes first in time, surely the knowl-edge of God comes first in importance. Christian readers will grant that our concept of God affects how we see everything. The case I want to make is that our view of ourselves as we stand before God is inextricably interwoven with our view of God.

Think it through with me.

Wrong Answers and the Damage They Cause

Self-image matters, but not in the way that pop psychology paints it. What one makes of the human condition—what you think you are now, and/or what you think you were when God found you and made you His—has a major ongoing impact on our approach to God, our view of Him, and our day-to-day relationship with God.

---

2. Calvin, *Institutes of the Christian Religion*, 35, 37.

Let's consider three different approaches to understanding ourselves, as embodied by three different characters. These certainly are not exhaustive, but they help us see the far-reaching significance of our self-estimation.

"Here, God, just sign this."

Suppose we have the belief that we are good people who simply need a bit of a leg up. We aren't really bad-hearted. People just don't understand us. Deep down inside we mean well and want good things. Oh, we may have a few bad habits, we sometimes make a bad call here and there—a mistake, a goof, an "oops" . . . but it's what's inside that counts, and what's inside is *good.*

Here's Bud Goodheart, for instance. Bud sees himself as a decent, moral, well-meaning guy. So naturally Bud is attracted to the sort of worldview that presents God as the grand Rubber Stamp in the Sky. This God loves us unconditionally, just as we are, and wants us to realize our deepest dreams and aspirations. "Go for it, child!" Bud's God cheers. "I'm right behind you!" That's the line from the pulpit . . . or stool, or "enablement stand," or whatever. "God wants you to pursue your dreams!"[3]

So Bud simply brings God his biggest and brightest dreams, and God signs off on them. *Whump! Whump! Whump!* goes the heavenly rubber stamp. *Approved!* God claps Bud on the back, gives a big thumbs-up—and off Bud trots. Pursuing *Bud's* agenda. Because God has Bud's back.

How will such a man, such a woman, see Christ? Not as a Savior, surely. As Facilitator, as Enabler, as Cheerleader inspiring him to

---

3. Do these preachers even wonder, as they speak, whether their hearers include any Adolph Hitlers, Dylan Klebolds, or Osama bin Ladens, dreaming their dark and malevolent dreams?

pursue his dreams, his goals, his ambitions. What is the Cross, to Bud? If anything, it is an expression of God's love and approval. The Cross proves how much Bud means to God, how worthy Bud is, how irresistibly adorable Bud is to God. The Cross tells Bud that he is okay—that God just wants to fulfill Bud and make him happy with himself. It's about affirmation, not execution.

Bud may view the Christian life as an ongoing negotiation with his partner, Jesus. Nothing radical, certainly. After all, Bud "invited" Jesus in, he gave Christ a "chance," he "tried Christ" (like the bumper sticker says). Jesus was a plug-in, an add-on, like some enhancement to a web browser—a really good and powerful plug-in that promises big things, but a plug-in nonetheless.

And Bud maintains control of the relationship.

But, you see, if Bud is wrong about himself, and he's wrong about God, and he's wrong about Christ, and he's wrong about the Cross—then Bud is wrong about the relationship, too.

It matters!

"I couldn't have done it without You—and vice versa."

Another fellow—Lodowick (Lodo) Legup—has been convinced that he needs Christ as Savior and Lord, and has come to be saved and led. Lodo knows he's a sinner, and looks to Christ to do something about that.

But, oddly enough, Lodo thinks that sin has disabled him, hurt him, wounded him—but not *killed* him as dead as, say, Julius Caesar. So Lodo has this inner notion that he still brings something positive to the equation. Lodo's Jesus holds out most of the makings of a nice big yummy Salvation Pie, but it's not really a pie until Lodo puts the "decision cherry" on the top, or the "faith sprinkles." Jesus is really a great help. He did a lot, all the heavy lifting and big stuff; but it's still nothing until Lodo does *his* part.

Jesus helps Lodo—but Lodo helps Jesus, too. In fact, without Lodo's help, nothing happens.

So, without in any way meaning to, Lodo has Jesus as Cosigner instead of Savior. Because the relationship is still partly based on Lodo's performance, on his works, he has the feeling deep down that God doesn't really like him much, or love him, unless he does his part. After all, He didn't save him until Lodo did his part first. God responded to Lodo then, so maybe He responds now. Lodo works so that God will like him, so that Jesus will love him and keep him. If Lodo stopped, he'd lose that relationship. That kind of fear motivates Lodo.

To Lodo, the Cross is where God did everything He could, made salvation *possible* and *attainable,* and then left it to Lodo to make it happen. The relationship started partly because of what God did, and partly because of what Lodo did. But Lodo added the decisive element. The relationship continues the same way.

Lodo may not be prepared to take up a cross himself, or do anything radical. After all, God didn't have to do anything too radical to save him. Lodo wasn't *so* bad off that Lodo himself couldn't provide the essential ingredient. Lodo kept *part* of the salvation package, and now he'll keep part of the Christian-life package.

But if Lodo is wrong about himself, and he's wrong about God, and he's wrong about Christ, and he's wrong about the Cross—then Lodo is wrong about the relationship, too.

It matters.

"Whimper words of 'wisdom,' let it be."

Our third person—an unmarried lass named Misty Call—is also convinced of her real, deep-down need of Christ. Misty comes to Christ as Savior and Lord. In that way, she's like the second model we just talked about.

Misty thinks she was spiritually helpless. Misty would say that. Yet she *also* thinks she had enough in herself to bring herself to Christ. And now there's *more* for Misty Call to do . . . and here it gets really confusing.

Misty believes she needs to empty herself of herself. Misty needs to yield. She needs to surrender, to make herself nothing, to wait for God to take control, pick her up, perhaps even talk directly to her, and move her about. Kind of like a living puppet.

Yet Misty Call still controls the relationship, since God is waiting for her to yield, surrender, and make herself nothing. Spiritually she isn't much until this great surrender happens. She's snagged in an odd state, what computer programmers have called an "endless do-loop." Commands circle and circle within her, but nothing happens. Nothing can. Misty is afraid to do anything, because she's not supposed to do anything. Well, she is. But she isn't. What she's supposed to *do* is surrender. This will make God make Misty do something. But until then, she'd better do nothing. Or God will do nothing.

Subtly, you see, Misty also controls the relationship.

The Cross, to Misty, is where she dies . . . and all but ceases to exist. It's the symbol of passive yieldedness to God, of absolute surrender and submission, of virtually vanishing as an individual, and melting into the divine. It isn't judicial;[4] it is *mystical*.

Misty Call's life will be a blur of muzzy mysticism. Misty will be suspicious of the rational, the objective, the external. Though Misty will grant that the Bible is God's Word, she'll really be straining her mystical inner ear to hear something better, higher, deeper. Faithful reasoning and obedience are not big themes to Misty.

But if Misty is wrong about herself, and she's wrong about God,

---

4. We will examine this more deeply in chapter 11.

and she's wrong about Christ, and she's wrong about the Cross—then Misty is wrong about the relationship, too.

It matters. *It all matters.*

Our Hearts Are Jacob

All three of our characters have something in common with the world. The world insists that we must "listen to our hearts"—and Bud, Lodo, and Misty partially agree. Each of them finds something that is of value, whether it's Bud's dreams, Lodo's activities, or Misty's muzzy inner light. The world won't care so much if they bring in a little religion, just so long as they continue to look within for their answers, their deliverance—their salvation.

God's view is exactly opposed to the world's—and here starts the tilting.

The Bible is absolutely emphatic about the fact that we will not find the truth by ourselves, within ourselves. We cannot diagnose ourselves. One telling statement is found in Jeremiah 17:9—"The heart is deceitful above all things, and desperately sick; who can understand it?"

Heart. God speaks here of our "heart." Perhaps you have been taught that the heart is the "center of the emotions." That sense may dominate English poetry and songs and movies, but it isn't the biblical idea. In the Bible, the heart is the fountainhead of the way we live (Prov. 4:23). It is the seat not only of our emotions, but of our calculated plans (Gen. 6:5; Prov. 16:1, 9, etc.), our intellect (Prov. 18:15), our values (Matt. 15:18), and our decisions (1 Cor. 7:37). Our heart is, in short, action central. It is where we do our thinking, cherishing, and deciding.

So you see this *heart* is not located in our chest. It is located between our ears.

Here is a graphic way to envision what the Bible means by "heart":

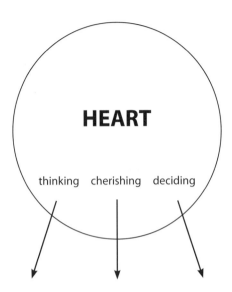

Deceitful. God says that our heart is "deceitful." That word translated "deceitful" merits a closer look. Jeremiah uses the Hebrew noun *ʿāqōb̲* (ah-COVE), which is related to the name "Jacob" (*yaʿᵃqōb̲*, ya-aCOVE). The prophet's readers might well have caught the connection right away: "Your heart is like a Jacob inside of you," the prophet says, in effect.

Clear? As mud? Stay with me. Let's look further.

Just think about the patriarch Jacob. What was he? He was a con artist. His very name means "heel-catcher," because he came out of the womb holding onto his brother's *ʿāqēb̲* (ah-CAVE), his heel. It was a colloquialism that meant someone who would come up on another person from behind and trip him up to take advantage of him.

Jacob was a pretty despicable fellow. He takes advantage of his brother's hunger in order to trick his birthright out of him (Gen. 25:29–34). He takes advantage of his father's poor eyesight to trick him out of the blessing (Gen. 27). Brother, father, no matter: Jacob is out for *Jacob.* He's a conniver and a trickster.

Above all things. God says our *hearts* are like that: conniving, deceptive. Not merely deceptive, but deceptive "above all things." The human heart is *intensely* conniving; it is that, more than it is anything else. Whatever capacity the heart may have for occasional goodness, honesty, good intentions—more than all that, the human heart is deceptive.

We've got our own Jacob living in our craniums, busily doing our thinking and cherishing and deciding.

So what is the effect when our most fundamental power of perception is deceitful?

It will affect the way you and I see *everything*.

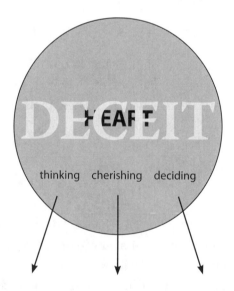

Desperately sick. Deceitful is bad enough, yet God adds that our heart is "desperately sick." How sick? The word *'ānuš* (ah-NOOSH) means *incurable*. It is used of incurable pain (Isa. 17:11; Jer. 30:15), and an incurable wound (Jer. 37:12). Our heart isn't annoyed by a passing cold. It doesn't have a summer headache. No, our heart is stricken with a spiritual cancer.

Who can know it? No wonder the prophet asks "who can know it?" The answer Jeremiah fully expects is "No one!"

That is why we cannot diagnose ourselves. What would we use as our instrument? Our minds, of course; which is to say, our *hearts*. Ah, but there's the problem, isn't it? The instrument is corrupt! It is irreparably out of whack. It skews the answers, it messes with the data. It gathers information like the mainstream media takes polls: "Are people who oppose abortion hateful or just ignorant?"

The heart sees what it wants to see, and conveniently finds inconvenient truths invisible. Self-diagnosis is hopeless.

The Case of Doctor Me

When I was seventeen, I had a dull ache in the pit of my stomach. Bothersome, but not agonizing. My mother prevailed on me to see the doctor, which I did reluctantly. I thought it would be wasted money.

I figured I had some minor nothing. Kindly Dr. Harry Kerber would poke and prod and look judicious, tell me to drink some antacid or laxative or something, pat my head, and send me home. Thus spake "Doctor" Phillips.

Wrong!

Kindly Dr. Kerber (a real doctor, not one on TV) did poke and prod—and he said it was serious. He said I should go see a surgeon right away.

I didn't care much for his diagnosis. It didn't match my own. It didn't make me happy. I didn't feel *that* bad. True, it hurt a bit to raise my foot to shift gears in my Pinto, but that was it. The good doctor sounded as if he were a bit of an alarmist. My diagnosis was much milder, much less radical, much less distressing.

What if I'd gone with "Doctor" Phillips's diagnosis instead of Dr. Kerber's?

For one thing, you'd not be reading this book.

As it was, I did bow to Dr. Kerber's judgment. He called up a surgeon, sent me right over to his office, and a few hours later I went under the knife. When I awoke, I was in far greater pain, but minus a red-hot appendix.

An appendix that would have killed me, if I'd gone with my self-diagnosis.

We are terrible at self-diagnosis. Our "knower" is broken! That is why the prophet says that no one can "know" the deceptive, incurably sick heart of man.

Who knows what lurks in the hearts of men? God alone. No *man* can know our heart. The next verse tells us, "I the LORD search the heart and test the mind" (Jer. 17:10a). God brings what we lack. His diagnosis of us is everything our self-diagnosis is not: It is objective, exhaustive, measured by an absolute and unimpeachable standard, and it is true. God searches the heart, He says.

In fact, earlier Solomon had written that "The spirit of man is the lamp of the LORD, searching all his innermost parts" (Prov. 20:27). God can compel our own spirit to be an internal informant, coughing up our deepest secrets on demand. Not that God needs such an informant. His understanding is infinite (Ps. 147:5). All things are visible, naked, and vulnerable before the One to whom we must give an account (Heb. 4:13). There is absolutely no fooling Him.

God alone has the goods on us. So if we want the truth about ourselves as individuals, or about humanity in general, we need to get it from God Himself.

What We Need: A Whole-Bible View

Our three friends share a common deficiency. Their understanding of Christianity is based on a reprocessed version based distantly on a few selected verses plucked hither and thither from

Scripture, mostly from the New Testament (hereafter NT). Those isolated scraps are reassembled according to worldviews not only *not* based on Scripture, but actually hostile to it.

They (and we) must understand that the whole Bible gives us the goods both on God and on us. It is God's unalloyed, inerrant disclosure of Himself, and His diagnosis of the human condition. What the Bible says, God says.

Where did I get that idea? I got it from Jesus. What we call the "Old Testament" came up constantly in Jesus' teaching ministry, and His attitude was always the same: What the Old Testament said, God said. Every bit of it was Scripture, and could not be broken (John 10:35). It was given by God the Holy Spirit (Matt. 22:43), so not the smallest part of it could be nullified (Matt. 5:17–18). Jesus treated its narratives as unerring historical fact (Matt. 12:40–41; 19:4–6). No human doctrine ever could outrank and set aside what the Old Testament said (Mark 7:6–13).

In all His teaching, Jesus confirms what the Old Testament (hereafter OT) says about itself. It claims to represent God's very words (Gen. 1:3). It quotes Him verbatim (Exod. 20:1ff.). It claims for itself qualities reflecting both its divine origin and its continuing power under God (Pss. 19:7–11; 119).

To understand Jesus, we must begin where His thinking begins: not with John 3:16, but with Genesis 1:1, and on through all that follows. There we find the truth that forms the basis of Jesus' teaching, truth that we would never find within our own deceptive, incurably sick hearts.

To understand who Jesus says that we *are*, we must understand who we *were*, and what we *became*, and how we *got* there.

For that, we're going to need to start at the beginning.

Chapter 2

What Happened in the Garden

Here We Are, Baby: Created, Tested, Ruined—We're Ours

To assemble a worldview based on God's truth rather than the world's lies or our hearts' self-serving deceptions, we must begin at the beginning—as in, "In the beginning."

The longer I study the Bible, the more I realize how crucial, pivotal, and *packed* its first three chapters are. Though terse, those pregnant passages convey an intense concentration of foundational revelation that is breathtaking in its depth and scope. It is here that we first encounter the truth of God, His nature, His word, His creation, and His plan for all the ages.

And we find ourselves in those chapters, as well. How did we originate? What were we? Why were we created? Where did everything go wrong?

Is there a plan to *do* anything about it?

We find all that and more in Genesis 1 to 3, and in what springs from those chapters. Get them right, and we're set to understand the rest of the Bible. But get them fundamentally wrong, and we get everything else fundamentally wrong. So let's not get them wrong!

Though a detailed exposition is beyond this book's scope, let me scoop out three highlights from these chapters:

1. Man's preparation
2. Man's probation
3. Man's prostration

Man's Preparation

If we want to know what God wants from us as Christians, we must have a firm biblical grasp of His intention in making man in the first place.

Everything in Genesis 1:1–25 is clearly preparatory for *something*. God creates, He meticulously designs, and He brilliantly sets a universe in exact order. But for whom, or for what?

Try to imagine that you are reading the text for the first time. Suppose that you have no idea where the story is leading. What do you see, step by step?

First we see the cosmos created by God, in the famous and sonorous verse 1—"In the beginning, God created the heavens and the earth." But in the next verse, we find the planet unfit for habitation—though God's Spirit hovers over the face of the deep, as if something big is about to happen.[1]

---

1. Genesis 1:1 narrates the creation of the universe out of nothing, initially unformed and uninhabitable (v. 2). Through six days, God makes the planet both formed and inhabitable. Picture the creation of a pile of Legos, followed by building those pieces into an intricate structure. The six days are meticulously structured to climax in verses 26–31.

And it does happen!

Step by step, by His word alone, God designs and prepares the earth as a habitat for something. Light is created and separated from darkness; waters are separated from waters; dry land is parted from bodies of water, and is filled with vegetation. Then light-bearers are put in the heavens; the waters below teem with marine life, and the sky above is filled with birds. Then, at the start of the sixth day, the land is populated with animals.

The narrative fairly quivers with anticipation through each stage, as God works and works, pausing at each point (except on the second day) to say "Good . . . good . . . good."

It's "good," but where are we going with all this? Where is it headed?

To the second act on the sixth day.

On the sixth day, God does something similar to what He had done on the third day, and yet different in a crucial way. Let's review a bit.

On the third day, His creation had been in two parts. God had given the word that the dry land was to separate from the waters, and it happened. He said it was "good." Normally, "good" means "good-bye" to that day's work. But then God gave a second word, commanding that plants and fruit trees grow from the new soil, which also happened, and which was also "good."

The third day, then, has a two-stage structure. We will see this same two-stage program recurring on the sixth day, but with a critical climax to the whole process.

The climactic narrative of the sixth day is the longest of all the days of creation. As with the third day, God starts with a single act of creation: He commands the emergence of land animals, and they appear. Also like the third day, after the first act we read that "He saw that it was good" (v. 25). But then on the sixth day, after the second act, He will take in all His creation, and pronounce it "*very* good" (v. 31).

That happy pronouncement tells us that this second act of creation on the sixth day is where it was all headed. Until then, the word in effect was, "So far, so good." Now all is done, all is finished, everything is *very* good!" The Master Artist puts down His brush and palette, steps back, and admires His work. "Done!" He says, with a delighted sigh.

So let us pause a moment to look at this crowning act of creation a bit more closely. In verse 26, God proposes to create the first and only finite being who is said to embody His image and likeness. God says, "Let us make man in our image, after our likeness. And let them have dominion over the fish of the sea and over the birds of the heavens and over the livestock and over all the earth and over every creeping thing that creeps on the earth." This creature is to be called *'āḏām* (ah-THAHM), "man." He will be God's representative on earth, God's finite likeness, a faithful representation of God, but in bodily form. *Adam* will be fully equipped with everything he needs to act as God's viceroy over creation.

The execution of God's plan follows in v. 27, where the image is shared by both man and woman—whose names, we will learn in the following chapters, are Adam and Eve. This verse is the first bit of poetry in the Bible:

> Then God created man in His *image*
> In the *likeness* of God, He created him
> Male and female, He created them. (DJP)

Note the threefold repetition of "created." While God fashioned man's body from dust of the ground (2:7a), his essence, his humanity, was a direct creation (2:7b). As God's image, Adam's physical attributes reflected spiritual attributes of God.[2]

---

2. God is spirit (John 4:24a), without literal hands, eyes, ears, and so on. But these physical attributes in man all represent powers that God does have, to

But at the same time, Adam was but the *likeness* of God. He was not God incarnate. Rather, man was to be an analogous, representative being. He was a finite, created, living mirror reflecting the glory of the infinite, uncreated God (1 Cor. 11:7).

Finally, God commissions the first family. God, who has previously addressed only marine life and birds (Gen. 1:22), now speaks to His image bearers. What is their charge?

> And God blessed them. And God said to them, "Be fruitful and multiply and fill the earth and subdue it and have dominion over the fish of the sea and over the birds of the heavens and over every living thing that moves on the earth." (v. 28)

In the beginning of a mediated kingdom over the earth, God puts the man and the woman in charge, under Him. Their task is to subdue and exercise dominion over the entire globe. They are not just like every other creature, as materialistic evolution preaches; they are *over* every creature and all creation.

To exercise this dominion, they have to create a staff. They have to be fruitful and multiply. They would have all they needed: They could eat any fruit and vegetation (1:29; 2:16)—with only one exception (2:17).

So the young couple had all the internal provision and all the external supplies they would require. What else did they need?

They just needed to *get going*: have kids and exercise dominion. But we'll develop that much more in chapter 3.

---

an infinitely greater and purer degree. The logic of Psalm 94:9 explains passages describing God in human terms (e.g., Genesis 6:8; 2 Kings 19:16; Isaiah 51:9; etc.). Our physical attributes are distantly analogous to spiritual realities in God, gracious gifts to help us better know and serve Him.

Man's Probation

If we want to know what God wants from us as Christians, we must have a firm biblical grasp of how we got to be in the mess we are in today.

The probation, strictly speaking, was twofold: God gave positive commands, and one negative command. Put another way, God told Adam to do some things, and He told him not to do one thing.

Multiply, subdue, chow down. As we saw, He told Adam to have a lot of kids, fill the earth, and gain control over it. Those are some pretty compressed commands! God did not spell out every detail of how to do what He told Adam to do. He set the goals, and left most of the specifics to Adam.

Those directives did, however, positively chart Adam's course. These things Adam must do.

God also told Adam that he could eat freely from any tree in the Garden (2:16). I am more of a carnivore than an herbivore, but I would love to have seen those fruits. Imagine succulent, full, bursting grapes and apples and berries, before the faintest breath of contaminant or insecticide had been introduced, fresh and straight from the hand of God.

I think we get the slightest hint of what that might have been like when we eat fresh fruit from a stand beside a farmer's field. The juiciness and flavor are so much brighter and bolder than what we bring home from the store. God's fruits and vegetables must have been far better still. And all of them were for Adam and Eve to eat freely.

With one exception.

There was one dietary prohibition, and one only: They must not eat from "the tree of the knowledge of good and evil" (v. 17).

What was that tree? The notion of an apple tree is sheer tradition, without any warrant in the text. The other common idea, that this tree was symbolic of sex, is just silly. God told Adam and Eve to make babies, and I'm pretty sure He knew how that was done. After all, He created that, too.

I take it that the tree was a sort of *dark sacrament*, if I may turn the phrase thus. As the bread and wine bring the blessing of Christ's presence to the Christian when partaken in faith, so the fruit of this tree would bring cursing to the man, when eaten in the only way possible—in unbelief. It was no more magical or physically enhanced than the bread and juice of Communion, but as an object of testing the fruit sealed Adam's unbelieving rebellion with the judgment of God.

The tree represented autonomy, the illusion of self-rule. It represented knowledge falsely gained, on man's own terms, born of rebellion. Had Adam and Eve walked with God in faith, they would have learned all they needed to know, under God's lordship. But this tree held out a knowledge premised on *rejection* of God's lordship, and specifically based on rejection of His word.

We can only speculate what would have happened had the pair continued in the obedience born of faith. It makes sense to think that they would have been confirmed in positive goodness and holiness, and their knowledge of everything would have expanded.

Alas, all we have is speculation, for it was not to be.

Instead, Eve found herself in *the one place* in all the universe where she had no useful business: in front of that prohibited tree.

Eve already knew everything she needed to know about that tree. She knew that God said it wasn't for her. That knowledge was sufficient.

Yet Eve was not satisfied with that knowledge. So she finds herself in a philosophical, theological debate with the one person in all of creation she had no business talking to: the Serpent.

A popular saying has it that the nine most terrifying words in the English language are "I'm from the government and I'm here to help." Yet we find here a far more terrifying sight. The Serpent presents himself in the guise of man's best friend, "here to help." He wants Eve to see that he only wants the best for her and her passive husband, that grand, should-be lord of creation, who perhaps is watching in impotent silence ("who was with her," v. 6). The Serpent's pretense is that he is concerned that the two young humans aren't fulfilled.

Though he is speaking to Eve, all the verbs are in the plural number. The Serpent is talking past her to Adam. It's Adam he really wants. He must bring down the leader God appointed. And oh my, does the Serpent have a sales line for Adam!

The Serpent starts with "Did God really say?" and ends in "God may have said, but He was wrong!" Challenge and disingenuous questioning swiftly morphs into denial and open rejection. To Eve's tepid, faltering defense, the Serpent counters with a scornful "You will not die!" Indeed, rather than die, "You will be as God"—or, perhaps more likely, "as gods." (The Hebrew text could be read either way.)

The young couple will be ultimate, not dependent (so goes the sales pitch). Their knowledge and values will not derive from God's truth and laws. They will know on their own terms, set their own values independent of God, as liberated from God. They will be self-ruled, they will be a law unto themselves.

The young humans are not enjoying life to its fullest—and they *should* be, the Serpent is arguing. They aren't realizing their potential, they aren't fully actualized, they aren't authentic. They aren't having their best life now! They are trapped, he hisses, by legalistic myths about God. They should burst their bonds asunder, reach out, and fulfill their destiny. It is *they* who deserve to be gods. Not God!

And so, *snap-crackle-squish!* goes the human brain. Against all sanity and reason, Eve "buys" the Serpent's slick line. No less astonishingly, her compliant husband shuffles meekly after her lead. (Far more astonishingly, people have fallen for the same line for millennia, and still do.)

My, that didn't take long. Just one negative test. And they fail it, *bang!*—right out of the gate.[3] Perfect Parent, perfect environment, perfect upbringing, perfect genes, flawless psyches, happy marriage, perfect society (except for the Serpent), and still they take one step and do an epic face-plant.

"Not fair," you say? Let me pause and have a word with anyone who finds it unfair that our fate hung on these two people.[4] "I never asked for them to be my representatives," some pout. "I think it would have been fairer if we'd all just stood our own tests, our own Gardens of Eden, one by one."

To that, two thoughts . . .

First, everything Adam and Eve were and had, you aren't and don't. *None* of us had perfect parents, genes, upbringing, environment, society. All the advantages Adam and Eve had, we lack. They were quite literally *model* humans, and they didn't last a whole chapter.

You really think you would have done better?

Second, by that very objection, you undo your argument. *God* evidently determined that this *was* a fair and just way to deal with mankind. In opposing our wisdom over against the wisdom of God, and insisting that we might have a better idea, *we do exactly as Eve did:* We prefer our judgment as superior to God's judgment.

---

3. Nothing in Genesis expressly indicates the passage of time between creation and fall. What matters is the text itself, which presents the events in rapid, trip-hammer succession: creation–commission–*corruption!*

4. This will be explained more fully in chapter 3. We will see that Adam was designated by God as the representative of all his natural descendants (cf. Rom. 5:12–21). Perhaps a workable analogy is athletes representing their countries at the Olympics. If they win, their country wins. If they lose, their country loses.

And so, pencils down. Test over. You already failed. Just as Great-gramma Eve and Great-grampa Adam did.

So what came of their failure?

Man's Prostration

If we want to know what God wants from us as Christians, we must have a firm biblical grasp of how extensive and how serious is the damage that sin has done to us as a race.

The next bit of the story puzzles us a bit. God has said quite emphatically, "of the tree of the knowledge of good and evil you shall not eat, for in the day that you eat of it you shall surely die" (Gen. 2:17). Eve eats, Adam eats. Now, they're supposed to die. We know what "die" means, and we expect them to get on with it.

We watch expectantly, like the Maltans in Acts 28 watched Paul after the serpent bit him. They expect Paul to swell up and fall down, or something. Not to keep eating his barbecued chicken.

In the same way, we watch Adam and Eve after they eat the fruit. Cue the "death scene." Any minute now they're going to gasp, maybe clutch at their throats, reel around a bit, cry out, then collapse in a heap, dead. Any minute now. Yes, sir. Soon. Really soon. Should be big.

So we watch, and we watch, and . . .

Nothing! They just go on. They make some itchy lame clothes. But them? They seem fine. Apparently air's still going in and out, heart's still pumping, blood's still flowing. Not so dead as all that.

What gives?

Not dead? Are you sure? You don't think they died right away? I think they did. Just like that. It simply took their bodies a few centuries to catch up to the fact.

It's all in what you mean by *death* and *life*.

What is life, anyway? In the Bible, *life* can denote physical existence (Eccl. 9:4), but it connotes far more than mere existence.

People in hell exist forever, but I can't think of any passages that refer to their existence as "life."[5] *Life*, in its fullness, connotes the enjoyment of God's presence, and the blessings that this enjoyment entails. To die is to be cut off—not from the bare reality of God's presence, which is impossible (Ps. 139:7–12), but from the enjoyment of His presence, from experiencing Him as other than terrifying (2 Thess. 1:8–9; Rev. 14:10).

Life isn't merely the length of the line on a chronology chart; it is the quality of that line. Moses elsewhere paints it so; when he preaches that man does not enjoy life merely by eating bread, but by feasting on what comes from Yahweh's[6] mouth (Deut. 8:3). When Moses lays before Israel the options of life and good, and of death and evil (Deut. 30:15), and urges them to choose life (v. 19), he means more than mere existence. Moses parallels "life" with "blessing" (v. 19), and says plainly that the Lord "is your life" (v. 20). Solomon will later describe life as the opposite, not only of death, but of sin (Prov. 10:16).

Waltke says that "the Old Testament represents 'life' as an unending spiritual relationship with God, not terminated by clinical death, and 'death' as total separation from God both in this life and after clinical death."[7]

Looking millennia ahead, we see a validation of this when the Lord Jesus prays, "And this is eternal life, that they know you the

---

5. The redeemed rise to a resurrection of "life"; the damned rise to a resurrection—not of life but—of "judgment" (John 5:29). John will elsewhere call this eternal existence the "second death" (Rev. 2:11; 20:6, 14; 21:8).

6. "Yahweh" is the probable pronunciation of God's personal covenant-name, which occurs over 6,800 times in the Old Testament. The consonants in Hebrew are *yhwh*, and most English versions hide it behind all-caps "Lord," or "GOD" (when it is "Lord GOD"). It's an ill-advised tradition, since "Yahweh" does not mean "Lord," for which there are two other main Hebrew words.

7. Waltke, *Old Testament Theology*, 964.

48

only true God, and Jesus Christ whom you have sent" (John 17:3). The essence of life is knowing God, relating to the triune God.

Real life, then, is a gift of God, and bears His presence and blessing. Likewise, if life is the enjoyment of God's intimate presence, then death will be the loss of the joy of that presence, and of all of the blessings that fellowship with God brings.

And so I say that Adam and Eve did die, right away. When the horrible reality of physical death eventually overtook them, it was the culmination of a ghastly process that began the moment sin touched them.

Disease produces symptoms. When she was a young girl, my dear and only daughter Rachael caught Chicken Pox. In those pre-vaccination days, we wanted her brother Matthew to catch it as well, to get over it while he was still young and the symptoms would be mild. When he became a bit ill and broke out in red spots, we knew he'd caught it. (And so did I, by the way, with a whole lot more misery!)

So we see Adam and Eve breaking out in death right away. The symptoms begin to appear immediately. What are they?

We see one "red spot" of death instantly in their self-consciousness and awareness of guilt (Gen. 3:7). Before, being naked had not been a problem. They were naked, and not ashamed (Gen. 2:25). Suddenly, now, being naked is a bad thing. They *feel* guilty because they *are* guilty; they are ashamed, because they are shameful. So they patch together some leaves.

But a worse and more extensive complex of "spots" is seen the moment Yahweh arrives for fellowship with the man. The presence of God really brings out the symptoms. Our bold, brave, pioneering godling-wannabes actually *hide* (3:8).

Isn't that just the most pathetic scene in the entire Bible? Adam hiding in the bushes from Him who made the bushes. As if God couldn't see him!

So, you see, this one wretched act is in truth an ugly constellation of "spots," and reveals the spread of death in their mental/spiritual makeup:

- God's presence is no longer beloved and welcome and sought-out, but excruciating and terrifying and repellant.
- Offending God, indeed insulting Him (by running and hiding from Him who fills heaven and earth) is an acceptable option; so
- God is no longer *God* in their universe; so
- God's glory is no longer their central heartbeat; it has been supplanted by their own self-preservation according to their own pitiful notions.
- Their very notion of God has become warped and inadequate. ("Hide here, honey! He'll never see us!")
- They are evasive about their sin, blame-shifting ("Maybe I can throw Him off!"), rather than openly confessing it, throwing themselves on His mercy, and pleading for a way back into His favor.
- Adam, in fact, has the dead/blind audacity to blame his sin not only on Eve, but also on God ("The woman whom you gave to be with me, she gave me fruit of the tree" [v. 12]; as if to say, "It's not my fault! You gave me a defective woman! You messed up!").

Adam and Eve, then, have *died* both in vertical relationship and in horizontal relationship. They've lost sight of God, and they've lost hold of each other. All that remains is their dead, blind, sin-ravaged selves. Thus, even after He redeems Adam and Eve, God will send ultimate physical death almost as a blessing to relieve them of an interminable existence in sin.

But what is infinitely more gracious and glorious, one day God will send a second Man, a last Adam, to win out where they so miserably failed (Gen. 3:15; more on this in chapter 3).

As the scene closes, God pronounces His judgments on the couple (Gen. 3:16–19), and they begin to ponder the repercussions of their act. Their responsibilities and structures—work and marriage—remain. But all will be more difficult, and physical death waits at the end. Childbirth will be an agony, and the relationship between husband and wife will become a difficult competition (v. 16). Man's work will be difficult and frustrating, until he returns to the dust (vv. 17–19).

From the Heights to the Depths

We have learned what the world does not know: what it means to be human. Our father Adam was created as God's image, a being apart, designed to rule for God. His wife was to be his partner in this adventure, working together in harmony to serve God.

Our first parents' characters were prepared to mirror God's, their spirits fashioned to commune with His Spirit. God gave them minds and wills and imaginations, to be fully employed in hearing His commands and prohibitions, and in figuring out how to carry them out to His glory.

Here is where we went wrong. Eve came under the sway of God's chief slanderer, the Serpent. She bought his lie that rebellion would lead to knowledge and Godhood, and Adam placidly followed along. In rebelling against God, Adam brought ruin on himself, his wife, and all his children. He left the fullness of life enjoyed in God's presence, and came to know guilt and death and fractured relationships with God and other humans. The brilliant mind crafted to think God's thoughts was turned into a ceaseless laboratory of deception.

So what comes next for our race? How far do the consequences of this one man's act go? Does his crime have any impact beyond the two of them? Can it possibly affect us, so many thousands of years later?

Read on.

Chapter 3

Like Father, Like Son

Any Hope That Was an Isolated Incident?

What we just studied is commonly called "the Fall." But I have long thought that *fall* is too mild a word for what happened in the Garden. It was a collapse, a catastrophe, a devastation. It was a disaster, a crash, a cataclysm.

But wasn't that just Great-gramma and Great-grampa? That was *them*, those two people. Long, long ago. You weren't there. I'm old, but even I wasn't there. What is the connection between them and us? Aren't we all our own Adams and Eves, facing our own tests in our own Gardens?

Hardly.

For one thing, Moses (the author of Genesis) does not present the story as if this were an isolated event. Some historical events are freighted with significance beyond the simple actions that narration relates: The crossing of the Rubicon, the signing of the Declaration of Independence, and the Supreme Court's 1973 ruling on *Roe v. Wade*, are three such events that spring to mind.

This event dwarfs them all.

Though we are reading about something that took place on this planet, in space and time, on a given day, the story's significance looms larger than the isolated elements of the narrative. The shadow cast by these events touches every man, woman, and child who has ever drawn breath on this big spinning ball—and some who haven't.

For one thing, our great-grandparents' very names are representative. "Adam" is simply the Hebrew word for *human being.* Adam is *a* man, and Adam is *Man*. As went Adam, so would go Man. And Adam's wife is first called simply "woman" (Gen. 2:22–23). Then she is called "Eve," which in Hebrew looks like the word for "life," because she was the mother of all living humans (Gen. 3:20).

For another, we read in Genesis 5:3 that when "Adam had lived 130 years, he fathered a son in his own likeness, after his image." This is a deliberate echoing of man's creation in God's image and likeness (Gen. 1:26; 5:1–2). God made Adam as His image and likeness, Adam had a child who was *his* likeness and image. Adam (finitely) resembled the perfect God; Adam's child (quite) resembled the fallen Adam. The image Adam received by creation was unmarred, until he rammed sin into it and wrecked it. The image was still there (Gen. 9:6), but it was disfigured. And that marred image was what every child of Adam then bore.

What is more, we see the spread through Adam's children, who commit murder (4:8), polygamy (4:19), and violence (4:23). And they keep dying, dying, dying (the sonorous refrain of Genesis 5: "and he died . . . . and he died . . . and he died"). The human history is a tale of the interweaving of sin and death.

"Sin"—Do you know what it means?

We discussed the meaning of "death" earlier, but we haven't yet opened up "sin." It is in this section that we first encounter the word in Scripture: "If you do well, will you not be accepted? And if you do not do well, sin is crouching at the door. Its desire is for you, but you must rule over it" (Gen. 4:7). Here, God is counseling Cain. He depicts sin as crouching like a wild animal, with a burning desire to dominate Cain.

What is sin, anyway?

The Hebrew verb is used in a literal sense of missing a target (Judg. 20:16). In the moral/spiritual arena, sin is missing the mark of God's holy character and law (which is an expression of God's character). Break God's law, and we assault God. Insist on our wills over God's, and we attempt deicide. Sin is a big deal.

Sin is lawlessness (1 John 3:4), being my own law and authority and god (cf. Gen. 3:5). It is a heart that hates God and His will (Rom. 8:7), which issues in love for things God hates, and hatred for things God loves, which in turn gives birth to doing things God forbids, and failing to do things God commands (cf. Matt. 15:18–20; Gal. 5:19–21).

Mark well: The "target" is not how well or poorly my neighbor lives. Being better than an ax murderer does not equal an automatic "pass." Nor does following my inner light. The target, the standard of testing, is the holy will and character of God. Miss that absolute standard even once—by ever once failing to love God above all (Matt. 22:37–38), or ever once sexually lusting after anyone other than your spouse (Matt. 5:28), or ever once lying (Col. 3:9)—and we are sinners, guilty and doomed.

Adam missed the mark, as did Eve. And that natural addiction to lawlessness passed on through his children, as we see in Genesis 4 and 5.

How far does it go?

Back to the narrative to find out.

The same bleak tale unfolds in Genesis 6, where God assesses the entire human race and finds "that the wickedness of man was great in the earth, and that every intention of the thoughts of his heart was only evil continually" (Gen. 6:5). That last phrase is literally "only evil all the day." It calls to mind the later observations of David, that the wicked "plots trouble while on his bed" (Ps. 36:4), and Isaiah speaking of those "who rise early in the morning, that they may run after strong drink" to get drunk (5:11). Every hour of every day is an opportunity for the effects of the Fall to show themselves.

Even after the Flood, when God wipes the earth clean of all but righteous Noah and his family, even among that select remnant sin shows itself. Noah gets drunk (Gen. 9:21), and Ham brings a curse on himself (v. 22f.).

Nor are any of the patriarchs without sin. In fact, you could simply bring this tale to a sum by saying that the whole rest of the Bible—in fact the rest of human history—traces the effects of the Fall in our race.

Beyond Genesis's narrative of sin and death, we have . . .

Categorical Biblical Diagnosis of Human Fallenness: Old Testament

It is sometimes said that the notion of "original sin" or "total depravity" (i.e., that every part of us is warped by sin) was either invented by the apostle Paul, or was made up later by Christian theologians. The claim is false. Prophets, sages, Christ, and the apostles all unite in reading off the dreadful effects of Adam's sin. Genesis itself treats sin as pandemic. So do all the narratives of the OT.

Beyond that, we have many categorical statements. To Genesis 6:5 (above) we may add 1 Kings 8:46, where Solomon confesses to God that there is no *'ādām*, no human being, who does not sin.

None? Not even one? That is what the sagacious sovereign says. Why is that? If the nature of all men is neutral or good, would not *fifty*, or *thirty*, or even *one* refrain from sin?

Solomon rules that out. "None," he says.

As if that were not clear enough, Solomon adds this in his book of thoughtful sayings: "Who can say, 'I have made my heart pure; I am clean from my sin'?" (Prov. 20:9). The answer Solomon clearly expects is, "No one." His diagnosis is categorical and absolute. He can make it without qualification. No natural-born son of Adam will ever arise, able to claim purity.

Why not? Because when our representative (Adam) fell, we fell too. When he was judged, the humanity he stood for was judged. When we were conceived, we bore his fallen, guilty, corrupted likeness.

Job agrees, asking, "Who can bring a clean thing out of an unclean?" and answering, "Not one" (Job 14:4). Dogs have puppies, cats have kittens, and large sinners give birth to little sinners.

Godly David, the man after God's heart, fell into shocking sin. Why? Was he born upright, but went wrong? No, he says, "I was brought forth in iniquity, and in sin did my mother conceive me" (Ps. 51:5). David is not talking about his mother's taint of sin, but his own; his first existence was in sin. Sin was David's by nature, and later became his by choice (v. 4).

Every department affected. People sometimes think of sin as strictly an issue of actions. It is not. The OT portrays sin as affecting every part of our makeup.

For instance, David depicts Yahweh making an inspection of humanity. Here are His findings:

> The LORD looks down from heaven on the children of man,
>   to see if there are any who understand,
>   who seek after God.

> They have all turned aside; together they have become corrupt;
>> there is none who does good,
>> not even one. (Ps. 14:2–3)

The psalm began with a remark about the fool (v. 1). However, lest we think that only one kind of person (the stupid kind) is in view, David broadens the scope to take in all of Adam's sons. The verdict is universal, sin has affected

> intellect/moral judgment (none understand);
> spiritual orientation (none seek after God);
> life orientation (all have turned aside); and
> morality (all have become corrupt; none does good).

In case we didn't get the message, David rewords it in Psalm 53:1–3. What he sings is actually quite comprehensive, isn't it? Intellectual and moral judgment, spiritual and life orientation, morality . . . what major area of life does that leave out? Sin has polluted every bit of us and every one of us.

In itself this statement rounds up Jew and Gentile alike—all humanity. But some might say, "Surely the chosen nation of Israel is an exception, isn't it?" Not at all; in fact, God finds their depravity all the more worthy of condemnation. The greater the privilege, the greater the condemnation when one goes wrong. God later says to Israel, "You only have I known of all the families of the earth; therefore I will punish you for all your iniquities" (Amos 3:2).

In fact, the verse that hit me between the eyes before my conversion to Christ was Isaiah 64:6, which reads:

> We have all become like one who is unclean,
>> and all our righteous deeds are like a polluted garment.

We all fade like a leaf,
and our iniquities, like the wind, take us away.

Did you catch that? Not merely "all our *sins* are like a polluted garment," but "all our *righteous deeds* are like a polluted garment"! Sin so contaminates every area of our being that deeds done in religious service are tainted with self-love, self-seeking, self-worship.

Further, the Hebrew word daintily translated "a polluted garment" actually refers to a used menstrual cloth. It is a deliberately rude, repellant image. From it, we should glean some idea of God's visceral reaction to the religious, moral deeds of a man or woman still enslaved to sin.

Not only do our evil deeds condemn us; even our moral deeds damn us.

Categorical Biblical Diagnosis of Human Fallenness: New Testament

We have seen that the teaching of human lostness is a broad and deep theme found throughout the OT. So much for the notion that any apostle or later church council concocted the doctrine.

What of the NT preachers and writers, movers and shakers? What was their position on man's inherent nature and his record before God?

People sometimes forget that Jesus and the apostles were not liberal Protestants. They were true Israelites who heartily accepted the OT's self-testimony. Jesus and the apostles all emphatically affirmed the God-breathed origin and inerrancy of the OT (John 10:35; 2 Tim. 3:15–17; 2 Peter 1:21). They accepted its teachings without reservation.

It cannot surprise us, then, to find that they all affirmed the OT's teaching about the universal spread and all-pervading nature of sin. Not only does the NT affirm this teaching of the OT, it builds on it and develops it.

Of course we must start with the teaching of Jesus. Everyone wants Jesus on his religious bandwagon, from "God wants you rich" preachers to "God wants you limp" preachers. What did Jesus say about the native human condition?

Let us start with His first recorded sermon in the first canonical Gospel. It was brief, seven words in Greek. Here it is, in full: "Repent, for the kingdom of heaven is at hand" (Matt. 4:17). Jesus' first word, "Repent," translates the Greek word *metanoeite* (meta-no-AY-teh), which indicates a change of mind so fundamental, so root-to-branch, that the life changes as a consequence.[1] "God's kingdom is hanging over your heads like an anvil about to drop," Jesus says in effect. "So everything about the way you think has got to change."

What is the premise of such a command?

- If we were naturally right with God and unconditionally accepted, would Christ have said "Repent"? No. He might have said, "Well done, lads! Carry on, I'm right behind you!"
- If we were basically okay and good-hearted, just needed to try a little harder, or think about God a little more, would Christ have said "Repent"? No. He might have said, "Come on, now; put your back into it!"
- If we were fundamentally sound, except for this and that sin, would Christ have said "Repent," categorically, with no qualifiers? No. He might have said, "Repent of your thievery," or "Repent of your immorality."

Instead, Jesus says "*Repent*. Change your most basic assumptions. Everything must be overhauled, from the ground up. *Repent!*"

---

1. We will study repentance more closely in chapter 7.

The premise? *Everything about how you and I think is fundamentally wrong.*

How did that happen to us? Jesus did not need to lay the foundation all over again. The OT—which Jesus assumed, remember—already explained it all for us. Nothing had changed. Man still was what man had become in Adam.

In fact, Jesus scopes out our hearts, and what He finds is dire and grim, and not at all hopey-changey. Jesus peers into the hearts of men, and what does He see?

> For from within, out of the heart of man, come evil thoughts, sexual immorality, theft, murder, adultery, coveting, wickedness, deceit, sensuality, envy, slander, pride, foolishness. All these evil things come from within, and they defile a person. (Mark 7:21–23)

What a nasty menagerie—but it is the same picture we got from the OT. It is a picture of *death,* of *spiritual* death. Adam was created in God's image. He sinned. He *died,* and since then, all his children have been spiritually stillborn.

That being the case, what would Jesus prescribe? What do we need? A program of good works, of self-effort, of self-improvement?

In chapters 4 through 6 we will study at length God's eternal plan to rescue humanity. We will learn from it that, for us to be rescued, *God Himself* must act personally and as a mighty king (cf. Matt. 20:28). Our natures are so ravaged by sin that we can contribute nothing, not a penny's worth, to what He will do to save us. That fact in itself will reflect eloquently on our sinful natures.

But here I focus on how Jesus' teachings reflect on our moral natures. Does He think we all have a spark of good within us, which needs only be nurtured and fed and cherished?

Hardly.

Jesus gives *two* extreme prescriptions, for what we need in the face of His teaching.

First extreme prescription: cross. Jesus tells His followers they must pick up their cross and follow Him (Luke 9:23). A *cross* is not a symbol of trying harder, of promising to do better, of really knuckling down, getting serious, and having "the eye of the tiger."

A cross is not where you go to *work out*, as if to build up what is already there.

A cross is where you go to *die*, which is the final negation of the sin-riddled nature we inherit from Adam.

That command alone tells us everything we need to know about ourselves, as God the Son sees us. We do not need to *try*; we need to *die*.

But there is more.

Second extreme prescription: new birth. When religious, legally righteous Nicodemus comes up to have a theological chat, Jesus says, "You must be born again" (John 3:7).

How does this reflect on human nature? Remember, Jesus is not talking to a moral derelict, a drunkard or a murderer or a prostitute. He is talking to a very proper, very religious man. But Jesus holds out no hope of the kingdom of God to Nicodemus if he goes on as he is. He must be born again.

Now, a man who is basically all right does not need to be born again. "Born again" means what is already there is *all wrong*, we need to start all over with something new.[2]

It is no surprise to learn that the apostles saw things exactly as Jesus saw them. Take the man who was the first among equals, the mouth that roared, the apostle Peter. What did he teach and preach about man's condition and his deepest need?

---

2. We will study what it means to be born again in chapter 8.

Peter's first sermon on the church's birthday climaxes in this call: "Repent and be baptized every one of you in the name of Jesus Christ for the forgiveness of your sins, and you will receive the gift of the Holy Spirit" (Acts 2:38). Like Teacher, like disciple: "Repent," Jesus says; "Repent," Peter echoes. The man called Rock has Jesus' same view of man's nature and man's need.

Peter preaching the need for repentance points to the fact that mankind is all wrong in our most fundamental thinking; only in Jesus Christ can we find forgiveness of sins. There is no hope whatever in self-reform or self-efforts, or in simply doing more of the same religious practices that had kept him from God. We must repent; we must belong to Christ.

Further, when he wrote his first letter, Peter affirmed that there is no spiritual life without being born again as an act of God's grace. He does not suggest that we can manufacture a new start by our own efforts. No, the apostle leaves no hope for us in anything we can produce. Rather, Peter writes that God *caused* us to be born again out of His own *great mercy* and by means of Christ's *resurrection* from the dead (1 Peter 1:3).

What Christ taught, Peter taught.

The apostle Paul also confirmed and developed the teaching of Jesus, and his extended development is particularly rich, theologically. A full development of his teaching would take us afield from our emphasis, but let's at least take a good running skim. We will focus on some of his teaching from two of his letters: to the Romans, and to the Ephesians.

Paul's most extended theological treatise, his most systematic setting forth of the good news of Christ, is the book of Romans. The apostle introduces the Gospel as God's saving power for all believers (Rom. 1:16), His way of giving perfect righteous legal standing through faith alone (Rom. 1:17). But before he dwells any more on that good news, Paul works very hard to demonstrate conclusively that all men, women, and children are involved in sin, in repressing the truth of God and turning aside from God (Rom. 1:18–3:20). "None is righteous, no, not one," Paul writes at the head of a litany of damning quotations from the OT (Rom. 3:10–18; cf. Pss. 14:1; 53:1). All stand guilty and condemned before the holy and righteous God.

Then Paul sets forth *how* sin came to hold us all in its vice-like grip, in one magnificent section.

Romans 5:12–21, Adam and Christ. This passage is a magnificent work of theological art.[3] Here, Paul the apostle, preacher, theologian, is led by the Spirit of God to pull out all the stops, as he frames the Garden and Golgotha side by side.

Paul sees in Eden's rebellion everything we saw earlier, and much more. Adam did not sin as a lone individual, affecting himself alone. Indeed, "sin came into the world through one man, and death through sin, and so death spread to all men because all sinned" (v. 12). Adam was the representative head of humanity. What he did, he did as our head; what he experienced, we experienced.

But Paul sets up another figure, another lone individual—the Lord Jesus Christ—as head of a new subset of humanity. As with Adam, so with Christ: What He did affects all of those whom He represents—but with vastly different results. Jesus Christ is, as Paul calls him elsewhere, the "second man" and the "last Adam" (1 Cor. 15:47 and 45, respectively).

In Romans 5:12–21, Paul sets the first and last Adam side by side, and does a compare and contrast. Consider the upshot:

---

3. My interpretation and application of this section assumes a good deal of challenging analysis of the text. For an excellent (but technical) study, I still know of no better than the late S. Lewis Johnson's masterful article "Romans 5:12—An Exercise in Exegesis and Theology," in *New Dimensions in New Testament Study*, ed. Richard N. Longenecker and Merrill C. Tenney (Grand Rapids: Zondervan, 1974), 298–316.

Compare
• First and last Adam are alike in that they did not act as lone individuals.
• First and last Adam are alike in that all whom they represented were affected by what they did (vv. 12, 14–19, 21).
• First and last Adam are alike in that they affected their dependents by one act (v. 18).

Contrast	
The first Adam sinned . . .	. . . the last Adam obeyed (vv. 12, 14–19)
The first Adam brought condemnation . . .	. . . the last Adam brought justification (imputed righteousness; vv. 12, 16, 18–19)
The first Adam brought death . . .	. . . the last Adam brought life (vv. 12, 14, 17, 18, 21)

Here and elsewhere, Paul clearly sees what Moses saw as well: Adam was the representative Man. When Adam was tested, all were tested. When Adam rebelled, all were condemned. When Adam died, all died—even the billions who had not yet been born.

This explains why all are born both guilty and sinful. Otherwise, there is no explanation for our natural, ruined state. Theologian S. Lewis Johnson points us to Ephesians 2:1–5 and says that man "was either tried in Adam and fell, or he has been condemned without a trial."[4] Clearly, only the former is true.

Another place in which Paul vividly depicts our natural condition is in the book of Ephesians generally, and chapters 2 and 4 specifically. In both, Paul's intent is the same as my aim in this chapter: to show the grandeur of God's salvation in Christ, by revealing the devastation from which He saved us.

Consider first, then, Ephesians 2:1–3:

---

4. Johnson, "Romans 5:12," 312.

And you were dead in the trespasses and sins in which you once walked, following the course of this world, following the prince of the power of the air, the spirit that is now at work in the sons of disobedience—among whom we all once lived [better *conducted ourselves*] in the passions of our flesh, carrying out the desires of the body and the mind, and were by nature children of wrath, like the rest of mankind.

Paul says that we are dead. Not "resting." Not "pining for the Fjords." Not "getting better."[5] Not "only mostly dead."[6] Not merely sick and weak, though we are that (Rom. 5:6; 8:3). *Dead.*

How bad off is "dead"? Well sir, it's bad. If a patient is "recovering," there's hope. If he's "stable," there's hope. If he's "critical," there's still hope. Even if he's "in dire condition," there's still hope.

But if he's dead, that's it. The music swells, the credits roll, the movie is *over.*

Notice that the word *dead* doesn't admit any modifiers. Someone might be "a bit lively," or he might be "very lively." But nobody is "a bit dead" or "very dead." There are not degrees of death. Death is an absolute. It is a toggle switch, not a dimmer.

My beloved father's death on New Year's Day, 1993, was very upsetting to me. His spiritual condition was uncertain, and the manner of his death infuriating (cancer, which had been long misdiagnosed and mistreated). After Dad died, the phrase, "We lost Dad," became very poignant to me. He was *lost* to me, irrecoverably lost in terms of this life. With every passing day, I felt Dad moving

---

5. If you don't "get" those three references, ask a fan of the 1970s British comedy troupe Monty Python.
6. And if you don't "get" *that*, ask a fan of the movie *The Princess Bride.* I will try to back away from the cultural references for a while, now that all that's out of my system.

farther away. It was as if he had gotten out of the car, and the car was moving inexorably forward. He was being left farther and farther behind.

In my dreams, I kept "saving" him; that is, he kept being *back*, thanks to this or that medical miracle or treatment.

But of course all those dreams were illusory. My dear dad was simply and finally gone from this world the moment his spirit left his body. There would be no recovery in this life. There was no backing the "car" up to let him back in. I would not find a cure. He was not more dead a week later; he is not more dead now, nearly two decades later.

This is how Paul describes our spiritual condition: *dead.* The Greek word for "dead" means "D-E-A-D." It doesn't carry any special, technical, secret nuance detectable only by professional lexicographers. It is used many times—in the NT of sleep-diver Eutychus after his fatal plunge from the third story (Acts 20:9), or in the Greek translation of the narrative about Sisera, after Jael nailed his head to the ground (Judg. 4:22).

What do these all have in common?

They're all *dead!* As dead as Moses. As dead as King Tut. As dead as Marcus Aurelius, Confucius, Augustine, and any other *dead* person you can name.

Do you really believe it? All Christians who say they believe the Bible have to say they believe this verse. But do they? I wonder.

I thought I believed it, once, as a younger Christian. But I also thought that I was saved by exercising my free will, by my deciding to choose Christ, by bringing something that made God's *offer* of salvation work, by coming up with the faith through which I was saved. Yet at the same time, I did have a vague notion that it was all of God . . . but then, there was my part.

A *dead* guy's part.

I was confused. I think a lot of Christians are confused.

But Paul says *dead,* and *dead* is what he means. In fact, ask yourself this: If Paul had meant to paint man as spiritually dead and absolutely powerless to help himself or move himself toward God in any way—what stronger word could he have chosen? What is deader than *dead?*

All are spiritually dead—yet we do have to say this is a strange sort of death. Notice how Paul says that we were "dead in the trespasses and sins in which you once *walked* . . . we all once [*conducted ourselves*] in the passions of our flesh, *carrying out* the desires of the body and the mind" (Eph. 2:1–3, emphasis added). So Paul does not mean "dead" in the sense of "inactive, motionless."

The apostle means "dead" in the sense we defined it above: the utter loss of spiritual life, of the joy and blessings of God's presence. Bereft of God and all of His traits that He can reproduce in us, such as holiness, righteousness, wisdom, purity, and love. Or as he puts it in Ephesians 2:12, "without Christ, alienated from the citizenry of Israel and strangers to the covenants of promise, not having hope and godless[7] in the world" (DJP).

So, in a way, we are like the undead of horror movie fame. We are like zombies. The brains we eat are our own (Prov. 1:7, 22; 10:21; 15:14; 18:2; 28:26; Jer. 8:8–9; Rom. 1:18, 21–22).

Or again, we are like dead people who keep stabbing themselves in the heart, shooting themselves in the head, hanging themselves, and drinking poison. How so? Because we are dead because of sin, and in our death we sin and sin and sin. So it is a dreadful sort of death-life, an animation, an active existence that parodies life. It is un-life: hopeless, helpless, shut off and cut off.

Further, we must not forget that sin affects every aspect of us, not just morality or spirituality. Paul says that the Gentiles walk

---

7. The word is *atheoi* (AH-theh-oi), whence we get "atheist." It means not to have God, not to have a real relationship with Him.

in the pointlessness of their *mind*, being abidingly darkened in their *understanding*, abidingly alienated from the *life* of God on account of the *ignorance* which is in them, on account of the *hardness* of their *heart*; who, having become *morally numb*,[8] delivered themselves over to *outrageousness* resulting in the working of every kind of *uncleanness*, with a hunger for more and more. (Eph. 4:17–19 DJP)

From the word translated "mind" in v. 17 (*nous*, nooce) we get the theological phrase "the noetic effects of sin"—the cognitive, or mental/intellectual effects of sin. That is, sin not only makes us behave badly, it makes us think badly. Sin puts a virus in our wetware, to adapt IT terminology. It throws a monkey wrench in our entire way of processing and valuing information. We may see things, but we do not see them as they are, do not know what they mean, do not rank priorities rightly. We look at the world through distorted lenses.

What's worse, we don't know it, and we can't help ourselves.

It is simply the way we are.

Thanks a lot, Great-grampa Adam.

The Upshot

We opened our exploration in chapter 1 with Calvin's conundrum: where to start. With God, or with ourselves? Calvin went on to say that it was essential that we come to the end of ourselves, be "stung" with our own unhappiness, and in that way we are led up to God:

Thus, from the feeling of our own ignorance, vanity, poverty, infirmity, and—what is more—depravity and corruption,

8. The word means to be past pain, past feeling.

we recognize that the true light of wisdom, sound virtue, full abundance of every good, and purity of righteousness rest in the Lord alone. To this extent we are prompted by our own ills to contemplate the good things of God; and we cannot seriously aspire to him before we begin to become displeased with ourselves. For what man in all the world would not gladly remain as he is—what man does not remain as he is—so long as he does not know himself, that is, while content with his own gifts, and either ignorant or unmindful of his own misery? Accordingly, the knowledge of ourselves not only arouses us to seek God, but also, as it were, leads us by the hand to find him.[9]

God's view of us summarized. Now we have seen ourselves as God sees us:

- God designed us to reflect Him and serve Him.
- Our representative/forefather sinned, and plunged us all into death, sin, guilt, and misery of every kind.
- We have willingly plunged down the path Adam opened up.
- Sin has left us helpless and hopeless, without either hope of natural recovery or hope of self-improvement.
- We're dead.
- Dead people don't and can't help themselves.

That is a grim analysis. What must be done to save us—if *anything* is to be done?

Imagine that you walk into a morgue. Corpses on every slab, right and left. Death everywhere.

---

9. Calvin, *Institutes*, 37.

Ah, but you bring them a precious gift! You have the elixir of life in your hand! One sip, and they will live!

So you preach to them. You "sell" the drink. You offer them the elixir. You appeal to them, beg them, plead with them. At the climax of your utterly convincing, flawlessly reasoned address, you set the golden chalice on a table in the center and issue an invitation. All who will may come, and drink, and live! Come! Come now! Your friends will wait for you!

And the response is . . . well, let's just say it's very peaceful. A cricket in the corner scrapes his lonely melody.[10]

My point: If there is to be a rescue operation for us children of Adam, aimed at bringing us to anything like God meant us to be, it has to overcome not only our sin and depravity, but the fact that sin makes us utterly uninterested in the solution. In fact, we would be repelled by it.

C. S. Lewis spoke for us all: "Amiable agnostics will talk cheerfully about 'Man's search for God.' To me . . . they might as well have talked about the mouse's search for the cat."[11]

Can You Handle the Truth?

This was all a crucial first step. We cannot understand what God has done for us, or wants for us, until we come to grips with where Adam put us, what sin has made us. After all, "our doing is rooted in our being. Who we are is more fundamental than what we do."[12] From the heart flows the details of life (Prov. 4:23), and the heart is absolutely hopeless left to itself (Jer. 17:9), because it is dead (Eph. 2:1), hates God (Rom. 8:7), and is unable to come to Him (John 6:44a).

---

10. This is a developed extension of a metaphor drawn from Cornelius van Til, *Defense of the Faith*, 18.
11. Lewis, *Surprised by Joy*, 227.
12. Wells, *Courage to Be Protestant*, 247.

That is not just bad news. It is terrible news. It is the worst sort of news.

But it is where we must start.

Now—ready for some really good news? Not just good news, but wonderful news?

So am I. But first . . .

Part One Summary

How does all this make me a world-tilter and a barrier-buster?

Tilting the world. We learned that the way man sees himself, and the way God sees man, are exact opposites.

The World	God
• People are basically good, and have basically good goals. Mostly, we just need help feeling better about ourselves and attaining our goals.	• People are sinners by nature and by choice, blissfully in love with ourselves, rebellious against God, and clueless about the true nature or depth of our problem.
• We should trust our hearts and look for the answers within.	• Our hearts are deceptive and incurable. We must seek the answers from God.
• We are becoming better and better, naturally.	• We will only grow worse unless something radical is done supernaturally.
• In sum: Our problems are external, and the answers are internal.	• In sum: Our problems are internal, and the answers are external.

Even many Christians shrink from the Bible's frank, bold, and shattering pronouncements about where sin has put us. They want to reserve something to us. They insist on seeing something in man that wants to reach out to the true God, though Scripture says he does not (Rom. 3:11). It is threatening and unsettling to think of man as that bad off. Plus, they know it would be offensive to tell anyone anything like that.

We must deal with the fact: The Gospel is offensive to human pride. If what we preach as "Gospel" is not offensive, we're doing it wrong. An inoffensive Gospel is a false Gospel, a damning Gospel— because the only Gospel that saves is the Gospel that offends (1 Cor. 1:18, 21, 23; 2:2; Gal. 1:10; 5:11; 6:12, 14).

It is time that we understood that offensive, saving Gospel.

So let's do.

Part Two

What Has God Done for Us?

The Eternal Plan Conceived, Predicted, Executed

Chapter 4

The God Who Plans

Can't Grasp the Deed Without a Glimpse of the Doer

Our eyes open on an operating room.

We've never seen such a scene. Impossibly complicated machines are busily engaged. We see blinking, flashing, pulsing; we hear beeping, buzzing, throbbing. A dozen measurements display on a dozen monitors. Tubes, wires, even arcing electricity fill the room.

One full complement of antiseptically garbed professionals rushes about, working intently on a patient in the center of the surgical theater. Instruments flash, experts lean in, all attention is riveted on this figure and the controlling machinery surrounding him. Off to their right stands another complete team, uniformed and equipped, waiting for their cue to dive in and begin their specialized assignment. On the other side, to the left, another squad reclines on cots, resting.

A clock on the wall reads Time elapsed, and gives a figure of eighteen hours, forty-seven minutes, nineteen seconds . . . twenty . . . twenty-one . . .

And we gasp, *Good heavens, what a desperate ruin this poor soul must be, that such a massive-scale operation was necessary!*

Blink. Our eyes open again on a garden.

It is nighttime. Before us, we immediately recognize the figure of Jesus Christ—but we are seeing Him as no one has ever seen Him. This man who has stared down thousands of hell's foulest demons without blinking, who has shut up storms with a curt word of command, who has reduced the human powers to babbling, loose-bowelled nonsense—is falling down in horror, and He is pleading with His Father.

Listen. What does He ask?

"Abba, Father, all things are possible for you. Remove this cup from me. Yet not what I will, but what you will" (Mark 14:36).

The Father has never through all eternity denied a request of the Son. Surely He will grant this! Yet Christ pleads it once . . . twice . . . three times. There is no answer. The Father says nothing.

Another first—and an alarming one.

An angel appears. We hear no words. But the Son rises. He squares His shoulders. He goes forth, meets a jittery and heavily armed crowd. He allows Himself to be arrested.

Too horrified to look away, we watch from afar as He is led off, as He is subjected to atrocious and repellant mockeries of justice; as He is beaten, whipped to a ragged walking corpse; as He is mocked, condemned, and sent off carrying a cross.

To that cross He is nailed. On that cross He bleeds. He groans under glowering, angry, darkened skies. Our gut clenches and we gasp to hear Him cry out in prayer once again, this time to the silent heavens, "My God, My God, why have You forsaken Me?" He lets out a loud cry . . .

And He—the resurrection and the life; the way, the truth, the life; the bread of life—*dies.*

Nauseated with horror, through numb lips we murmur, "Dear God, why? What a desperate ruin must we be, that such a massive-scale operation was necessary!"

For, you see, the Bible is clear that the miserable, lonely death of the Son of God was *absolutely necessary* for the recovery and redemption of men and women. If such extreme measures were an absolutely necessity—and they were—then the ruin from which we needed to be rescued must have been far worse, and far more comprehensive, than many imagine. As we are about to see, the cross of Christ underscores the truth of what we just learned about man, and our need for what we are about to learn.

Where We Are

We have taken a brief but unsparing look at God's assessment of man. It wasn't pretty. Our rebellion in Adam has left us dead, doomed, and not only helpless but positively disinterested in helping ourselves back into a relationship with God as God and Lord. What is worse, everything we dream up to improve our situation actually worsens it.

That being the case, how can we get to be on good terms with this God before whom we must "give account" (Heb. 4:13)? We must have a directly biblical understanding of that God. Otherwise, human-viewpoint barriers will prevent us from grasping His plan of rescue and restoration, and how that makes us world-tilters.

The Predicate in God

What kind of God is God? Cults that are influenced by Eastern thought dismiss the notion of God being a *person.* In its place, they substitute gauzy notions that make God out to be a sort of cosmic fog bank: vaguely comforting, gray, malleable, shapeless, and well-nigh featureless. (Though even in this attempt, they cannot avoid descriptions; their God is a person, too—just a bland, boring, unthreatening, uninvolved person.)

The God of the Bible is starkly different in every regard.

The living God of the Bible is described repeatedly and emphatically in moral terms, in language bristling with that element we hate in our postmodern culture: value judgments. Yet even the fullest list scarcely brushes the outermost edge of the universe-overflowing reality that is God. Were I—or a far better writer—to compose a hundred books about Him, none could ever sum up (let alone explain) God.

For our purposes, I am going to single out three of God's traits: His holiness, His love, and His wisdom.

First Central Truth: God Is Holy

The trait of holiness, though absent from much modern preaching and writing, is a central character trait of God in the Bible. It may even be *the* central essential facet of God. Holiness virtually defines God.

How can I say that? The prophet Isaiah writes "thus says the One who is high and lifted up, who inhabits eternity, whose name is Holy" (Isa. 57:15). When Isaiah says that God's "name is Holy," he is saying that holiness is a fundamental defining trait of God. It is essential to His moral existence.

And well might Isaiah say that! When he was commissioned as a prophet in chapter six of his book, Isaiah finds himself in the heavenly throne room, and he sees the Lord God Himself, lofty and exalted. The very air creaks and groans, the atmosphere trembles with the immense presence of God.

Before this great King are seraphim—bright, burning angelic creatures, creatures without sin or shame or guilt. Yet even these radiant beings cover their eyes and feet with their wings, overawed by the sight of God, crying out again and again, saying . . .

"Loving, loving, loving is the LORD of hosts"?

"Gracious, gracious, gracious is the LORD of hosts"?

"Merciful, merciful, merciful"?

"Forgiving, forgiving, forgiving"?

No, though all these things are true, those are not the traits that overwhelm these luminous entities. "Holy! Holy! Holy!" They cry out "Holy!"—but once is not enough, so they say a second time "Holy!" Yet even twice does not catch it, so they shout a third time—befitting the triunity of this God—"holy is the LORD of hosts; the whole earth is full of his glory!" (Isa. 6:3). In all the Bible, *holiness* is the only attribute of God that is marked by a threefold repetition. Holiness is an overwhelming and all-encompassing trait of God. We cannot understand the first thing about God unless we have some glimmer of His holiness.

What is more, this truth about God will never change. In his prophecy, the apostle John sees other angelic creatures in heaven, and "day and night they never cease to say, 'Holy, holy, holy, is the Lord God Almighty, who was and is and is to come!'" (Rev. 4:8). Think of it: God has beings whose whole ministry forever is to shout out the praise of His attribute of holiness!

God was holy. God is holy. God will always be holy.

Many verses resound with this truth. The book of Leviticus contains frequent assertions of Yahweh's holiness, with phrases to the effect of "you shall be holy, because I, Yahweh your God, am holy" occurring over and over again (Lev. 11:44, 45; 19:2; 20:26; 21:8; 22:2).

The anonymous and undated Psalm 99 echoes Isaiah 6 (or is it the reverse?), by saying *three times* that the majestic King Yahweh is holy (vv. 3, 5, 9).

Clearly, a conscious awareness of this truth must control the way we understand everything else that can be said about God. If we do not see everything about God in the light of His holiness, we do not see God as He is.

Holiness must never be set over against other truths, nor isolated from them. It controls them. By that I mean that God's holiness is not merely a lone attribute. God's holiness overarches and gloriously radiates through all of His attributes.

If we want to understand God's love, we must know that it is a *holy* love. If we think of His goodness, it is a *holy* goodness. His righteousness is a *holy* righteousness, His wisdom a *holy* wisdom, His power a *holy* power. There is no "God is holy, *but*"; there is only "God is holy, *and*."

What is holiness, then? Both the meaning and use of the words teach us that the basic idea of *holiness* is *separation, apartness, transcendence.* In His holiness, God is indeed the Wholly Other. He has no rival, no peer, no equal. All analogies to God are necessarily distant and incomplete. This is true both as to His being and His moral character.

Moses sang,

> Who is like You among the gods, Yahweh?
> Who is like you,
> majestic in holiness,
> fearful in praises,
> doing wonders? (Exod. 15:11 DJP)

This note of the incomparability, the holy *otherness* of God, is a large and recurrent theme in Scripture (cf. Exod. 8:10; 1 Sam. 2:2; Pss. 35:10; 71:19; 77:13; 89:6; 113:5; Isa. 44:7; etc.). He is high and lofty, removed from mankind, and His name is Holy (Isa. 57:15).

That is, unlike everything else, God is self-existent and dependent on absolutely nothing for His being. By contrast, all created things are dependent from the first nanosecond of their existence, and so they continue onward through every subsequent moment. In their every thought and breath, every last creature depends upon God (Ps. 104:27–30; Dan. 5:23). All things hold together, even at the subatomic level, only by the sustaining work of God the Son (Col. 1:17).

The reverse is not true (Acts 17:24–25). God is independent of creation.

Perhaps some illustrations of the impact of God's holiness will help us break this truth down. Recall Moses' encounter with Yahweh at the burning bush. In that moment, Moses was warned to take the sandals off his feet, since the manifest presence of Yahweh made it "holy ground" (Exod. 3:5). How so? Super-soil? Dyno-dirt? Not at all. That plot of ground was set apart from all other ground, because God was appearing there, at that moment. His holy presence hallowed the site. No "historical marker" along America's highways can approach the dignity of this place, made holy by the visible manifestation of the very presence of God.

Or again, God set apart ("made holy") the seventh day as the day on which He rested (Gen. 2:3), and He later told Israel to do the same, to set it apart from all others (Exod. 20:8). Saturday, for the Jew, would be different from Sunday, Monday, Tuesday, and the rest. It must be distinct, different.

An even more vivid illustration is the tabernacle. The whole structure was called a "holy" building. God called for a special ceremony, involving holy anointing oil (Exod. 30:25–26). This oil was of a distinctive mixture, and thus was set apart to God, withheld from common use (v. 32) on pain of being cut off from Israel (v. 33). This oil was applied to the tabernacle structure, which made it *holy*, set it apart from all other structures in Israel (Exod. 40:9).

The tabernacle wasn't a lounge, a pool hall, a coffee shop. It was not a community center, where everyone could just stroll in and hang out. It was set apart to God's ownership and service. It was separate, distinct.

But back *within* that set-apart building was a smaller structure that was divided into two compartments. The first compartment was called the "Holy Place" (Heb. 9:2). It was doubly set apart/holy/ sanctified: a set-apart compartment *within* the set-apart building. Priests (and *only* priests) entered in pursuit of their daily duties (v. 6).

Beyond the "Holy Place" was a second compartment called "the Holy of Holies," which in Hebrew syntax means "the Most Holy Place" (Exod. 26:33; Heb. 9:3). How was this partition "most set apart"? Virtually nobody in the world could enter it (Lev. 16:2)— certainly no Gentile, no common Israelite, no common priest, no king nor ruler. Only one man could ever enter that compartment: the high priest from the descendants of Aaron, who wore a crown engraved, "Holy to the LORD" (Exod. 28:36). Only he could cross the threshold, and even he could enter only on one day of the year, and that only with special ceremonies and offerings (Lev. 16:3ff.; Heb. 9:7).

So you see: "*most* holy" = *most* set apart.

The whole tabernacle was constructed after a pattern that Yahweh showed Moses on the mountain (Exod. 25:40). That pattern communicated realities above and beyond the earthly structure. The tabernacle symbolically represented the throne and dwelling place of Yahweh (Exod. 25:22; cf. Heb. 8:5; 9:23–24; 10:1, 19–22), the thrice holy God of Israel.

How can a *thing* such as a tent or a glorified barbecue be called "holy"? They have no special, magical properties in themselves. They are all created objects. What makes them "holy"?

They are "holy" by virtue of association with God.

God is the original; He is the definition; He is the source. God naturally possesses holiness by virtue of being God. Holiness is not conferred on God, or achieved by Him. He is holy because He is who He is. He is "the Holy One of Israel." When we give Him a holy place as Lord in our hearts (Isa. 8:13; 1 Peter 3:15), we add nothing to Him. We are only crediting Him with being what He is in truth.

Because of this perfection of beauty in God's being, He is ethically or morally apart. I think we can say that God is not holy because He does holy things; but God does do holy things—and only holy things—because He is holy. God alone is permanently, utterly, and immovably consistent with His moral excellence, His righteousness. He does only what is right and good; He is capable of doing only what is right and good (Deut. 32:4; 2 Sam. 22:31; Pss. 92:15; 97:2; Jer. 9:24; Hab. 1:13).

In connection with this, we notice how anyone and everyone who receives a vision of God in Scripture is overwhelmed with His holiness. Consider how Isaiah the prophet is overcome by God's radiant, transcendent purity. Everything we know about Isaiah is positive. He is a godly man, a faithful prophet, a literary genius. Yet when Isaiah beholds the angels celebrating God's holiness, he spontaneously cries out in terror and shame, and needs to have atonement applied to him (Isa. 6:5).

Consider Job, who was "blameless and upright, one who feared God and turned away from evil" (Job 1:1). Nonetheless, the sight of God drove Job to unconditional self-loathing repentance (42:5–6).

As Yahweh affected OT believers, so did the Lord Jesus in the New Testament. A brief glimpse of Christ's nature drove Peter to his knees, unable to bear His presence (Luke 5:8). And neither can we bear His presence.

The tremendous reality of God's holiness gives us a glimpse of our massive dilemma. It is easy to sum up our dismal predicament in two succinct points:

1. God is holy.
2. We aren't.

And there is our nightmarish quandary. We are unholy. How can unholy creatures have a relationship with such a holy God?

We are heading toward the answer to that question. At present, however, we are still talking about who God is in Himself.

Second Central Truth: God Is Love

If God's holiness receives little mention in modern preaching, His love receives almost exclusive focus.

Love is indeed a grand attribute of God. After all, the apostle says, "God is love" (1 John 4:8, 16)—which, let us note, is very different from saying "love is God." Scripture portrays love as central to a truthful vision of God. We do not know God rightly if we do not know that God is love.

We see God displaying His love in His goodness and mercy from the opening pages of Scripture. The first five and one-half days of creation served not only to make earth a home for man, but to make it a beautiful and delightful home. The munificence of Creation's bounty was and remains a testimony to the love of God.

God lovingly trusted this gorgeous, rich masterpiece to Adam and Eve to subdue and rule for Him, equipping them with every internal and external asset they'd need (Gen. 1:26–28). God told them to have lots of kids, and designed it to be loads of fun for them to do so (Gen. 1:28). He put them in the Garden and bid them eat freely of all His fruits and vegetables (Gen. 1:29–30). He only made one exception—the single fruit that would bring them death if they ate it (Gen. 2:16)—and He lovingly warned them about that fruit. Further, God spoke to them, He communed with them, He gave of Himself to them. All these gifts and commands alike are displays of His love.

This extravagant generosity teaches us much about God. His love is never a mere emotion, a cheap greeting-card sentiment that spurs no action. Nor is it a frustrated longing that lacks the will or power to deliver.

God's love is a bursting, robust, dynamic rushing river. It moves Him to act, it overwhelms barriers, it smashes obstacles, it topples powers. It throws a vivid, gorgeous, delicious universe onto a blank canvas as a love-gift for His image bearers.

God's love is a mighty, powerful thing.

Having said that, having taken just a peek at the force of super-nature that is the love of God, it's important that we at least attempt to construct a biblical definition of God's love. To know God we must understand Him as well as we're able, sticking to what He reveals of Himself as closely as we can. Here, then, is the definition I'd propose: As an attribute of God, love is *that motivating excellence which moves Him to plan and act to accomplish what is for His greatest glory, and what is for His people's highest good.*

This is a shocking, world-tilting definition all in itself. Men want to see themselves as the center of the universe. We do not think of God as having Himself first in His affections. That thought offends us. We think such self-love is selfish and unworthy of God.

Yet it is undeniably true.

Love defines. A person is defined by his loves. We think that someone who loves entertainment above all is shallow and silly; someone who loves child pornography at all is sick and evil; someone who loves money above all is materialistic and grasping. God is the infinitely majestic one. Whom or what should God love above all? What worthier object of His love is there than Himself? What object of affection does God have that is worthier than God Himself?

After all, God's laws flow from His being, and His prime law is to love God with our all, *then* to love our neighbor (Matt. 22:36–40).

We are to imitate God in our love (Matt. 5:44–45; Eph. 5:1–2). If we are to love Him first, can it shock us to learn that He does the same? If we were to love any creature more than God, it would be idolatry for us. Would it not be the same for God?

"But," someone objects, "if we see anyone else loving himself first, we say he's a selfish pig. How is God not a selfish pig if He loves Himself first?"

The key to the answer comes in the two words "anyone else." With those qualifiers, the statement is absolutely true. Self-love in anyone else would be a ridiculous sin. Why? Because no one else is the center of the universe! No one else is the sum and essence of perfection and beauty. No one else is worthy of that kind of love.

Because no one else is God!

And that's a world-tilting truth.

It is not merely a factoid to be tucked away somewhere in our brainiums. This truth has momentous applications to our entire worldview, which we will ponder together later.

Before we move on, I would highlight three germane truths:

1. God can no more not love, than He can not be God; however, we must remember . . .
2. God's love must be a holy love, since all of God's attributes glow with His holiness; and
3. God's love always and necessarily and rightly has Himself as its first object.

Without a biblical grasp of these truths, our view of God is skewed and sentimental, and disastrously sub-biblical. Seeing man at the top of God's love suits the world fine; seeing *God* as God's first love—and His love for man as expressed in that light—is world-tilting.

God is holy and He is loving. We might say that these describe His *character* and His *heart*, but what of His *intellect* and *judgment*?

Third Central Truth: God Only Wise

We are looking at the character of God with an eye to our dilemma. His holiness, in isolation, makes our plight worse. God can tolerate neither sin nor sinners per se, and still be God. His holiness could be satisfied by the instant, unsparing, and eternal condemnation and punishment of every last rebel.

But God's love gives us a glimmer of hope. Perhaps God, in love, could look for a way to deal with our plight without compromising His holiness. But working out something of that magnitude—dealing with sin as the catastrophic offense that it is, while accomplishing and applying some sort of rescue and restoration—would take a degree of intelligence and wisdom that we can only imagine.

While we can only imagine it, God embodies that kind of wisdom. Wisdom is so characteristic of God that Paul can say in Romans 16:27—"to the only wise God, through Jesus Christ—to Him be the glory forever! Amen" (HCSB). God the Father is "only wise." Christ is the wisdom of God (1 Cor. 1:24). The Holy Spirit is "the Spirit of wisdom and understanding" (Isa. 11:2). God alone is the font, the source, the unalloyed original of wisdom. He is not simply "the wise God"; He is "the *only* wise God."

We cannot speak of the living God of the Bible without speaking of His wisdom. In *The Existence and Attributes of God* (1682), Stephen Charnock says that "Wisdom is the royalty of God; the proper dialect of all his ways and works. No creature can lay claim to it; he is so wise, that he is wisdom itself."[1]

Thomas Watson, in his *Body of Divinity* (1890), says that God's wisdom "is one of the brightest beams of the Godhead."[2] But, since

---

1. Charnock, *Existence and Attributes of God*, 1:506.
2. Watson, *Body of Divinity*, 50.

we cannot see God's wisdom as if it were a physical thing, can we see displays of His wisdom? Indeed we can.

Once again, we need to run our minds back to Genesis 1:1, and view it from another angle. "In the beginning, God created the heavens and the earth." God the Creator acts alone and without counsel. He does not need input from exploratory committees or expert consultants.

If Creation is an act of unimaginable power, it is no less a work of immense wisdom. Every vast and staggeringly complex movement issues from His mind. He needs no manual, counsel, or outside authority. "I, the LORD, am the maker of all things, stretching out the heavens by Myself, and spreading out the earth all alone" (Isa. 44:24b NASB).

When you watch those marvelous nature specials, you are beholding an exhibition of God's wisdom. Though the narrator blathers on about "Mother Nature," you should know better: These are the works of God's hands, and He made them all in wisdom (Ps. 104:24).

Do you ever do anything right the first time? Anything really hard? Genesis 1 narrates the first time God ever created anything—and He got it perfect. In fact, everything God does, He does perfectly, even the first time.

That is because God's wisdom, unlike ours, is immeasurable. As Job said, "With God are wisdom and might; he has counsel and understanding. . . . With him are strength and sound wisdom . . ." (Job 12:13, 16a).

Or as the psalmist says, "Great is our Lord, and abundant in power; his understanding is beyond measure" (Ps. 147:5). The Hebrew phrase for "beyond measure" is literally "there is no counting." It envisions God's understanding as broken down into specific items. In effect it says, "Try to count all those items of God's understanding. You can't!"

Theologian Louis Berkhof well says, "The knowledge of God may be defined as *that perfection of God whereby He . . . knows Himself and all things possible and actual in one eternal and most simple act.*[3] Only the God who created all things could have such knowledge. God even knows all possible things!

In 1 Samuel 23, God tells David what the people of Keilah would do if he stayed there—which David then didn't! Contrary to some new perversions of biblical teaching, there is literally nothing that God does not know exhaustively about any aspect of the future, whether in its indicative or its subjunctive mood. God equally knows what will be and what could be.

God has this knowledge because He is God, and such knowledge is definitional of the God of the Bible.

Also, God has this knowledge because of Genesis 1:1. He created all things in heaven and on earth, including heaven and earth themselves. In doing so, God created all facts. And thus God assigned meaning, value, and significance to everything. That means, then, that there are no "brute facts," only created facts, with their meaning designed and assigned by God.

God has not only infinite knowledge, but infinite *wisdom.* Knowledge is possession of data—but that is not wisdom. Wisdom is knowing what things mean, what things weigh, what is their significance.

My computer "knows" a lot. It "knows" far more things than I do. It has the Bible memorized—in Hebrew, Greek, and dozens of translations! My computer has whole libraries committed to memory.

But my computer possesses no wisdom. It does not know what any of those things mean, what they're worth, whether they're true or false, evil or righteous. It has a sort of knowledge, but no wisdom of its own, whatsoever.

---

3. Berkhof, *Systematic Theology*, 66; emphasis in original.

God has both an infinite array of facts at His command, and infinite wisdom concerning the meaning, significance, and weight of all those facts in every possible arrangement. He has that knowledge, because He created them and rules over them.

All of this is also a world-tilting truth. The current mind-set makes much of the supposed meaninglessness of "life, the universe, and all that." The common subtext of many media's storylines is that life is meaningless in itself; that we must choose our meaning and define ourselves. But history itself has no aim, meaning, or purpose.

This truth demolishes that notion, insisting that we have neither the right nor ability to redefine the universe, since it is a created universe, and since every fact has a value assigned by the Creator. Including us. We have neither the right nor ability to assign meaning to the universe. Its Author is the one who assigns definition and meaning. At best, we discover and uncover that meaning.

So how does God's wisdom combine with His holiness and love to have any impact on us in our plight?

The answer is one of the most world-tilting truths of all.

Chapter 5

God's Rescue Operation Outlined

God's Holy, Loving Wisdom Confronts Our Hopeless, Desperate Need

The attributes of God we just highlighted set the stage for the jaw-dropping majesty of God's eternal plan of rescue. We would be far from the truth if we imagined that Adam's suicidal collapse caught God off guard. Surprise God? Can't be done! God's knowledge, as we just saw, is literally infinite. He *cannot* be caught flat-footed, ever.

Nonetheless, from time to time, well-meaning (but dreadfully unbiblical) sorts have sometimes spoken as if Adam's rebellion put God in a fix, requiring that He put on His thinking cap and come up with something. Nothing could be further from the truth.

The Bible traces the origination of God's rescue plan back to the dim eons of eternity past. As we proceed, I am particularly going to stress the truth that this is not an obscure, seldom mentioned thought, hidden in the margins of the Bible. It can't be categorized and rejected as merely a Pauline thought, a Johannine thought, a Lutheran thought, or a Calvinist thought.

It is a *whole-Bible truth*.

Remember: This is *God*. The God we meet in the first verse of Scripture is a planner, not an improviser. As we noted in chapter 1, the six days of creation are beautifully and deliberately structured and targeted. When God spoke the first "Let there be," He knew exactly where He was going. The light is for man; the heavens and earth are for man; the dry land and animals and food are for man.

And man is for God, for His glory and for His plan.

How could God not have a comprehensive plan that encompasses absolutely everything? After all, He is not just Creator, but also the sovereign designer of the cosmos. While we are familiar with texts that point to God as Creator of all, we mustn't overlook the broad biblical emphasis on the fact that He is no less designer of all.

A number of OT verses use the verb *yāṣar* (yot-SAR) of God's activity. That verb is used of people carving or otherwise designing and creating idols (Isa. 44:9–10; Hab. 2:18). A form of this word is used of a potter, a skilled artisan who shapes vessels from clay (Isa. 41:25; Jer. 18:4). Used of God, the verb (emphasized in the verses below) shows that He is forming and shaping and fashioning, as an artist:

- "Then the LORD God *formed* the man of dust from the ground and breathed into his nostrils the breath of life, and the man became a living creature." (Gen. 2:7)
- "Now out of the ground the LORD God had *formed* every beast of the field and every bird of the heavens and brought them to the man to see what he would call them. And whatever the

man called every living creature, that was its name." (Gen. 2:19)

• "Have you not heard that I determined it long ago? I *planned* [formed] from days of old what now I bring to pass, that you should turn fortified cities into heaps of ruins." (2 Kings 19:25)

• "You have fixed all the boundaries of the earth; you have *made* [formed] summer and winter." (Ps. 74:17)

• "Everyone who is called by my name, whom I created for my glory, whom I *formed* and made." (Isa. 43:7)

• "Woe to him who strives with him who *formed* him, a pot among earthen pots! Does the clay say to him who forms it, 'What are you making?' or 'Your work has no handles'?" (Isa. 45:9)

Other verses speak of God founding and establishing the universe (including man) in wisdom (Prov. 3:19; Jer. 10:12; 51:15), of making all things with wisdom (Ps. 104:24) and skill (136:5). The extended poem in Proverbs 8 portrays Lady Wisdom as God's partner in the creation of all things (see especially vv. 27–31). The Hebrew word translated "wisdom" is *ḥokmâ* (<u>CH</u>OK-mah). It means (among other things) skill, the knowledge of the best way to get done what needs to be done (e.g., Exod. 36:1–2, where "skill" translates *ḥokmâ*).

Given that all creation is designed by God, it cannot surprise us to learn that God has a design—a controlling plan—that encompasses everything, from the topple of an empire (Dan. 2:21) to the tumble of a pair of dice (Prov. 16:33) to the fall of a sparrow (Matt. 10:29).

This, too, is world-tilting. The modern conception that history is meaningless and aimless is wrong. History is meaningful, and it is on target and on schedule.

This is in stark contrast to human schemes. All of the wisdom and planning skill in the world, in a creature, still could amount to nothing but nice intentions and frustrated, failed efforts. "Great idea. Too bad it didn't work," is a frequent refrain among the frail mortals residing in my house.

But God is no frail mortal! In fact, He is not a creature at all. He's massively huge beyond the borders of the universe (1 Kings 8:27), and He's powerful to the extent that He can do absolutely anything He chooses to do (Dan. 4:35). Unlike us, in God, the scope of His will and the scope of His effective power are coextensive—or, in plain English, everything He pleases, He does (Pss. 115:3; 135:6; Isa. 46:10; Rom. 9:19; Eph. 1:11). It is simple to envision graphically:

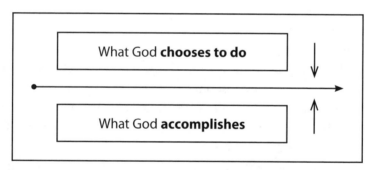

So you can actually work this both ways. Find out God's will, and you find out what is going to happen. Equally, look at what happens, and you find out God's will.

God's Eternal Plan

Put this all together, and we are unsurprised to find that God has a plan that goes back to eternity past. Paul writes of God's "plan of the ages which He made in Christ Jesus our Lord" (Eph. 3:11 DJP).

More fully, Paul said that God

selected us in Him [i.e., Christ] before the foundation of
the world, for us to be holy and unblemished before Him,
in love having foreordained us for adoption through Jesus
Christ unto Himself, in accord with the benevolence of His
will, to the praise of the glory of His grace with which He
graced us in His Beloved. (Eph. 1:4–6 DJP)

We could spend the rest of this book simply teasing out the meaning of these three verses but for now, five brief observations must
suffice.

First, this plan is eternal. That is, it was formed, laid, and determined before the first planet had spun, before the first star had
twinkled, before the first atom had popped into being.

Second, this plan addresses our major moral/spiritual problem. God "selected us . . . to be holy and unblemished before Him."
Assuming us to be unholy and blemished (see the third point), God
made a plan that would deal with our moral and spiritual deficit.
Something would be done about our crimes against Him, our brokenness, our guilt, our rebellion. Whatever would be done would
put us right in His eyes ("before Him"), and every objection that
His infinitely searching, white-hot-pure justice could raise.

Third, if He selects us to be holy, then He selects us as unholy.
That is, He is not foreseeing our decision for Christ or our faith
or our conversion. In that case, Paul would have to have said, "He
selected us as holy," or "because He knew we would become holy."
Instead, He selects us to be holy. Paul assumes that God viewed us
as unholy—which is Bible shorthand for saying that we are morally and spiritually ruined, offensive to God, under God's judgment,
without access to God and without real interest in God. But by this
plan God selects some people ("us," Christians, see verses 1 and 2)
to be holy. God is seeing us in our unholiness. Therefore, His plan is
that we become holy as a result of His selection, not as a reason for it.

Fourth, God's eternal plan also addresses our relational problem. The apostle will tell us later that we were rebels against Him in full sympathy with His enemy, the Devil (Eph. 2:1–3), and thus were aliens and estranged from God (v. 12). But God "foreordained us for adoption through Jesus Christ unto Himself, in accord with the benevolence of His will." This plan accords with the entire narrative of the Bible, which keeps cycling around the theme of man's flight from God and God's pursuit. God's plan will bring us into the most intimate relationship with Himself. He will not merely make us servants or subjects—which would be a terrific privilege—but sons, reconciled to Him, adopted into His family with full rights and privileges (John 1:12–13; Rom. 8:15; Gal. 4:5).

Fifth, His plan is that all of this reverberates to the praise of God's grace alone, or in the Latin phrase, *soli Deo gloria* ("to God alone be the glory"). The triune God formulated the plan; the triune God will execute the plan; to the triune God belongs all glory and credit and praise and thanks for every aspect of the plan. Any understanding of salvation that reserves or allows one iota of credit to man runs afoul of Paul's central thought and does it great violence.

God had a strategy set before the first tick of the first nanosecond. His plan would address both our unholiness and our spiritual deadness and distance: He would set His kingly love on us, deal with our guilt and sin, graciously bring us to Himself as adopted sons in Christ, and transform us.

But this idea did not originate with Paul. We actually find it earlier in the words of the Lord Jesus. He prayed to His Father, saying:

> Father, the hour has come; glorify your Son that the Son
> may glorify you, since you have given him authority over all
> flesh, to give eternal life to all whom you have given him.
> And this is eternal life, that they know you the only true

> God, and Jesus Christ whom you have sent. . . . I have manifested your name to the people whom you gave me out of the world. Yours they were, and you gave them to me, and they have kept your word. (John 17:1–3, 6)

Thus our Lord, in a prayer whose scope reaches back to eternity past (v. 5), speaks of a transaction between Father and Son. As Paul later assumed that all men were unholy, our Lord's words assume that all men are dead, that we lack spiritual life.

And so, the Father gives a vast subset of all mankind to the Son, that the Son may in turn give them what they lack and need: eternal life. They don't procure or extract it from Him by some ritual or program. He gives it to them as a royal grant. As in Paul's later writing, Jesus portrays the Father's actions as coming first, and as the cause of our response of faith.

God's Rescue Operation Unfolded

As we might expect, we can witness the unfolding of God's eternal plan throughout the OT, as the majestic opening words of Hebrews declare:

> Long ago, at many times and in many ways, God spoke to our fathers by the prophets, but in these last days he has spoken to us by his Son, whom he appointed the heir of all things, through whom also he created the world. (1:1–2)

Revelation was unpacked bit by bit and in various formulations. It was progressive and increasing and varied. But it was one revelation, because one God was speaking one multifaceted message. Focusing on the aspect of redemption—the plan for the rescue of mankind to God's glory—we can draw out three factors.

The Conquering Seed

Whole books have been devoted to tracing the plan of redemption through the OT. We can only briefly survey highlights. Beginning in Genesis 3:14, God announces the consequences and curses flowing from Adam and Eve's sin. God's first curse falls on the Serpent. In God's pronouncement of a curse for the Serpent, we find a promise of hope for mankind. Genesis 3:15 has long been called the *protevangelium*, which is a Latin word meaning the first preaching of the Gospel. Is that designation warranted? Here is my very literal rendering of the verse:

> And hostility shall I place between you and the woman,
>> and between your seed and her seed;
> He Himself will strike you on the head,
>> and you yourself will strike Him on the heel.

In this narrative, we notice three arresting features: different pairs, different languages, and different outcomes. We can display this graphically:

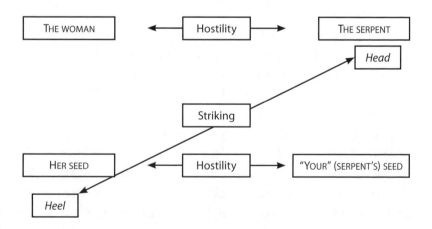

First, the different *pairs*. Initially we see two pairs in "hostility" (v. 15a): There will be hostility between the Serpent and the woman, and also between the Serpent's seed and the woman's seed.

But notice a jarring shift in conflict. Twice God speaks of "striking" in v. 15b, using the same Hebrew verb each time. Who would you expect to strike whom? Well, given the pairs in hostility, I think we'd expect the woman and the Serpent to strike each other, then the woman's seed and the Serpent's seed to strike each other.

But no. There is a startling change-up. The Serpent is struck— not by the woman, but—by the woman's Seed. And in being struck, the Serpent strikes not the woman, but the woman's Seed Himself! So it is the Seed of the woman who is to be the Champion and Deliverer of the human race.

Second, note the different *language*. Our Champion is described as "*her* seed"—the Seed of the *woman* (v. 15). The Hebrew word *zera'* (zair-AH) literally means *seed*, or *sperm*. From there, it comes to mean what is produced by the sperm, descendants. The word can by collective or singular, like our "progeny."

So perhaps you see that "*her* sperm, *her* seed" is an odd expression. That is true not only in English, but in the Hebrew OT, where the exact term "her seed" never occurs again.[1] Now, if God had spoken of the *man's* seed, we'd not bat an eyelash. Or if He'd said this of the seed of the man and woman, none would find anything unusual. But when God makes this prophecy of her seed, He seems to suggest that the Seed is conceived by a woman in some unique way.

The woman, who was deceived and subsequently transgressed God's command, is graciously made the vehicle for her race's salvation.[2]

---

1. "Your seed" is said to a woman in Genesis 16:10; 24:60; "*her* seed," here only.
2. I would not argue that this proves the virgin conception of Christ. At the very

Third, notice the different *outcomes.* The Serpent strikes the Seed on the heel, which will be painful, but not lethal. However, presumably with that heel which has been bitten, the Seed strikes the Serpent on the head—which as we all know is in snake-language means "S-s-s-s-see ya later!"

In this conflict, the woman's Seed is hurt, but in the act of being hurt, He destroys the Serpent. So here, at the dawn of human history, we have a prophecy that hints:

- A human being will avenge and deliver mankind.
- It won't be Adam, or Eve.
- It will be a male descendant of Eve.
- The conception of that human may be remarkable, unusual, perhaps miraculous.
- The way He will work salvation is by being Himself wounded, and in the wounding He will destroy the Serpent.

I believe that you could say that all the rest of the Bible, from Genesis 4 to Revelation 22, is about who and how: a Son traced through from the lineage of Abraham, who will summarily crush the Serpent's head.

Penal Substitutionary Atonement by Blood

As with the Seed, we see a twinkle of this theme immediately after the Fall. Adam and Eve had fabricated some makeshift veggiewear to cover their shame (Gen. 3:7). God tacitly rejects this covering and substitutes animal skins (v. 21). That this is a bloody

---

least, however, this prophecy sets the stage for it. When later prophecy and fulfillment features that birth, there is no excuse among biblical readers for shock.

bestowal only stands to reason. Unlike snakes, cattle and the like do not part with their sins without bloodshed.

Therefore, God was the first to shed blood in order to deal with the effects of man's sin, and bloodshed by another to deal with human guilt becomes a theme that is steadily developed as revelation moves forward. Presumably on the basis of a word from God, the pre-Flood patriarchs know that God is to be approached through bloody sacrifice (Gen. 4:4; 8:20; etc.). These animals were victims whose blood was shed to enable the human worshiper to approach God.

The Passover is perhaps the consummate example of this. The full description of the event and celebration of the Passover is found in Exodus 12. In the pivotal event of the Exodus, a flawless and innocent victim—a lamb—is separated and its blood is shed. That blood is applied to the doorways of believing Israelites' houses. Due to the shed blood of this innocent, substitutionary victim, God does not visit death on the household. The nation is saved by the blood of the unblemished lamb who died that they might live.

After the nation passes through the blood of the lamb and arrives at Sinai, God makes His covenant with the nation of Israel and constitutes them as His people. There is a ceremony to commemorate this new reality. At this event, Moses built an altar (Exod. 24:4), offered a variety of bloody sacrifices (v. 5), collected the blood, and threw it both on the altar and on the people (vv. 6, 7–8). He said, "Look! The blood of the covenant which Yahweh cut with you concerning all these words" (v. 8 DJP).

Bloody substitutionary sacrifice lay at the foundation of the nation, and was a main feature of its worship. Leviticus details a number of bloody sacrifices, as well as the climactic yearly Day of Atonement. In Leviticus 17, which narrates the ceremonies marking that day, the Hebrew word translated "blood" occurs nine times, and plays a major role. This is the only time that one man, the high priest, is allowed to enter the Holiest Place in which God's presence is manifested—and that only with blood (Lev. 16:14–16; cf. Heb. 9:7).

Why all this blood? Here, in the entire institution of bloody and substitutionary sacrifice, is the first hint of what an extensive and extreme operation is required to rescue us. It was hinted at in the fact that the Seed must be wounded (Gen. 3:15). Now, in these bloody sacrifices, the truth is made more explicit: *Innocent blood must be shed in death.* The wages of sin is death (Gen. 2:17; Rom. 6:23a), and that debt must be paid.

God explains how blood accomplishes this substitution in Leviticus 17:11, 14, "For the life of the flesh is in the blood, and I have given it for you on the altar to make atonement for your souls, for it is the blood that makes atonement by the life. . . . For the life of every creature is its blood: its blood is its life."

In God's pedagogy of Israel, His chosen nation, He aimed at creating a Pavlovian response: sin—blood—atonement. Yahweh wanted those concepts indissolubly linked in believers' minds. So, in the case of the Russian physiologist's famous experiment: ring a bell, Pavlov's dog thinks, "Food!" Thus also with Israel under God's instruction: sin, and the believing Israelite thinks, "Bloody sacrifice."

The intended lesson is clear. People who commit sin should expect to find forgiveness and atonement only by an innocent creature being punished to the point of bloody death in their stead (Lev. 1:4; 4:15, 20, etc.).

This representation was a true picture, but it was just that: a picture; a shadow; not the reality. In Hebrews, chapters 9 through 10, the author masterfully opens up the designed obsolescence of the sacrifices of the Mosaic Covenant. His case is expressed forcefully in 10:1–4:

For since the law has but a shadow of the good things to come instead of the true form of these realities, it can never, by the same sacrifices that are continually offered every year, make perfect those who draw near. Otherwise, would they not have ceased to be offered, since the worshipers, having once been cleansed, would no longer have any consciousness of sins? But in these sacrifices there is a reminder of sins every year. For it is impossible for the blood of bulls and goats to take away sins.

Now we are ready to understand the terms used in this section's heading—*penal substitutionary atonement:*

Penal means that the sacrifices were means of justice. They were not giving God something He lacked or needed. Man was liable to God's judgment, and morally guilty. The penalty for sin has always been *death* (Gen. 2:17). So these sacrifices were given to address the penalty for sin.

Substitutionary points to the fact that the animal suffered this penalty so that the offerer need not do so. The animal was presented in the offerer's stead. When the offerer pressed his hands on the head of the victim (Lev. 1:4; 3:2, 8, 13; 4:4, etc.), it was a little like a tag-team move. He was designating that animal as his substitute. The penalty for his sin would fall on the animal instead of falling on him.

Atonement describes the sacrifice as making peace between God and the offerer.

From the beginning to the end of the Bible, we observe the reenactment of these terms in God's unfolding plan of redemption.

Prophesied Fulfillment

Predictive prophecy is a major factor in the Bible, which contrasts biblical Christianity rather sharply with other religions. It has been estimated that 27 percent of the Bible was predictive prophecy, when first uttered.[3] Some of the most striking prophecies deal with the coming of mankind's deliverer-champion—Messiah.

We already discussed the first such prophecy in Genesis 3:15. The body of Messianic prophecies, direct and indirect, is such a massive topic that I will only focus on what is arguably the most arresting and unambiguous prediction. I speak of Isaiah 52:13–53:12, usually (and rightly) called the prophecy of the Suffering Servant of Yahweh. This is the same passage that the Ethiopian eunuch was reading in Acts 8, concerning which he asked Philip, "About whom, I ask you, does the prophet say this, about himself or about someone else?" (v. 34). Let's fasten on *three* aspects of this prophecy.

First, He is an individual. Though it has often been suggested that the servant is Isaiah, or a personification of Israel (cf. the eunuch's question), neither of these approaches satisfies the text.[4]

* He is not Yahweh the Father, but is His Servant (52:13; cf. 53:4, 6, 10).
* He is not Isaiah (contrast with how the prophet speaks of himself in chapters 6–8; and 20:2–3; 38–39; also contrast 53:9 with 6:5, and 53:10 with Lev. 6:6–7).
* He is not Israel in general (53:2–6, 8; also contrast 53:10 with Lev. 6:6–7).
* He is not the elect remnant within Israel (53:11).

---

3. Cf. Busenitz, *Reasons We Believe*, 87–90.
4. There is a very readable discussion of this prophecy in Ankerberg, Weldon, and Kaiser, *Case for Jesus the Messiah*, 50–61.

Second, He has what it takes. Back in Isaiah 7, the prophet had taken up the old prophecy of the Seed of the woman and moved its fulfillment into view. It turned out that the words of Yahweh would find real fulfillment, perhaps beyond all of Adam and Eve's expectations. Eve seems to have hoped that her first child might be the conquering Seed. She specifies that Yahweh was involved in the child's birth, strikingly calling newborn Cain a "man," a word nowhere else applied to a baby (Gen. 4:1).[5]

But Cain fell far short of that expectation, being spiritually more a seed of the Serpent than the Seed of the woman (1 John 3:12). And so did every successive child afterward. The birth of this delivering Seed is again and again pushed forward into the future.

But now Isaiah mentions a "holy seed" in 6:13, in the context of the remnant of Israel. Does the prophet mean "seed" collectively, as it is often used; or does he mean it of an individual holy Seed, as in Genesis 3:15? The question is not so easy to answer. Israel had a strong concept of "corporate unity," that is of one person standing for a group. Adam was such a person, whom God had appointed as a representative of all mankind. Similarly when Achan sinned, Israel suffered as if they were all guilty (Josh. 7); when David sinned, again Israel as a whole suffered (1 Chron. 21).

These are unhappy examples of corporate unity, cases where many suffered because one sinned. When the conquering Seed came, corporate unity would be the root of a very happy outcome. Because of His connection with mankind, the Seed would also be called "the Son of Man," and would be both human and divine (Dan. 7:13–14, where the title underscores His humanity while the clouds of heaven point to His deity). For this reason, the Seed stood in for all the people He would rule and represent (Dan. 7:18). One, yet many.

---

5. Cf. Greidanus, "Preaching Christ from the Cain and Abel Narrative," 390.

Thus in the very next chapter Isaiah prophesies of an individual who would be called "Immanuel," meaning "God with us" (Isa. 7:14). His birth would be a great sign such as God Himself would choose, for He would be born of a virgin mother.[6] "God with us" would not be a mere figure of speech, since He would later be given the name "Mighty God" (Isa. 9:6). This is no less than a direct assertion of His Godhood, since the same name is used of Yahweh Himself (10:21).

I take it that this is the same figure who appears in the Servant of Yahweh passages in Isaiah, of which 52:13–53:12 is the most remarkable. He is the virgin-born Davidic King, God in human form, deliverer of Israel and Savior of the world (49:6).

So this One is fully qualified to do everything set forth in Genesis 3:15. He is human; and since He is virgin-born, He is uniquely the Seed of the woman. He is utterly righteous, as mankind is not (Isa. 6:13; 53:9, 11). Yet He would be of infinite power and worth, as God incarnate. He could both be holy Yahweh's representative *and* ruined mankind's representative.

Third, He does what was needed. This individual would do what no man had ever done: He would live a perfectly righteous life as a human being, fulfilling every divine requirement of seamless righteousness. And then, at the climax of His earthly career, He would deal with our deepest need.

We have seen that universal need. What is it? What do we need for our deliverance, our redemption? Do we need more rules? Rules

---

6. Though some argue for the translation "young woman," the Hebrew word is never clearly used of a married or sexually active woman. Well over a century before Christ's birth, the Septuagint unambiguously rendered it by the Greek word meaning "virgin," so I would argue that this prophecy speaks directly of Jesus' virgin conception by Mary. (For further documentation and argumentation, see the respective commentaries on Isaiah by Edward J. Young [Grand Rapids: Eerdmans, 1960] and J. Alec Motyer [Downers Grove, IL: InterVarsity Press, 1993].)

can be good, but they cannot redeem. We just break them (cf. Rom. 7:5–14)!

Do we need a perfect King? Truly mankind does need such a king. Yet we already had a perfect King in the Garden, and we spit in His face. The mere presence of a perfect King would not redeem us, but would provoke our hatred. The same happened the next time the King came (Matt. 27:22–23). Give us another in our present, unredeemed condition, and we would rebel again (cf. Luke 19:14)!

Do we need a just and perfect society? Indeed we do. But we had one in Eden, and raced for the nearest garbage chute as fast as our idiot-feet would carry us. And now all the more, such a society would not redeem us, as long as it was populated and led by unredeemed people still in our sin. External perfection will not do a thing for the sin we carry and nurture and indulge.

What we really need most of all is for something to be done about our *sin*. And that is precisely what Yahweh's Servant, God incarnate, does.

Earlier in this chapter, we saw that God had painstakingly laid the predicate for the necessity of penal substitutionary blood atonement through the centuries of biblical history. At the same time, we saw that animal sacrifice was but a picture and a shadow.

The Servant, in Isaiah 52:13–53:12, accomplishes the *reality* of which all else is but a shadow. Let's detail it out:

1. "So shall he sprinkle many nations; kings shall shut their mouths because of him; for that which has not been told them they see, and that which they have not heard they understand" (52:15). "Sprinkle" is used of ritual application of blood in such passages as Exodus 29:21 and Leviticus 5:9. By this language, Isaiah denotes right at the outset that the Servant has a priestly function that affects not only Israel, but the whole world ("many nations").

2. "Surely he has borne our griefs and carried our sorrows; yet
   we esteemed him stricken, smitten by God, and afflicted. But
   he was wounded for our transgressions; he was crushed for
   our iniquities; upon him was the chastisement that brought
   us peace, and with his stripes we are healed. All we like
   sheep have gone astray; we have turned—every one—to his
   own way; and the LORD has laid on him the iniquity of us
   all" (53:4–6). In the plainest language one could hope for,
   this designates the penal and substitutionary nature of the
   Servant's sufferings. *We* are guilty, but *He* suffers the just
   penalty. *He* is innocent, but *His* sufferings bring *us* peace and
   healing. *He* is righteous, but *He* carries *our* iniquity away.

3. "By oppression and judgment he was taken away; and as for
   his generation, who considered that he was cut off out of
   the land of the living, stricken for the transgression of my
   people? And they made his grave with the wicked and with
   a rich man in his death, although he had done no violence,
   and there was no deceit in his mouth" (53:8–9). This suffering is not merely a burdened or painful life; it is a burdened
   and painful death, which goes as far as burial. (See also verse
   12—"because he poured out his soul to death.") The wages
   of sin were, are, and remain death, and the Servant pays that
   bill in full.

4. "Yet it was the will of the LORD to crush him; he has put
   him to grief; when his soul makes an offering for guilt, he
   shall see his offspring; he shall prolong his days; the will of
   the LORD shall prosper in his hand. Out of the anguish of
   his soul he shall see and be satisfied; by his knowledge shall
   the righteous one, my servant, make many to be accounted
   righteous, and he shall bear their iniquities. Therefore I will
   divide him a portion with the many, and he shall divide the
   spoil with the strong, because he poured out his soul to death

and was numbered with the transgressors; yet he bore the sin of many, and makes intercession for the transgressors" (53:10–12). The phrase "the will of the LORD" tells us that *this* is the denouement of the eternal great plan of God for man's redemption. It centers not on an event or a place, but on the person of Jesus Christ. Then "crush him . . . put him to grief . . . his soul makes an offering for guilt . . . he shall bear their iniquities" stresses the penal substitutionary nature of this suffering. The Servant suffers *not* for Himself, but for His people.

And the suffering is not a gesture, or a side effect of sin, or part of His identification with creation. It is an offering for sin—which is to say that it pays the price due for our sin and our objective guilt and our rebellion against God. Even more, it is God Himself crushing God Himself for our sin, to bring us deliverance. This brings about marvelous good news, "by his knowledge shall the righteous one, my servant, make many to be accounted righteous." Not only does the Servant bear our iniquities and pay our moral debt; by so doing, He also pays the debt for our *failure* to live perfectly righteous lives. So by His knowledge (or "by knowing Him," a possible translation) He makes many to be counted righteous. The righteousness we need in order to have a relationship with God, the Servant has in overflowing abundance; and He earns for us a verdict of "righteous" in God's eyes.

Finally Isaiah writes, "He shall see his offspring; he shall prolong his days; the will of the LORD shall prosper in his hand. Out of the anguish of his soul he shall see and be satisfied. . . . Therefore I will divide him a portion with the many, and he shall divide the spoil with the strong." He—who died! He—who was buried! That very One sees offspring (people who have life because of Him), prolongs His days, is satisfied with the results of His penal substitutionary death. He will Himself carry out the eternal plan of Yahweh. That very One is given a position of power. This can only be fulfilled by the bodily resurrection of that One from the dead.

Let us stop, catch our breaths, and recognize where we are. We have just learned in some detail the good news of the marvelous salvation that Jesus Christ accomplished—and we're still over seven hundred years before the angel breaks the news to Mary!

I have approached it this way so that we all can see that the Gospel is a *whole-Bible* message. The dilemma of man, and God's plan for bringing men back into a relationship with Himself, does not begin with John 3:16. It begins with Genesis 1:1, it goes all the way on to Revelation 22:21, and it never lets up in between.

Now that the stage is all set, and the players are in place, it is time to see the drama played out.

Chapter 6

God's Rescue Operation Executed

God Enters Enemy Territory
to Seek and to Save

From the first tick of the cosmic clock, God guided every event, from the micro to the macro, toward His determined goal. There has always been a divinely determined time for everything (Eccl. 3:1–8), and God works all after His own will, according to His plan for the ages (Eph. 1:11; 3:11).

When history had finally been shepherded to just the ripe moment (Ps. 75:6–7; Dan. 2:21; 4:32; Mark 1:15; Eph. 1:11), God sent out His Son to accomplish redemption (Gal. 4:4–5). What was taking place was exactly in accord with what the OT had set out over the millennia: God the eternal Son humbled Himself by taking to Himself human nature in the form of a servant—the Servant of Yahweh (Isa. 52:13–53:12; John 1:1, 14, 17–18; Phil. 2:5–7; see chapter 5).

Christ's reason for doing this was singular: In love, the Father had commissioned Him (John 3:16–17; 10:18) to come and save lost sinners (Luke 19:10; 1 Tim. 1:15). It was for this reason that He was given the name "Jesus," which in Hebrew would suggest *salvation*—because He Himself would save His people from their sins (Matt. 1:21).

What of the divinely-appointed rule of man over the world that had been the climax of creation (Gen. 1:26–28)? Was the world a lost cause? Had God given up on it altogether? Was Christ just tagging people for some future, gauzy, misty heaven after the planet winds itself down or blows itself up?

Far from scrapping the concept of perfect human rule over creation, Jesus is the Agent of its realization. Jesus' first recorded sermon in Matthew is short and to the point: "Repent, for the kingdom of heaven is at hand" (Matt. 4:17). This planet still would come under the rule of God, with *a man* at the helm—but that man would not be Adam the first, but Adam the *last* (1 Cor. 15:45).

Where our father Adam failed miserably in every respect, Jesus would succeed. Jesus would subdue the earth and rule it. He would eventually people the earth with His "staff," as it were. He would fill the earth with His spiritual seed, those alive because of Christ (Isa. 53:10). Christ would succeed in every way in which Adam failed.

How did God accomplish the rescue of His people, and the redemption of the planet? I'll paint out four broad strokes that unveil what Jesus did to accomplish the plan of God for mankind and for earth.

Jesus Accomplished His Work by His Life

The moral and supernatural qualities of Jesus' life were crucial to the accomplishment of God's plan. As we saw earlier, when Adam sinned, all his natural progeny were condemned and corrupted.

But in his announcement of Jesus' conception to Mary, the angel Gabriel says of Jesus, "The Holy Spirit will come upon you, and the power of the Most High will overshadow you; therefore the child to be born will be called holy—the Son of God" (Luke 1:35). Jesus would not be a naturally conceived child of Adam; therefore, He would be free from the taint of Adam's sin.

He would have the holiness we lack, and so desperately need. This was the testimony of all who encountered Jesus in the course of His ministry, the first of whom was John the Baptist. John was a relative of Jesus (Luke 2:36), and would have known of His family and upbringing. Jesus' godly Jewish mother and stepfather raised Him according to the Law of Moses (Luke 2:27). He was a model child (Luke 2:51–52). So well known was His character that, when He came up to be baptized by his relative John, the Baptizer recoiled in horror. Overwhelmed by his own sense of unworthiness, John was unwilling to apply his baptism of repentance to Jesus, who needed no repentance (Matt. 3:14). Rather, he felt it was Jesus who should baptize him!

Yet Jesus' reply is telling: "Let it be so now, for thus it is fitting for us to fulfill all righteousness" (Matt. 3:15). In the modern American expression, Jesus was "all about" righteousness. John knew it. That is why he could see that Jesus was the holy and spotless Lamb of God who, so far from being involved in the sin of the world, came to carry it away (John 1:29).

This aspect of Jesus' character never changed. It overwhelmed Peter who, when he saw a display of Jesus' power, fell at His feet and cried out, "Depart from me, for I am a sinful man, O Lord" (Luke 5:8). The demons even recognized it in Jesus, shrieking that they knew who He was—the Holy One of God (Luke 4:34). With this judgment, Peter and all the apostles would concur (John 6:69).

That last is worth a moment's further reflection. These men traveled with Jesus. They saw him early in the morning and late at night.

They saw Him tired, hungry, and badly overworked. They saw Him physically worn out, and under the fire of a thousand outrageous accusations and immense, tireless, merciless opposition. They saw Him in private and in public, on the land and at sea.

How would you fare under that sort of scrutiny? When folks who read my blog posts say nice things about me, I instantly think, *Yeah, brother, sister . . . you don't really know me!* But these men did know Jesus. They knew Him intimately, over the space of years, and in every conceivable circumstance. Yet they—His closest associates—called Him "holy" (John 6:69), and perfectly spotless and pure in every aspect of His character (1 Peter 1:19; 2:22–23; 3:18; etc.). Even His half-brother James came to see Him as worthy of being called the glorious Lord and Messiah (James 1:1; 2:1)!

Perhaps the ultimate test comes when Jesus has the nerve to ask this question: "Which one of you convicts me of sin?" (John 8:46). The response? Crickets. Beyond accusing Jesus of breaking special nonbiblical rules, the best the Jewish leaders can do is pay witnesses to come up with lame lies and slanders that don't even hang together. Even corrupt Pilate has to admit, "I find no guilt in him" (John 19:6b). The gutless governor condemns Jesus in order to get himself out of a bind, not to serve justice.

It's important to note that Christ's testimony extends beyond merely His outer actions. Jesus' righteous deeds spring from a heart that is wholly given to love for God. Which of us could make statements like these without blushing, embarrassed laughter, or immediately reading off a lawyer's laundry list of qualifications?

- "My food is to do the will of him who sent me and to accomplish his work." (John 4:34)
- "Truly, truly, I say to you, the Son can do nothing of his own accord, but only what he sees the Father doing. For whatever the Father does, that the Son does likewise." (John 5:19)

- "I can do nothing on my own. As I hear, I judge, and my judgment is just, because I seek not my own will but the will of him who sent me." (John 5:30)
- "And he who sent me is with me. He has not left me alone, for I always do the things that are pleasing to him." (John 8:29)

So we must recognize in Jesus the quality that every other human being since Adam has lacked: utter, comprehensive, all-consuming love for God that flowed from a sinless heart and issued in a flawlessly, perfectly holy life.

Visualize a vast scale indicating God's requirements for holiness from mankind. The moment Adam sinned, wherever the needle had been previously, it hit bottom at that very moment and never budged.

"Never?" you ask.

Never.

Remember: God's requirement is not "best effort." God demands and expects absolute holiness, womb-to-tomb, 24/7/365. One speck short of that is a *fail*.

Then comes Jesus. In His case, the moment of His conception, the needle shot to the top and never wavered.

"Never?" you ask.

Never. Not when He'd gone forty days without a meal. Not when He'd been serving others all day and could not get fifteen consecutive seconds to Himself. Not when He was surrounded by human jackals slavering to catch a misspoken syllable. *Never* a reading other than 100 percent righteous in God's eyes, both in heart and action.

While it's true that Jesus accomplished the eternal plan of God by the moral and spiritual perfection of His life, it's also essential that we appreciate the supernatural quality of that life. Had He been a perfectly good man as defined above, that would have been miracle enough. But He also had to show that He was more—and mercy sakes alive, *was* He!

I was about to write that Jesus' life bore a supernatural mark from conception to death and beyond. That is true. But in a way, it began long before. To be the Messiah who fulfilled prophecy, Jesus would have to hail from the line of Abraham, Isaac, Jacob, Judah, and David—but not Jeconiah (Jer. 22:24–30). He would have had to be born of a virgin, in Bethlehem, under Gentile rule, *before* the fall of Jerusalem and 400–some-odd years after the decree to restore and rebuild Jerusalem after the Babylonian Captivity.[1]

All of this, *for starters*, was required to fulfill the pattern of OT Messianic prediction. And Jesus did tick off every one of those items, simply by being born when and where and to whom He was born.

Nice trick, given that these are particulars over which no mortal has the slightest hint of control.

Thus, it couldn't have been a trick.

The miraculous is a major element in Christ's earthly life. He is conceived and born of a virgin. The movements of Jesus' parents are directed by angels. At His baptism, the sky opens up, God the Father speaks to Jesus, and God the Holy Spirit descends visibly upon Him.

Then Jesus immediately faces down, not just any garden-variety nasty demon, but the prince of the dark powers, the original and chief of the demons, Satan himself. This is he before whom our great-grandparents collapsed like a house of cards in a high wind.

How did that confrontation with Jesus work out for Satan?

Jesus sent him yelping like a scalded dog.

But all this is only the beginning, as you well know.

---

1. This compendium synthesizes the following Scriptures: Genesis 12:1–3; 21:12; 49:10; 2 Samuel 7:12–14; Psalm 2; Isaiah 7:14; 9:1–6; 11:1; Daniel 9:24–26; Micah 5:2.

When it came to Jesus' public ministry, His miracles were unparalleled and unambiguous. Think of their scope and extent.

Jesus . . .

> healed visible and congenital illnesses (John 9:1ff.);
> bent the "laws" of nature to His service (now *that's* "dominion" over the created world! Matt. 14:25–32);
> shut up an earthquake of a storm with a sharp command (Matt. 8:24–26);
> scattered demons as if they were scared little girls (Matt. 8:16, 29, 31–32); and
> knew things no mere man could know (Matt. 17:27; Mark 14:13; John 4:17–18).

Jesus Christ's miracles were so in-broad-daylight and primary-colored that He simply left His critics sputtering and spitting and coming up with lame cover stories ("Could it be . . . *Satan*?").

They were stung by Jesus' miracles, threatened by Jesus' miracles, bothered by Jesus' miracles, forced to pathetic evasions by Jesus' miracles. But deny them? They just couldn't do it (Matt. 9:34; John 11:47). It simply was not an open option to them.

They had to leave that little stunt to self-styled brainiacs, millennia later, who hadn't actually been there. Jesus' contemporary enemies knew they could never get away with it.

Jesus' miraculous works were significant in that they authenticated Jesus as being who He claimed to be—the divine Messiah (John 10:25, 37–38)—and in that they were harbingers of the kingdom that Jesus would one day bring to earth (Isa. 29:18–19; 42:7), which will be a restored, global Eden as it should have been—and more (Isa. 2; 11).

These qualities mark Jesus as the only one fit to head up the new humanity, a vast throng consisting of all the men and women He saves from their sins.

Jesus Accomplished His Work by His Teaching

Though we focus extensively on Jesus' miraculous and holy life, the Gospels characterize Him just as chiefly by His teaching.

The gospel of Mark, known for its action sequences and constant use of the word "immediately," lays a very heavy emphasis on Jesus' *teaching*. Mark writes of Jesus' *doctrine* in four verses (1:22; 4:2; 11:18; 13:28). He describes Jesus as *teaching* in another sixteen (1:21–22; 2:13; 4:1–2; 6:2, 6, 30, 34; 8:31; 9:31; 10:1; 11:17; 12:14, 35; 14:49). He is called "the teacher" in another twelve verses (4:38; 5:35; 9:17, 38; 10:17, 20, 35; 12:14, 19, 32; 13:1; 14:14).

So Jesus' teaching is a big theme! The impact is well summed up in Mark 1:22: "And they were astonished at his teaching, for he taught them as one who had authority, and not as the scribes."

Why was this important? Because as the King, He had to announce, explain, and apply the agenda of His kingdom. To this end, He needed to confront any tendency (ancient or modern) to think of that kingdom as primarily a dramatic, special-effects extravaganza. True, there would be outward phenomena and events affecting the entire planet; but that kingdom would have a particular spiritual and moral character at its very core.

Jesus needed to clarify the will of God and issue directions that were to characterize the lives of His subjects in the coming age, under the New Covenant.

The Lord Jesus, in His teaching no less than in His person, *is* God's final word (Heb. 1:1–2). And so, He must have the final word. In fact, one of Christ's divine titles is "the Word" (John 1:1), who took on human nature for our salvation (v. 14). Jesus is the living and personal and incarnate expression of God the Father (v. 17). In Him, we meet God (John 14:9).

The personal (Christ the Word) and the propositional (the words Christ spoke) unite to bring us into this relationship. That is, Jesus is the Word, but He also spoke words. We must hear those words, must learn them and believe them and take them to heart, in order to have a relationship with Him and with the Father (John 8:19; 14:21, 23; 1 John 1:1–3). Conversely, to reject Him *and His teaching* is to reject the Father (John 3:34–36; 5:37–38; 7:16–17; 8:46–47; 12:47–50; 15:23–24). The two elements are inseparable.

In His teaching, Christ had to clash head-on with many of the hand-me-down beliefs and practices of the most powerful and influential leaders of His day: the Pharisees. In a misdirected zeal for holy living, the Pharisees had tamed God and reduced Him to a system of rules: burdensome, yet concrete, manageable, and workable rules. Keeping the rules often produced spiritual pride and arrogance (Matt. 23; Luke 18:11–12; Phil. 3:4–6). This proud, self-righteous attitude was the very opposite of the spirit of a man who enjoys God's favor and presence. In an arresting clash of images, we read that the loftiest and exalted One can only be known by the lowest and humblest (Isa. 57:15). The pride of man must be abased and humbled (Isa. 2:11ff.).

To this end, for mankind's own salvation, Jesus must finally shatter man's pride. The anointed leaders had so handled the Law of Moses and so stressed the external that it seemed possible to check outward boxes and feel righteous. Jesus would rip off the façade and reveal the truth about righteousness and a genuine relationship with God.

Jesus did more than assure that the holy Law did its full work. The Law and the Prophets pointed forward to Jesus (Matt. 11:13); He embodies their fulfillment (Matt. 5:17–18). And so, Christ announced His own law ("But I say to you," Matt. 5:22, 28, 32, 34, 39, 44), which fulfills the righteousness of the Law with a particular focus on its heart impact (cf. Matt. 5–7; Mark 10:17–22).

All this would have the effect of bringing us to know our spiritual bankruptcy before God (Matt. 5:3). Only in this way could we become citizens of the kingdom of heaven, and live in a way that glorifies the King.

Jesus Accomplished His Work by His Atoning Death

Perhaps it seems a lovely sentiment to hear Gabriel tell Joseph, "and you shall call His name Jesus; for He Himself will save His people from their sins" (Matt. 1:21 DJP).

But those "lovely" words are a death sentence, for there was no other way to save His people from their sins, than by Jesus' death. More teaching, more moral examples, more commandments, and even more divine blessings, would simply leave them—and us!—more condemned, more guilty, more damned, more hopeless.

Remember the lesson we learned in the first three chapters. Our problem is internal. We are sinners, alienated from God. The salary sin pays is death (Rom. 6:23). The life of a sinner is forfeit, period. We are sinners, we must die, eternally. The holiness of God demands it. For Him to "let it go" would be for God to un-God Himself.

Yet it would be a marvelous expression of the *love* of God if some way could be found to redeem such guilty sinners. Not that God needs to do any such thing. He already showed His love in His gift of life, of creation, even of His law. He was under no compulsion or obligation whatever to do one more kindly thing for His rebellious, ungrateful creatures.

Yet could there be a way to save sinners as a free expression of God's love, without damage to His holiness? He could not do anything that appeared to compromise His purity, His separation from and hatred of sin. No amount of love could right the wrong that would be done to God's name in such a case. How could a *holy* God express His free love in saving His rebellious creatures?

This is where the wisdom of God (discussed in chapter 4) comes to the fore. Seventeenth-century writer Thomas Watson was right to call redemption "the masterpiece of divine wisdom." His language is old and quaint, but give a careful listen to how Watson works it out by depicting the eternal counsel of God as a conversation among God's attributes:

> Mercy had a mind to save sinners, and was loath that the justice of God should be wronged. It is a pity, says Mercy, that such a noble creature as man should be made to be undone; and yet God's justice must not be a loser. What way then shall be found out? Angels cannot satisfy for the wrong done to God's justice, nor is it fit that one nature should sin, and another nature suffer. What then? Shall man be for ever lost? Now, while Mercy was thus debating with itself, what to do for the recovery of fallen man, the Wisdom of God stepped in; and thus the oracle spake:— Let God become man; let the Second Person in the Trinity be incarnate, and suffer; and so for fitness he shall be man, and for ability he shall be God; thus justice may be satisfied, and man saved. O the depth of the riches of the wisdom of God, thus to make justice and mercy to kiss each other![2]

And so Jesus knew and accepted that He would have to die for the sins of His people. There was no other way. What the wisdom of God had brilliantly conceived, the Son of God would willingly achieve. This was utterly mind-blowing to Jesus' disciples and contemporaries—which is probably why He often discouraged people from saying out loud that He was the Christ,[3] or to tell of

---

2. *Body of Divinity*, 51.

3. "Christ" and "Messiah" are (respectively) Greek and Hebrew transliterations;

His miracles (Matt. 8:4; 16:20; 17:9; Mark 1:44). Jesus knew that, to His contemporaries, "Messiah" simply meant "Tough-guy-who-will-smash-Rome-and-make-life-peachy-for-us." But that was not Christ's mission. Jesus came to save His people from their sins (Matt. 1:21; 1 Tim. 1:15), not from Rome. Before deliverance from outward and political oppression, His people desperately needed personal and spiritual deliverance from the guilt and power of internal corruption.

So Jesus told His baffled, horrified, unbelieving apostles again and again that He was about to be rejected, condemned, and killed on the cross (Matt. 16:21). In spite of His repeated teaching on the subject, when it finally happened they were thunderstruck. The cross was *that inconceivable* to them.

Was all that really necessary? Scripture requires that we be absolutely dogmatic: Christ's death on the cross was absolutely necessary for the completion of God's eternal plan. How can we know that?

Return to the second scene with which we opened chapter 4. Christ falls on His face, pleading with His Father, "My Father, if it be possible, let this cup pass from me; nevertheless, not as I will, but as you will" (Matt. 26:39). He prays it *three times* (vv. 42, 44), using the startling Aramaic intimacy "Abba," which would mean something like "Papa" or "Daddy" (Mark 14:36).

Each time, Jesus receives the same tacit answer: *It is not possible, and the cross is My will.*

Never before, never since. This is a historical first. *Never* had the Son made a request to which He'd received a "No." But here He says in effect, "Father, if there is any other way to accomplish their

---

both mean "Anointed." Since prophets, priests, and kings all could be anointed as part of their inauguration to office, the Coming One—who would be Prophet (Deut. 18:15), Priest (Ps. 110), and King (Ps. 2)—was called The Anointed One: the Christ, or the Messiah.

redemption and fulfill Your plan, no matter how extreme—grant Me that way!"

Question: Who would not spare Jesus? Answer: the Father.

And if there had been such a way, don't you think the Father would have leapt at it? Would not any person who loved Jesus have spared Him this? Remember, when Jesus announced His coming death to the apostles, Peter was so aghast at the thought that he forgot himself, and actually took it on himself to *rebuke* Jesus for saying such an appalling thing (Matt. 16:22). What Peter says in Greek is hard to bring over to English; too literally, it is "Propitious[4] to You, Lord!" The idea actually drips with unintended irony: Peter is saying, "May God be propitious to You, Lord! May God turn His wrath from You and spare You!"

Yet "spare Jesus" is precisely what God the Father did not do. Had God done that, had God been propitious to Jesus, then His wrath would remain unpropitiated. All humanity would continue forever helplessly and hopelessly under His wrath. We would face an eternity of unrelieved suffering, paying the unpayable and infinite debt of our sins.

But God was *unpropitious* toward Jesus, that He might be *propitious* toward us.

Such is the Father's stunning love for those who hated Him: God is the One "who did not spare his own Son but gave him up for us all" (Rom. 8:32). Such was the Son's love as well (John 13:1). Jesus knew and accepted that His self-offering in this particular manner was an absolute necessity. What was coming was no "cosmic child abuse," as a biblically clueless writer once sneered. It was the Son willingly embracing the will of the Father for our salvation. So

---

4. The related Greek word translated "propitiation" in such texts as Romans 3:25 means *a sacrifice offered to absorb and deflect the wrath of God* (cf., e.g., Morris, "Propitiation," 975).

He sharply rebukes *Peter*. He who had changed Simon's name to "Peter," now changes it again: "Satan" (Matt. 16:23).

But can't we sympathize with Peter, wrong though he was? Who could love Jesus, and wish Him to go to such torment and shame?

The Father could. And the Son willingly complied. "Not my will, but yours, be done," He says.

No one has ever loved anyone as purely, deeply, and profoundly as the Father loves the Son. Yet heaven was silent to Jesus' plea. There was no word of reprieve from the Throne.

And so, to the cross went the Son.

The Cross According to Jesus

Jesus told us exactly what He would do there. He said that "the Son of Man came not to be served but to serve, and to give his life as a ransom for many" (Matt. 20:28). Every word is important, but I'll force myself to be brief:

- *Son of Man* marks Him as the divine/human Messiah and head of the new humanity, who is envisioned in Daniel 7:13–14.
- *Came not to be served but to serve, and to give* reveals that this was the mission of the Lord Jesus: not to be served by being carried to the Messianic throne on the shoulders of adoring crowds, but to serve by doing what His students did not want, but did need—by freely *giving . . .*
- *His life* a bit more literally is "His *soul.*" That is important to note because it takes our minds back to Leviticus 17:11 and 14, which revealed that the *soul*[5] of the flesh was in the blood. This

---

5. The Hebrew uses the equivalent of "soul" (*nepeš*, NEF-esh) and the pre-Christian Greek translation renders it by the word Jesus uses here (*psuchē*, psoo-KAY).

was why God had appointed the blood as the means of giving life for life, soul for soul, in redemption. This is why it had to be a bloody death such as the death on the cross: That was the appointed means of shedding a life in the stead of a life.

- *A ransom* translates the Greek world *lutron* (LOO-trone), which means a price paid to free a prisoner, hostage, or an indebted slave. A ransom is by nature substitutionary, as it takes the place of the hostage or slave. The ransom is given, the captive goes free. In this case, we are the captives, and the ransom price paid is Christ's life, given by means of the shedding of His blood in death.

- *For many* uses a preposition that means "in the stead of." Christ thus places a double emphasis on the truth of substitution. Substitution is an unpopular idea in some circles today, but Jesus is quite emphatic about it. It is as if He is saying that He would be a substitutionary substitute. Christ does for us and in our place that which we could not do for ourselves, and thus by interposing Himself in our place He wins our freedom.

In this way, Matthew 20:28 answers the otherwise unfathomable question as to why Christ suffered so, why He who knew no fear recoiled, then groaned so and cried out, "My God, My God, why have You abandoned Me?" He, the sinless Son, would bear sin before His beloved Father.

Other than Jesus, none can put it better than the apostle Paul later did: "For our sake he made him to be sin who knew no sin, so that in him we might become the righteousness of God" (2 Cor. 5:21). Christ hung and suffered as a substitute. He took on Himself the sin of all His people, absorbed the wrath of God they so richly deserved, put His perfectly righteous life between us and God, satisfied the judgment of God, and so died.

But, before He died, Jesus cried, "It is finished" (John 19:30). These three English words translate one Greek word: *tetelestai* (teh-TELL-ess-tie). With this marvelous word, Christ says, "It stands accomplished." Everything that needed to be done has been done; every bit of the mission the Father gave Him for His glory, the redemption of His people, the defeat of Satan, and the reclamation of the planet, has been brought to completion.[6]

Jesus is saying that everything necessary for the completion of God's saving plan has been accomplished. At that moment, the great curtain that separated the Holy Place from the Most Holy Place tore in two, from top to bottom (Matt. 27:51; these compartments were discussed in chapter 4). This was an act of God, trumpeting that the way into the Most Holy Place had been thrown open by the sacrifice of Jesus (Heb. 9:8; 10:19–20).

The reality that all the sacrifices had foreshadowed throughout the many centuries of OT history now had come to fulfillment. The picture gave way to the reality, the shadow to the body, the promissory note to the full payment. God's very presence was open to sinful man through the substitutionary atoning death of the Son of God.

Yet how could the observers on earth know that this sacrifice had been accepted by the Father? How can you and I know that our sins are finally and fully dealt with by Christ's cross? How do we know that the eternal plan worked?

Our answer comes with the aftermath.

Jesus Accomplished His Work by His Bodily Resurrection

"Resurrection" doesn't mean anything unless it is a *bodily* resurrection. The Greek word very literally means to "stand back up."

---

6. It is interesting to note as well that the Greek word was used in ancient receipts, bills, to indicate "Paid in full" (cf. Tenney, "John," 185).

What is it that stands back up if not the body that had lain down in death?

So it was in Jesus' case. His body was nailed to the cross. His body died. His body was pierced with a spear, and shed blood and water (John 19:34). His body was taken down from the cross, wrapped in linen, and laid in a tomb (Mark 15:46).

If Jesus did not rise bodily, He did not rise in any meaningful sense of the word.

Ah, but what did the women come seeking on that Sunday morning? They sought His body for further burial treatment. And what did they not find? His body (Luke 24:3).

The body was missing, though the grave clothes were left behind (John 20:6–7).

And what was it they encountered that convinced them of Jesus' victory over death? The living, resurrected, glorified *body* of the Lord Jesus. In fact, though cults and false teachers have sought out ways to deny it, the historical narratives go to great pains to stress the physical, material reality of Jesus' resurrected body. He still bears the trophies of His contest (Luke 24:40; John 20:27), He can be touched (Matt. 28:9), He eats (Luke 24:41–43)—He has flesh and bones (Luke 24:39). Though His glorified body could be called a "spiritual body" (1 Cor. 15:44), it is a body, nonetheless.

But why was it important for Jesus to rise from the dead in a material body?

First, this is what Jesus predicted. At the very outset of His public ministry, Jesus announced that He would raise up the "temple" that the Jews tore down (John 2:19). Though His hearers thought He spoke of the physical temple building, He was speaking of the temple of His body (John 2:21). That body would be torn down; and that same body would be raised up. The same body that was whipped, beaten, and mortally crucified, would rise (Matt. 20:18–19). If that did not happen, Jesus' prediction was false, and His whole case is undone.

Second, Jesus' bodily resurrection would prove to be the ultimate divine validation of Jesus' person and work (Rom. 1:4). Think it through. What would God have had to do to the dead body of Jesus in order to invalidate everything He said? The answer? *Nothing!* Simply let Jesus' corpse lie there dead, as corpses have characteristically done since Adam, and the entire structure of Jesus' claims would collapse with a horrendous crash. Jesus' resurrection is His Father's seal of approval on everything He said and did.

Third (and central for our purpose here), His resurrection shows that His sacrifice for us was accepted. As Paul puts it, Jesus "was delivered on account of our trespasses, and was raised on account of our justification" (Rom. 4:25 DJP). "On account of"—in other words, the resurrection of Jesus attests to the fact that God had declared His people righteous because of Jesus' sacrifice. We are not justified by His resurrection; His resurrection proves that we are justified by His death.

Unless Satan can get Jesus back in the tomb—and I don't see that happening—I know that God sees me as righteous for Jesus' sake. (More on that in chapter 7.)

Where Is Jesus Now?

With all this in mind, take a quick look at Hebrews 10:11–14:

> And every priest stands daily at his service, offering repeatedly the same sacrifices, which can never take away sins. But when Christ had offered for all time a single sacrifice for sins, he sat down at the right hand of God, waiting from that time until his enemies should be made a footstool for his feet. For by a single offering he has perfected for all time those who are being sanctified.

You think a *woman's* work is never done? Consider first the futile, endless repetition so masterfully set forth in verse 11, as the writer depicts the priest's ministry. *The Christian Standard Bible* renders the Greek text a bit better: "Now every priest stands day after day ministering and offering time after time the same sacrifices, which can never take away sins." The author, a true word-artist, tells us that

> *Every* priest stands
>> day after day
>> ministering
>> and offering
>>> time after time
>>> the same sacrifices,
>>>> which can never take away sins.

Did you catch all that? Every word is meaningful. What is the one piece of furniture missing in the tabernacle? There's a washbasin, a couple of altars, the table for the Bread of the Presence, the Ark . . . what's not there?

A chair!

There is no chair in the tabernacle because the priest's work was never done! Nor could it be, because the blood of bulls and goats could never take away sin (Heb. 10:4).

Finished! Ah, but contrast all that with the work of Christ (according to the equally masterful Heb. 10:12–14), who,

> when [he] had offered
>> for all time
>> a single sacrifice
>> for sins,

he sat down
    at the right hand of God,
    waiting
        from that time
        until his enemies should be made a footstool for his feet.

    For by a single offering
        he has perfected
        for all time
          those who are being sanctified.

Why say more? I could never top that, not in my wildest literary or sermonic dreams. Such is the marvel, the splendor, the wonder of Christ's sacrifice, that one sacrifice for all time achieved what centuries and millennia of every other ritual and effort could never accomplish.

A Man of infinite worth, offering a soul of infinite worth, to a God of infinite holiness, for rebels with infinite guilt—and *bang!* just like that, they are saved and reconciled and set apart to God by that one sacrifice.

That is where Jesus is, then. At the Father's right hand—sitting!—having accomplished full redemption, waiting for the day He will come again to reign.

Part Two Summary

How does this make me a world-tilter and a barrier-buster?

The truth of God's saving plan and its culmination in Christ makes us world-tilters because we now know where our rescue comes from. What did mankind contribute to this operation? What was our part?

We contributed:

- The traitor
- The corrupt politicians
- The religious hypocrites
- The lynch mob
- The soldiers
- The whips
- The thorns
- The cross
- The nails
  . . . and, most especially . . .
- The *sins* under the burden of which Christ groaned, suffered, bled, and died

So we know that *the world* is wrong in looking for deliverance within its own corrupt and deceitful heart. We know that the world is wrong in whistling past the graveyard, kidding itself that sin is not a big issue to God. The world is equally wrong to deny God, or to seek Him within or in nature.

We know that God is transcendent and holy. And we know that He has launched one and only one rescue operation. We know that the plan was laid in eternity. And we know that it was executed by the Lord Jesus Christ

We know that He accomplished what we could not.

But too much of *the church* is wrong, too. Those parts of the church that sideline Christ's saving work, His Gospel, this age-spanning rescue plan of God, are terribly wrong. They have erected barriers by their addiction to popularity, an addiction that has led them to accommodate the world's hopeless self-misdiagnosis. Eager to be accepted by the world, they offer the world what the world wants on the world's terms with just a light sprinkling of God-dust.

Given that Christ and His cross are central to God, they must be central to the church of God as well. Given that God pivots everything on the person and work of Christ, the church of Christ should do the same in its preaching, thinking, worship, and practice.

To put it bluntly: If we think we have something better to offer, then we think we know something God doesn't know.

Which . . . dude. Seriously. Whoa. *Think* about that.

Up to this point we've concentrated on the objective facts of this rescue.

Now let us examine how *we* get a share in it, and what difference it makes to, in, and for us.

Part Three

How Do We Get In?

A Tale of Two Towering Truths

Chapter 7

First Towering Truth—
Declared Righteous

How God Deals with Our Bad Record

In chapters 4 through 6, we learned about who God was, about His eternal plan, and about what God accomplished in Christ. But you may well have felt that most of that was "out there." Perhaps it was a bit like reading about our grandfathers storming the beach at Normandy. It may seem remote.

So, let's say we're convinced. Here are we, dead in sin, helpless and hopeless. There is Jesus, full of life and truth and grace and glory (John 1:14; 11:25). Out here, all is lost (John 3:36; Eph. 2:1). In Christ, we can be filled full (Col. 2:10).

The big question: How do we get from here to there?

I'll endeavor to answer that question by setting out two towering truths of our redemption: one in this chapter, the second in the next. The truths are *justification* and *regeneration*. These two will serve as a useful biblical model for gathering together and laying out in broad strokes what the Bible teaches about how God brings His salvation to folks like you and me, answering to our miserable condition. After all, we do bad things because we are bad people. So, if we've any hope of a God-blessed life, something has to be done about *what we've done*, and something has to be done about *what we are*.

Which is precisely what God has accomplished in Christ.

First Towering Truth: Justification

When Job asked, "How can a man be in the right before God?" (Job 9:2), he posed the million-dollar question. How indeed? We rebel against God by nature and by choice. We have broken God's laws from our first opportunity. He is pure and holy, and He cannot abide the presence of sin.

How can such as we ever have a relationship with such as He? It isn't a mere pairing of opposites. It's worse. It is a meeting of mutual repellants.

What is "justification"? In short: Justification is the answer to Job's question. It is the answer to the question we should be asking. Justification is at the very heart of the good news about Jesus Christ. Justification is what men and women need most.

Listen: The very next second after you, I, Richard Dawkins, Barack Obama, Donald Trump, Oprah Winfrey, Bill Gates, or Deepak Chopra breathe our last and find ourselves standing before a holy, righteous, unstoppable, and inescapable God, we won't be asking trivial questions about big rocks God can or can't lift and Cain's wife and the fate of distant tribes.

Trust me on this. Infinitely better, trust the Scriptures.

Instead, we'll be wondering about *our* fate. We will be wondering how we can possibly survive the encounter. We'll be wondering how we could ever lay claim to the *righteousness* that the infinite, all-knowing God rightly demands of us.

That is *the* question: How can guilty sinners stand before the holy God without eternally disastrous consequences? How could we ever amass the perfect righteousness we need to come to know and be accepted by Him?

Justification is how God meets that need for us. And in biblical contexts bearing on man's standing before God, the words usually translated "justify" or "justification" in the Hebrew OT and the Greek NT mean one and the same very specific thing: *to declare righteous.* It is a courtroom-type word. It is meant to call to mind a judge, in effect pounding his gavel and pronouncing his verdict: "This person is righteous!" It is often a legal ruling; its sense is to declare that someone lines up with the law. He is just. He is righteous.

You will find words like these scattered through English translations of the Bible:

- just
- justify
- justification
- right
- righteous
- righteousness

In truth, all these words usually render the same Hebrew and Greek words. To be just is to be righteous; to do justice is to do righteousness; and to be justified is to be declared righteous.

Let me be very clear: To justify is not "to make righteous." It is "to declare righteous." It is a pronouncement, not an accomplishment. We see that very clearly in many texts and usages.

We see this regularly in the OT uses of the Hebrew word. Consider Deuteronomy 25:1—"If there is a dispute between men and they go to court, and the judges decide their case, and they justify the righteous and condemn the wicked" (NASB). The judges are not *making* the righteous righteous, but *declaring* that they are righteous. Or again, we read that Elihu "burned with anger at Job because he justified himself rather than God" (Job 32:2). Again, Elihu doesn't see Job making himself right, but declaring himself to be in the right, instead of God. Examples could easily be multiplied.[1]

The NT uses the Greek equivalents in the same way. For instance, Paul quotes Psalm 51:4, "Let God be true though every one were a liar, as it is written, 'That you may be justified in your words, and prevail when you are judged'" (Rom. 3:4). Paul is using the Greek word in the same sense as the Hebrew original. To both David and Paul, it is God who is being "justified" here. Clearly neither writer means that God is being set straight or made righteous. It means He is being declared righteous, found to be in the right.

Or again Paul says that it is "the doers of the law who will be justified" (Rom. 2:13). Well, if they do the law, it cannot mean made righteous, can it? After all, they do the law, so they already are righteous. What it means is that they are ruled righteous, declared to be in the right, to be in line with the righteous law. This is the regular meaning of the Greek term.[2]

So "justified" means "declared or pronounced righteous," and this is precisely what the Gospel is about. In the verse that set Martin Luther (and many others) free and fueled the Reformation, Paul says that in the Gospel "the righteousness of God is revealed

---

1. See Genesis 44:16; Exodus 23:7; 1 Kings 8:32; Job 27:5; Proverbs 17:15; Isaiah 5:23.
2. Cf. Matthew 12:37; Luke 7:29; 10:29; 16:15; 18:14; Romans 3:20; 1 Corinthians 4:4.

from faith for faith, as it is written, 'The righteous shall live by faith'" (Rom. 1:17). The Gospel is about God's free gift of a righteous legal standing before His judgment seat. It is a status He bestows on sinners. It is a declaration that they are in good standing as far as His righteous law is concerned.

How can God do that? How can He count the guilty righteous, and still be righteous Himself?

The Great Transfer

Paul uses the most daring language in 2 Corinthians 5:21: "For our sake he made him to be sin who knew no sin, so that in him we might become the righteousness of God." This verse stands out in every regard. Even the Greek wording is unique. Unlike the surrounding verses, it stands without any connecting words such as *therefore, and,* or *but.* While it fits in with what Paul is saying about his ministry of reconciliation, the verse itself stands out like a tower jutting up from a plain.

What is more, Paul's emphasis in the original Greek text has a more "raw" and powerful feel to it, as if the apostle himself could scarcely believe what he was writing. Hear him more literally: "The One who did not know sin, on our behalf, sin He made, in order that we—we might become the righteousness of God in Him" (DJP). The word order reflects amazement over at least four marvels:

1. *Who* Paul is talking about: "The One who did not know sin." Paul cannot mean that Christ was unaware of what sin was, or of the ruin it caused (cf. Mark 7:21–23). Jesus knew all about sin. However, Jesus did not "know" sin in that He had no experience of it, it never once touched His character, stained His record, marred His life. Jesus was tempted in every way, as we are, yet He never yielded to temptation, as

we do (Heb. 4:15). Christ was spotless, pure, and righteous to an infinite degree (John 8:46; Heb. 7:26; 1 Peter 1:19; 2:22; 3:18; 1 John 2:1).

2. *For whom* the Father acted: "on our behalf." This is the realization of the ages-long symbolism we observed in the OT, where an unblemished and innocent victim stands in for the sinful offerer, and dies in his stead. So Christ died as a substitute for His people, and received in their place the action Paul is about to describe (Isa. 53:5–6, 8, 12; Matt. 20:28; 26:28; Gal. 3:13; Titus 2:14; Heb. 9:28; 1 Peter 3:18).

3. *What* God the Father did to the sinless One: "sin He made." Incredulously, Paul sticks that ugly, offensive, scandalous word right out in front: sin. We might have expected the Son to be made king, to be made ruler, to be made glorious. Ah, but no; He had come to save sinners (Matt. 1:21; 1 Tim. 1:15), had humbled Himself unimaginably to accomplish the task (Phil. 2:6–8). To save them, sin is what He must be made, and sin is what He was made. This alone answers the forlorn, desolate lament: "My God, My God, why have you forsaken me?" (Matt. 27:46). As He hung on the cross, the sins of His people were billed to Christ, as it were; they were reckoned to Him, imputed to Him. Though in His pure and pristine person Jesus Christ knew no sin, sin was laid on Him, that He might absorb the Father's holy and just wrath and fury for all the sin of all His people (Isa. 53:4–6, 10; Rom. 3:24–25; 1 John 2:2; 4:10).

4. *Why or for what end* the Father acted: "in order that we—we might become the righteousness of God in Him." Paul lays some grammatical emphasis on the "we." That is, the Father's design in all this is that such as we—such guilty lawbreakers as we—might become God's very righteousness in Christ. Now, as the sin that Christ was made was alien to Him, was

from outside of Him, so is this righteousness alien to us, coming from outside of us. The sin Christ was made was our sin; and so, the righteousness that we become is God's righteousness—credited to us in Christ, and declared so by the Father (Rom. 3:21–28; 4:2–6, 24–25; 1 Cor. 1:30; Gal. 2:16).

So then, in that awesome moment on the cross, God considered Christ as if He were the very embodiment of sin—because of us! To what end? So that He might then consider us as if we were the very embodiment of righteousness—because of Christ!

Surely such redeeming and rescuing grace from the Father and the Son defies the most eloquent speaker or writer's attempts even to graze the outer edges. A lesser light feels himself capable of doing little more than pointing and marveling, in the hopes that others might adore such a Savior.

The grand truth that we are touching on here is called *imputation*. That word comes mostly from the King James Version of the fourth chapter of Romans, verses 6, 8, 11, 22, 23, and 24. Those verses speak of the imputation of righteousness through faith alone, apart from any works. Modern translations use words such as "count" (ESV), or "credit" or "charge" (HCSB). The Greek word has the idea of reckoning, charging, or crediting to someone's account. In fact, it was used as an accounting term, referring to putting something on another's bill, or crediting an amount to his account.

In Romans 4, Paul develops the truths about justification that he'd brought out in the previous chapter. The apostle depicts God as crediting divine righteousness to the believing sinner. To show that this truth accords with the whole OT (Rom. 3:31), Paul adduces Abraham as his first witness. Quoting Genesis 15:6, Paul notes that God credited righteousness to Abraham simply through the patriarch's faith, and irrespective of any good deeds done, promised, or foreseen. Then, to make the point as plain as a billboard, Paul says, "Now to the one who works, his wages are not counted as a gift but as his due. And to the one who does not work but believes in him who justifies the ungodly, his faith is counted as righteousness" (Rom. 4:4–5).

Faith, then, is not a human work. Faith is the God-ordained instrument of receiving the gift of perfect righteousness, credited to our accounts before God. Through faith alone, God considers us as righteous.

On what basis? How can God regard the guilty as righteous? We have already seen it: because of Jesus Christ fulfilling all righteousness, then standing in our stead to receive the wrathful justice due our sins. Our sins are debited to Him; His righteousness is credited to us.

Paul celebrates that very reality in Philippians 3. Paul lists out some of his points of pride as a purebred, lawkeeping Pharisaical Jew in verses 3–6. Then he says that he had turned his back on all that, and had come to consider it both loss and manure in order that he might instead gain Christ (vv. 7–8). Paul's great aim was no longer to check all the legal boxes the Pharisees had identified, but to "be found in him, not having a righteousness of my own that comes from the law, but that which comes through faith in Christ, the righteousness from God that depends on faith" (v. 9).

This is the repentant, believing sinner's stance before God. The things he has done can only serve to damn him. Even the repentance and faith he brings are pale, flickering things, more like a mustard seed than a monument. He has no hope in himself; in fact, he doesn't even have a hope of hope in himself.

Here the Gospel enters and tells hardened career criminals such as we that we can be perfectly righteous in God's eyes. The Gospel shows how a sinner can stand before God, clothed in the perfect righteousness of Jesus Christ. Jesus Christ does what the law could not do, in accepting in Himself the full tale of God's justice on our sin (Rom. 8:3), and thus delivering us from every bit of God's just condemnation (Rom. 8:1).

The Gospel shows how God can be—equally and at the same time—*both* righteous *and* the One who declares sinners righteous (Rom. 3:26).

Our need of this righteous standing in God's eyes should be beyond rational argument. But how do we get it? How do we get from *here* (guilty, condemned, hopeless, doomed) to *there* (forgiven, counted righteous, rejoicing, at peace with God)?

How Can a Guilty Person Be Justified?

First of all, the answer is found in Christ. We saw that He became a human being, and by nature and choice He was the opposite of what we are. Jesus was righteous, untainted by Adam's sin. He actively fulfilled all the law of God from the heart, from conception to death. So Jesus Himself personally possesses that righteousness we lack and need.

Objectively, we saw that Jesus bore the sins of His people on the cross, and thus satisfied the justice of God. He took their place. He bore their penalty.

How, then, do they come to partake of His righteousness?

It might help us to clear away some conceptual debris first. People have heaps and piles of misunderstandings about how to be right in God's eyes. Every one will send a soul to hell, if relied upon.

Thank God the Bible is absolutely emphatic and crystal clear about how *not* to be righteous in God's eyes. Here are a few absolutely disastrous, doomed, hopeless ways:

- Whistling along gaily and imagining that God is whoever we make Him to be (Ps. 50:21–22; cf. Exod. 20:3–5).

- Banking on the unconditional love of God to accept us just as we are in our unrepentant, unbelieving, defiant state (Nah. 1:2; John 3:36; Rom. 1:18–32; 2:8–9; Eph. 5:6; Rev. 6:16–17).
- Holding to absolutely correct theories on a sheerly intellectual basis (James 2:14, 19).
- Having the finest parents (Phil. 3:5, 7–9).
- Having believing parents (John 1:13).
- Being a bit (or a *lot*) better than the other guy (Luke 18:10–14).
- Keeping every commandment of God, except for just one time in all my life (James 2:10).
- Doing truckloads of good works (Phil. 3:6–9).
- Merely holding some correct ideas about Christ (Mark 1:24).
- Banking—*to any degree whatever*—on my keeping God's law (Rom. 3:20; Gal. 3:10).

You see, there's *nothing* that we can do to be right with God! Not one thing. We cannot be righteous before God by anything we produce ourselves. Period. Not works, attitude, philosophy. The tree is bad, so the fruit is bad (Matt. 7:17–18). You can't pull a white T-shirt out of a mud pit (cf. Job 14:4). All of which explains one of the most shocking verses in the Bible, a revelation that helped me see my need for Christ:

> We have all become like one who is unclean,
>   and all our righteous deeds are like a polluted garment.[3]
> We all fade like a leaf,
>   and our iniquities, like the wind, take us away.
>
> (Isa. 64:6)

---

3. As mentioned in chapter 3, the Hebrew words refer to a used menstrual garment, which was not only an offensive figure, but denoted someone unable to enter the presence of God in Israel's worship.

Did that grab you? "All our *righteous deeds* are like a polluted garment"! If that is how God sees our *righteous* deeds, how must He see the rest?

If everything we can do is excluded, what does that leave?

God's way: by grace alone, through faith alone. The Bible is also clear as a pane of glass about the means by which God declares sinners righteous. Take the marvelous statement in Romans 3:22b–25a: "For there is no distinction: for all have sinned and fall short of the glory of God, and are justified by his grace as a gift, through the redemption that is in Christ Jesus, whom God put forward as a propitiation by his blood, to be received by faith."

To rephrase the apostle: We sinners keep falling short of God's glory by our own doing, but we are declared righteous by God's grace as a gift received by faith. Justification costs! But it does not cost us! Justification cost God the Father giving His Son. Justification cost God the Son giving His life, His blood, and bearing our sins.

But to us? No cost! Free of charge! It was not earned by anything we did before turning to Christ; it is not earned by anything we do as we turn to Christ; it will never be earned by anything we do after we trust in Christ. It is a gift by grace, received by faith. And even that faith is itself "bundled," as they say in the IT industry. It is part of the package. Saving faith is a work of God and a gift of grace as well (Acts 16:14; Eph. 2:8–10; Phil. 1:29). Paul says faith is the opposite of a human deed, the opposite of a work (Rom. 4:5).

Since our eternal destinies depend on coming to God on God's terms, we had better be very clear on what those terms are. As we examine what is involved in receiving this gift of righteousness, I will single out three components of how God brings sinners to Himself by grace alone through faith alone. But before I do, let me stress, these are like three inseparable sides of the same object. They may happen instantaneously, or they may take weeks, months, years, or even decades.

But these three will always be present in justification: *hearing the Word, repentance,* and *vital faith.*

Hearing the Word

We are not born thinking in terms of God's truth. We do not come out of the chute (as it were) with a God-honoring worldview. It does not naturally bubble up from within a God-hating sinner. What does bubble up is the compulsion to suppress the truth of God we see in nature and elsewhere (Rom. 1:18ff.), to resist the law of God (Rom. 8:7), and to create a worldview that serves our own twisted interests (Prov. 12:15; 14:12; 16:2, 25; Jer. 17:9).

So we need to hear what we do not know and could not figure out. We need to hear the Word of God. The truth will not unearth itself from the tomb of our deceitful, blind, darkened, self-serving hearts. We have too many distorted lenses. The truth has to shine down on us from heaven.

This is precisely what has happened. God took the initiative. He was the first speaker (Gen. 1:3). He has spoken to mankind from the start (Heb. 1:1–2). He selected individuals as His mouthpieces, called them "prophets" and "apostles," and enabled them to receive and relay His word without error (Exod. 4:15–16; 7:1–2; Deut. 18:15–22; John 16:13–14; 1 Cor. 14:37).

This is what gives Scripture its unique qualities: It is the Word of God, breathed out from Him as surely as your words are breathed out by you (2 Tim. 3:16; 2 Peter 1:21). Being God's Word, it is living, powerful, and piercing (Heb. 4:12), and true (John 17:17).

God has commanded that His Word be taken to the farthest corners of the world (Matt. 28:19; Acts 1:8; Rom. 15:20). He wants everyone to hear the good news about Jesus (Luke 24:47). The call is to go out to all.

With that in mind, hear the crucial role God has given to His

Word: "Faith comes from hearing, and hearing through the word of Christ" (Rom. 10:17; cf. 2 Tim. 3:15). You knew this would end up being about faith, I'd wager. But see how we get to faith. Not by philosophy; not by miracles; not by experiences; not by feelings; but by the Word of God.

Why is the Word so crucial? Because what the Word says, God says. And God uses His Word to speak to individuals. When He wants to save a man or a woman, He sends His Word—whether by a Bible, a tract, a sermon, or a person quoting the Word. But the power is in the Word of the Gospel.

Hear Paul:

> So I am eager to preach the gospel to you also who are in Rome. For I am not ashamed of the gospel, for it is the power of God for salvation to everyone who believes, to the Jew first and also to the Greek. For in it the righteousness of God is revealed from faith for faith, as it is written, "The righteous shall live by faith." (Rom. 1:15–17)

Rome was the center of corrupt political power in Paul's world. Paul knew that he could lose his life at Rome. (In fact, eventually he did.) But that didn't matter. He was eager to preach the Gospel there.

Why? Death wish? Hardly. It wasn't the low estimate Paul had of life; it was the high estimate he had of the Word, of the Gospel.

Follow the text backward. In verse 17 Paul talks about how God's gift of a righteous standing is revealed to be a matter of faith alone. Revealed in what? In the Gospel, which is God's power resulting in salvation for all believers (v. 16). So you see:

- Righteousness comes by faith alone.
- That truth is revealed in the Gospel alone.

- The Gospel alone produces that faith which alone leads to saving righteousness.
- It is God alone who gives the Gospel that power.

The Bible, however, never depicts the Gospel as magic, as if we could get "results" simply by pronouncing the words. Jesus told a parable specifically designed to illustrate the fact that the very same preached word can receive four different kinds of reception, only one of which represents a saving response: the person who takes the Word to heart (Luke 8:5–15).

What will characterize the person who does take the Word to heart? So glad you asked.

Repentance

Jesus' inaugural sermon in Mark is a brief one: "The time is fulfilled, and the kingdom of God is at hand; repent and believe in the gospel" (Mark 1:15). When Jesus sent out His disciples to preach, they preached that people should repent (Mark 6:12). On another occasion, Jesus lamented the fact that so many had not repented despite His many miracles, and foretold dire judgment on the unrepentant (Matt. 11:20–24).

Jesus took the occasion of the death of some people by Pilate's hands, and others' death in an accident, to warn His hearers twice: "Unless you repent, you will all likewise perish" (Luke 13:3, 5). On a happier note, in Luke chapter 15 Jesus told His beloved parables of the one lost sheep (out of 99) who was recovered, the one lost coin (out of 10) which was found, and the one lost son (out of two) who repented and returned to his father—all to make and vividly illustrate the point that there is great joy when a sinner repents (Luke 15:7, 10).

In another parable (if it was a parable), we find a money-grubbing rich man in torment after his death. It is too late for him to repent.

He pleads with Abraham to send poor Lazarus to preach to his brothers, insisting that they would repent if such a miracle occurred (Luke 16:30).

In fact, repentance features in one of Jesus' statements of His own mission. He did not come to pat the pious on their fat little heads, or congratulate the complacent. "I have not come," Jesus says, "to call the righteous but sinners..." (Luke 5:32). Call them to what? To rejoice in God's unconditional acceptance and approval of them just as they are? Let Jesus finish: "... to repentance," He says.

This accords with the mission on which Jesus then sent His apostles. After His resurrection, He told them "that repentance and forgiveness of sins should be proclaimed in [Christ's] name to all nations, beginning from Jerusalem" (Luke 24:47). It was part of their core message, a message that would be universal in scope.

Unsurprisingly, the apostles and early Christians took up the exact same theme. See it right off the bat, at the church's birthday party. When Peter's hearers ask, "What shall we do?" (Acts 2:37), Peter's response is direct: "Repent and be baptized every one of you in the name of Jesus Christ for the forgiveness of your sins, and you will receive the gift of the Holy Spirit" (v. 38). Peter reissues the same call to the nation in 3:19, and he and other apostles echo that call again in 5:31.

Is this call to repent addressed only to Israel? Hardly. Peter calls Simon in Samaria to repent of his wicked heart-intentions in Acts 8:22, and some Jewish Christians in Jerusalem hear of Peter's effective preaching to Cornelius (Acts 10), and conclude, "Then to the Gentiles also God has granted repentance that leads to life" (Acts 11:18). "To the Gentiles also" in addition to whom? In addition to Israel. From the Jews' perspective, that wrapped up the whole human race, which consisted of Jews and Gentiles.

As if all that weren't clear enough, Paul tells the Greek philosophers on Mars Hill that God now "commands all people everywhere to repent" (Acts 17:30). Who is excluded in "all people everywhere"? Nobody. It is no surprise, then, that Paul characterizes his ministry as calling Jews and Gentiles—which is to say every human being—alike to repentance (20:21; 26:20).

And . . . maybe you're thinking, *Great. Repentance, repentance, repentance. Got it. So . . . what is repentance?*

Again, glad you asked!

Sticking with just the words translated "repent/repentance" in the Greek NT, we start with the term's fundamental idea: "Change your mind." However, I must issue an immediate warning: Beware mistaking "change your mind" as meaning simply "shift an opinion or two." The "change" is a radical, top-to-bottom change; and it is the "mind" that must change, not merely some individual notion.

First, let me give some evidence to support that warning, illustrate it, and then briefly explain and apply it.

Evidence. John the Baptist preached repentance first. In fact, his baptism was called a "baptism of repentance" (Mark 1:4). And how did the prophet flesh out "repentance"? He exhorted his hearers to "Bear fruit in keeping with repentance" (Matt. 3:8; Luke 3:8). Ah, so this change of mind necessarily issues in a change of life. In fact, you could say that only a changed life shows a changed mind.

What's more, when the crowds responded by asking, "What then shall we do?" (Luke 3:10), John responded in this way:

"Whoever has two tunics is to share with him who has none, and whoever has food is to do likewise." Tax collectors also came to be baptized and said to him, "Teacher, what shall we do?" And he said to them, "Collect no more than you are authorized to do." Soldiers also asked him, "And we, what shall we do?" And he said to them, "Do not extort money from anyone by threats or by false accusation, and be content with your wages." (vv. 11–14)

John is not preaching that his hearers will be able to work their way to heaven by taking these actions. But he is showing that repentance necessarily results in specific changes of attitude, priority, and behavior (Matt. 3:8). So we read that those who received this message from the prophet were baptized in the Jordan, "confessing their sins" (Matt. 3:6). It is very clear, then: Genuine repentance—a genuinely changed mind—would issue, without fail, in a changed life.

This is exactly what Christ and the apostles meant by it as well. Remember, Peter had said, "Repent and be baptized every one of you in the name of Jesus Christ" (Acts 2:38). Baptism was no magical act, but it was an outward expression of their inner transformation. Their radical reevaluation of Christ would immediately show itself in public and final identification, through baptism, with Jesus the Messiah whom they had recently rejected. Baptism was the public declaration of a 180-degree course change.

In the next chapter of Acts, we see that this change of mind would involve turning back to God by trusting His Messiah (3:19). Later, Simon must repent of the wickedness of his heart (8:22). That is, he must change his mind and values about this wickedness, and disown it, so that he no longer embraces and pursues it.

Paul preached the same message. In the context of Paul's address to the Mars Hill philosophers, God's call to repentance (Acts 17:30) comes at the end of a concise sermon addressing the way they thought about God, the world, history, and Jesus Christ. If they repented, all those aspects of their worldview would change.

And finally, in his summation of his ministry, Paul said that he had "declared first to those in Damascus, then in Jerusalem and throughout all the region of Judea, and also to the Gentiles, that they should repent and turn to God, performing deeds in keeping with their repentance" (26:20). That is, real repentance would issue in deeds.

Let me offer an illustration of what repentance is and is not, then return to explanation and application.

Walking in your neighborhood, you round a corner and are startled to find a house catching fire. Flames are beginning to lick hungrily everywhere. To your horror, peering through the front window, you can make out two men sitting in the living room. They're watching TV.

No time to waste! You burst in the front door and race to the TV room. "Your house is on fire!" you shout in alarm.

The gents look at you in polite interest.

"Oh?" says the man on the left, setting down his pop can and politely muting the TV. "How do you know?"

"I saw flames starting everywhere!" you gasp. "Look, look out your window! Do you see the smoke?"

They look, glance at each other, then nod at you. "Yes. We see that. Yikes!" murmurs the man on the right, extending a languid hand for his doughnut.

You gape a half-moment, but time is wasting. "Don't you see, if you stay here, you'll burn to death!"

Again they glance at each other, and Left Man concedes, "Yes, that makes sense. The house is on fire, you're right. Anyone in a house on fire will be burned to death. That'd be awful." He considers a moment, then inquires, "So, what do you think we should do?"

"Do?" you fairly scream. "You should get up off your backsides and run outside with me, right now, while you still can!"

"Yes, you're right," Right Man assents. "We really should. I see that." Left Man nods his hearty agreement.

Beside yourself now, and out of time, you holler Schwarzeneggerly, "Come with me if you want to live!"—and you run out the front door.

Right Man hops up and follows. Left Man watches a moment, shrugs, unmutes the TV, picks up the doughnut his friend dropped, goes back to the game.

And burns to death.

Now, both changed their minds, in a manner of speaking. Both came to mental assent with your assertion that the house was on fire. Both intellectually grasped that they'd be doomed if they did not flee the burning house.

But only one acted on those truths.[4]

Which one repented, in biblical terms? Right Man, of course.

So while it is essential that we change our minds, and while God's Word will cause us to change our opinions about a great many things—primarily about Jesus Christ—perhaps that isn't the best way to explain the Greek noun *metanoia* (meh-tah-NOY-ah), or the related verb.

Maybe a better explanation of repentance would be a transformed mind, or a transformed way of thinking that issues in a transformed life.

We are exposed to the Word of God; and as a result, the way we look at and think about everything is transformed.

The churches at Ephesus and Thessalonica provide vivid examples of repentance.

In Ephesus, the apostles made *Jesus* and His Gospel the issue. Paul spent two years there, preaching and teaching the Word (Acts 19:8–10), and the name of the Lord Jesus was raised to great prominence (v. 17). As a result, believers confessed their involvement in the occult (v. 18), and took practical steps to burn those bridges behind them. They brought together all the writings they had about dark arts, and burned them (v. 19).

Books were expensive; this collection was worth about fifty-thousand pieces of silver, Luke says. In buying power, think of that as around 137 years' worth of salary—with no days off! With *that* practical witness, the word about Jesus spread powerfully (v. 20).

---

4. Please note: This is not meant as an illustration of *salvation*. Clearly salvation *is not* accomplished by God telling us something so we can save ourselves. Like most parables, my little story has one aim: In this case, the aim is to demonstrate what repentance looks like.

Even the local economy felt the impact of these Christians' changed lives (vv. 23–27).

Their fundamental beliefs changed, and their lives changed—in costly, practical ways. That is repentance.

Or again in Thessalonica, Paul boldly and effectively preached Jesus Christ, making Him and His Lordship the issue (Acts 17:1–4). Unbelievers made such an uproar that Paul had to leave town (vv. 5–10)—but even in that brief time, the seeds of a church were sown. That preaching of the Gospel was enough to change their lives.

Hear Paul tell it: "You turned to God from idols, to become slaves to the living and true God, and to wait for His Son from the heavens, whom He raised from the dead: Jesus, who rescues us from the coming wrath" (1 Thess. 1:9b–10 DJP). This held true, even though their conversion meant persecution and suffering (2:13; 3:1–6).

Their fundamental beliefs changed, and so their lives changed. They turned from the dead, false idols they served, and to the living and true God, to a life centered around their hope in the Lord Jesus. That is repentance.

Old Testament passages, having been written in Hebrew, do not use the Greek word to express repentance. Perhaps the most common word is the simple Hebrew verb *šûb* (SHOOV). This term means to turn back, or turn around. It is used of repentance in many verses throughout the OT.[5] Again and again men and women are called to turn from-and-to. That is, they are to turn from their horrid idols, and turn to the true and living and forgiving God. Isaiah 55:6–7 calls on Israel to seek Yahweh, to call on Him, to turn away from their sinful ways and plans and throw themselves on the mercy of God.

One cannot seek God or turn to Him without by that act turning

---

5. Including 1 Kings 8:48; Psalm 7:12; Proverbs 1:23; Isaiah 1:27; 6:10; 31:6; Jeremiah 3:22; 4:1; 26:3; Ezekiel 18:21, 23, 32; Daniel 9:13; Hosea 6:1, to list but a few.

away from sin. It is impossible to lie in the arms of sin as a lover, or serve sin as a master, and at the same time love and serve God. One cannot turn to God without turning from sin.

Let us examine this dynamic more closely.

The fundamental element in repentance is both propositional and personal. That is, repentance involves a proposition about a person.

The person is *Jesus Christ*. Wherever they went, the apostles and early believers made *the Lord Jesus Christ* the issue. This carries through the entire book of Acts. They taught and proclaimed in Jesus the resurrection (4:2), they gave powerful testimony to the resurrection of Jesus (4:33), they taught and preached Jesus as the Messiah (5:42), they preached the good news about Jesus' name (8:12), told the good news about Jesus (v. 35), proclaimed Jesus as the Son of God (9:20), proved that Jesus was the Messiah (v. 22), preached boldly in Jesus' name (v. 27), preached the good news of peace through Jesus as Lord of all (10:36), preached Jesus as Lord (11:20), proclaimed Jesus as Messiah (17:3), testified that Jesus was the Messiah (18:5), showed by the Scriptures that Jesus was Messiah (18:28), testified to all about faith in Jesus (20:21), spoke about faith in Jesus (24:24), asserted that Jesus was alive (25:19), tried to convince Jews about Jesus from the Scriptures (28:23), and taught about Jesus with boldness (28:31—the last verse in the book).

Jesus was the aim and heart of their message.

Specifically, the proposition about Jesus is, "Jesus is Lord." This is the central and fundamental Christian confession (Luke 6:46; John 13:13; Rom. 10:9; 1 Cor. 8:6; 12:3; Phil. 2:11; 1 Peter 3:15). And no wonder, since everything hangs on Christ's lordship, and everything pivots on it.[6]

---

6. Some say that repentance is merely christological. What they mean by that is that all repentance means is shifting one's opinion about who Christ is. As I will make very clear, that is not at all my understanding of Scripture.

In Jesus' case, "Jesus is Lord" is the affirmation that Jesus alone possesses absolute authority. It is the central admission that He has the right to inform and command (Luke 6:46; John 13:13). That being the case, it is the tacit acceptance not only of Jesus' person, but of His teaching, as utterly authoritative. It is the admission that Jesus is, as He taught, God incarnate; and that everything He teaches is the binding truth of God. Jesus' lordship is the hub from which all the other specifics of Christian faith are spokes.

Think it through. If Jesus is not Lord, then—whatever! Make it up. Party. Retreat. Embrace. Hide. Sober up. Zone out. Whatever!

If Jesus is not Lord, pick your worldview, if you still imagine you have freedom to do so. Of course, if you're just matter in motion, you don't actually have freedom . . . but you do have the illusion. So, go with that. Embrace the absurdity. Run around, little cockroach. I'll join you. Because if Jesus is not Lord, then He is irrelevant, except as an odd historical footnote.

On the other hand, if Jesus really *is* Lord, that truth changes *everything.*

The issue of Jesus' lordship lies at the heart of how we view everything. Two entirely different and mutually exclusive worldviews follow from our conviction about the lordship of Jesus Christ.

How do we construct our worldview, naturally, apart from Christ? From birth on, we have made things up according to our own views and leanings and preferences, what we pick and choose from our parents, or from values culled from some false god.

If Jesus is Lord, everything changes. We've done it wrong. We must unlearn and relearn. Everything has to be thought through all over again, from basement to rooftop. We must, as it were, sit at Jesus' feet, and consciously learn from Him how to view everything.

To be even more specific, if Jesus is Lord, then it means that we have been wrong in how we approach God, the world, ourselves, others. (What does that leave?) It means we have been living wrong. We have been treasuring the wrong things. Every aspect of our thinking—not only *what* we think, but *how* we think—has rested on the wrong premise, the wrong foundation. So everything has to be re-thought, re-tooled, re-worked.

We need to repent and the issue of Jesus' lordship is far more than merely intellectual. I want to be sure we're absolutely clear on this.

Say you took the same test on Monday and Tuesday, featuring the question "Is Jesus Lord?" Monday you check "No." Tuesday you check "Yes." Does that mean you repented between the two tests?

Not necessarily.

Now it is true that your answer Monday was incorrect, and Tuesday's was correct. Formally. But all that measures (at best!) is an opinion. You can change an opinion, without transforming your mind.

The issue is whether your whole way of thinking pivots, from a world in which you and your wants, needs, biases, and desires are paramount ("lord") to you, to a totally different world in which Jesus is Lord, and you are His slave and student. Consider more fully Isaiah 55:6–7: "Seek the Lord while he may be found; call upon him while he is near; let the wicked forsake his way, and the unrighteous man his thoughts; let him return to the Lord, that he may have compassion on him, and to our God, for he will abundantly pardon."

The issue is seeking and finding God in Jesus Christ. We are heading in the wrong direction, so to seek Him we must turn to Him. In so doing, we must abandon our own self-absorbed, self-ruled lives; we must turn from our self-serving, self-centered thoughts. We must embrace God the Lord in Jesus Christ. Only in this way can we find Him and His rescue and forgiveness.

Bottom line. Here is where the rubber meets the road. There is a very tight relationship between this proposition and repentance.

Where we stand—where we rest our weight—in relation to that proposition ("Is Jesus Lord?") affects the way we see, value, and approach everything. When I say everything, I mean it literally enough that you can run it both ways:

- When we come to be gripped by the truth that Jesus is Lord, everything in our lives begins to shift. How we think, evaluate, cherish, make decisions, relate: Everything begins to change. There is a seismic shift, a sea change, and it echoes through every day of the rest of our lives. That shift both is, and is caused by, repentance.
- If nothing has shifted—if we basically look, see, perceive, reason, love, and live exactly like others to whom Jesus is not Lord—then there has been no repentance. "Jesus is Lord" is at best an opinion, not a conviction. We have not repented. We are not Christians. We have no relationship with Christ, and no right to hope for forgiveness or life or heaven or any other blessing that is found in Christ alone. We have no vital, saving faith. Clearly, then, it becomes essential that we understand the third component always present in justification: faith.

Vital Faith

I need to say at the outset that repentance and faith, in the Bible, are like a couple deeply in love: inseparable. You can distinguish them, but you can't part them. That is, if the "faith" we claim is not a repentant faith, it isn't real faith; it's merely a change of opinion. And if our "repentance" does not have faith at its heart, it is not real repentance; it's merely a change of tactics.

So intertwined are the realities of faith and repentance, that apostles might use either term—without excluding the other. For instance, what does Peter answer when his Jewish hearers are struck to their heart with their guilt and Christ's reality, and they ask "What must we do?" Peter says, "Repent!" (Acts 2:38). Does he mean they should not believe in Christ? Hardly. Peter calls them to get baptized "in the name of Jesus Christ," clearly confessing their faith in Jesus as Messiah. He can say "repent" because godly repentance is believing repentance.

Later, the Philippian jailor asked Paul and Silas, "Sirs, what must I do to be saved?" How did they answer? They said, "Believe!" (Acts 16:31). Did they mean that he should believe a fact or two about Christ, but go on clinging to his gods and ungodly ways? Hardly. Paul and Silas say, "Believe in the Lord Jesus." The one in whom he is to believe is Lord. To surrender to Christ's lordship necessarily will result in a transformed mind and life.

What is faith, then? Well, you probably know the description: "Faith is the assurance of things hoped for, the conviction of things not seen" (Heb. 11:1). Faith brings conviction and assurance that reach beyond what is immediately perceived. But does that mean that faith is a blind leap from darkness to darkness?

Not at all. Not biblical faith.

First of all, faith is focused on information, on truth—on statements of truth. The notion that Christianity is primarily a feeling or an experience is terribly misleading. Christian faith is distinguished by its focus on certain specific affirmations of truth.

That is why Christianity itself can simply be called "the faith" (1 Cor. 16:13; 2 Cor. 13:5; Gal. 1:23; 1 Tim. 3:9; 4:1, 6; 5:8; 6:10, 21, etc.). That is also why the Bible so often commands and commends believing that certain things are true (Exod. 4:5; Ps. 27:13; Matt. 9:28; Mark 11:24; Luke 1:45; John 8:24; 11:27, 42; 13:19; 14:10; 16:27, 30; 17:8, 21; 20:31; Acts 15:11; Rom. 6:8; 1 Thess. 4:14; Heb. 11:6; James 2:19).

Faith needs a base to stand on. As presented to us, that base is statements of truth, or propositions.

But we must immediately add that these are far from arid conclusions reached at the end of a syllogism. I am not talking about deduced facts, but revealed facts. Though the truths we must believe are reasonable and rational, they are not products of reason; they are products of revelation. They do not come up from within; they come down from above. Every one of the statements I speak of has behind it the true and living God who cannot lie (Titus 1:2). If God says it, it is true, it corresponds to reality.

Faith is a response to a word from God. We see this illustrated countless times. Let us start with the very first express statement of faith, in the narrative of Genesis 15:4–6.

> And behold, the word of the LORD came to [Abram]: "This man shall not be your heir; your very own son shall be your heir." And he brought him outside and said, "Look toward heaven, and number the stars, if you are able to number them." Then he said to him, "So shall your offspring be." And he believed the LORD, and he counted it to him as righteousness.

This is pivotal and definitional. Abram is the man the Bible points to as an example of what faith is (Rom. 4:12–16; Gal. 3:7–9; Heb. 11:8–19).

So what are the elements of faith, in this incident? Happily, the fundamentals here are simplicity itself:

1. A word from God (Gen. 15:4–5).
2. Human embrace of that word as true (v. 6).

If I wrote another twenty thousand words on the topic, we'd end up right back with those two points: Faith is embracing a word from God as true.

Of course, as with "repentance = a change of mind," the elements inside of that reception are a bit more complex. I think that the way theologians have long explained this is very useful, so here are faith's three Rs:

1. Recognizing
2. Realizing
3. Resting

In *recognizing* we get a view of the facts, the statements of truth. This is the basis of everything that follows. The modern silliness that says we need a "relationship" but not doctrine is just that: silliness.[7] Doctrine is teaching, a rational statement of truth, based on facts. Relationships rest on facts, on knowledge. If you don't *know about* someone, you don't *know* someone, and you have no relationship.

If we are to believe, we must know what or whom to believe. Paul asks, "How are they to believe in him of whom they have never heard?" (Rom. 10:14). This is why the whole Bible stresses the importance of information, of knowledge, of understanding—of facts. Every biblical statement about faith assumes knowledge of facts. If we are to "believe that" certain things are true (as we noted a moment ago), we must know what those things are.

For instance, the apostle John describes the purpose of his gospel: "Now Jesus did many other signs in the presence of the disciples, which are not written in this book; but these are written so that you may believe that Jesus is the Christ, the Son of God, and that by believing you may have life in his name" (John 20:30–31).

---

7. I say "modern," but it really isn't new. J. Gresham Machen shot this fantasy all to doll-rags back in 1925 (J. Gresham Machen, *What Is Faith?* (Grand Rapids: Eerdmans, 1925). Read it sometime. You'll get shivers.

What John had written supplied truths, facts, information necessary to come to the conviction that Jesus was Messiah and Son of God.

To have saving faith, then, we need to know the facts of the Gospel. This involves exposure at least to basic truths about the triune God of Scripture, about man, about God's world, about sin, and about the cross.

No facts, no faith.

Frankly, it boggles my mind how many don't even get past this first element. For instance, they won't even admit that Jesus in fact taught differently than what they believe, or that the Bible doesn't go where they want to go. They've made up a Cheerleader Jesus, or a Bobblehead Buddy Jesus, who's okay with their pet sin or perversion. They have yet to come to Square A—and that's the square where we realize what Jesus actually taught and was, and how radically different that is from where we've been.

But mere possession of facts is not enough. Men innately "know" important things about God, but they suppress that knowledge and rebel against it (Rom. 1:18ff.). King Agrippa "knew" a lot of things about prophecy and the Gospel, but that knowledge fell short of saving faith (Acts 26:26–29). Darkest of all, Judas "knew" more information about Jesus than we possess, yet went off into eternal darkness (John 13:2; 17:12).

What else is essential to saving faith? Possession of truths must lead to a realization about those truths.

Secondly, in *realizing*, we accept that those essential, revealed facts are true. The Bible repeatedly emphasizes the importance of accepting the facts of the faith as true:

- ". . . that they may believe that the LORD, the God of their fathers, the God of Abraham, the God of Isaac, and the God of Jacob, has appeared to you." (Exod. 4:5)

- "... unless you believe that I am he you will die in your sins." (John 8:24b)
- "I knew that you always hear me, but I said this on account of the people standing around, that they may believe that you sent me." (John 11:42)
- "Believe me that I am in the Father and the Father is in me, or else believe on account of the works themselves." (John 14:11)
- "... we believe that Jesus died and rose again." (1 Thess. 4:14a)
- "And without faith it is impossible to please him, for whoever would draw near to God must believe that he exists and that he rewards those who seek him." (Heb. 11:6)
- "Everyone who believes that Jesus is the Christ has been born of God." (1 John 5:1a)

In *realization* we come to see that these truths the Word of God asserts are in fact true truths, and not merely hollow truth-claims. God really is the almighty, holy, wise, loving, just Creator. We really are His fallen, corrupt, guilty, liable creatures. Christ really is the only hope and Savior, and salvation really is available only through Him, on the basis of His work on the cross, and achieved and offered by grace, and receivable by repentant faith alone.

But even correct information plus the opinion that the information corresponds with reality is not full-orbed biblical faith. The demons correctly believe that God is one (James 2:19). What's more, they admitted out loud in front of everyone that Jesus Christ was the holy Son of God (Matt. 8:29; Mark 1:24; 3:11). Mere consent to the facts is not all that the Bible means by that faith through which a person is declared righteous in God's eyes.

What is the third critical element? Recognition of the Bible's statements of truth must issue in realization that those statements are in fact true, and that must issue in personally resting on those truths.

Finally, we have the third R. In *resting*, we take the truths to ourselves and rest our weight on them. We embrace them, we bank on them, we lean on them. This is the catalyst. We do not merely recognize the meaning of the claim that the house is on fire; we do not stop with realizing that it really is on fire and that we will die if we stay in the house. We accept those things as true for us, resulting in action.

The Bible does not speak only of believing that, but of believing in, and into, and believing upon God or Christ.

- "Believe me," Jesus says in John 14:11. He is calling His students to trust Him, to rest on what He says as true.
- But more, He uses an arresting phrase when He says "Believe in God; believe also in me" (John 14:1). The Greek preposition translated "in" usually means "into." This is a frequent and characteristic expression in the Greek NT of our need to rest ourselves on God in Christ.[8]
- A number of verses also use a Greek preposition (emphasized in the verses below) that means direction toward, or resting upon. "And they said, 'Believe *in* the Lord Jesus, and you will be saved, you and your household'" (Acts 16:31); as if to say, Rest your faith on the Lord Jesus. Paul writes that "to the one who does not work but believes *in* him who justifies the ungodly, his faith is counted as righteousness" (Rom. 4:5). This man does nothing to try to earn or deserve salvation; he does not trust to his goodness or sincerity or virtue. Rather, he rests his faith on God, who declares the ungodly to be righteous by grace alone and through faith alone. Later in the chapter, Paul again affirms that righteousness "will be

---

8. Cf. Reymond, *New Systematic Theology*, 729. Reymond's discussion on 726ff. is very helpful.

counted to us who believe *in* him who raised from the dead Jesus our Lord" (Rom. 4:24).

It is a mistake to parcel off this or that proposition and make it the Gospel. I squirm when I hear people say, "Believe that Jesus died for you, and you will be saved." I am afraid that someone will think, "Ah, so, if I just believe that one thing, I'm 'in'!" Then that same person will feel free to *disbelieve* Jesus when He talks about sexuality, about the OT, or about a host of other things— because, after all, he believed that one thing he had to believe, so he's saved.

The Gospel does call us to hear and understand truth. It does call us to accept certain propositions as true. But it also calls us to believe in Christ, in the person of the Lord Jesus Christ—all of Him; and, believing, to rest on Him wholly.

My favorite biblical illustration is found in a familiar scene of Peter and Jesus on the sea (Matt. 14:24–33; also Mark 6:47–52; John 6:16–21).

Jesus' students had been having an absolutely miserable time. They had apparently set off to row across the lake at its widest point, where it is some six or seven miles across. They were now two or three miles out, right in the middle. It is somewhere around three in the morning. They had been working all night, toiling and struggling against a contrary wind. Since none of them was Jack Bauer, they weren't accustomed to pulling all-nighters.

All is pitch black. Then suddenly, out in the gloom of the night, these exhausted, dispirited men hear an unexpected sound. They look up, look all around. There? No, no—I think it's . . . yes, it's over there.

From the gloom, a dim figure approaches them.

Walking *on* the water.

It is a spine-jellying sight. They didn't know what they were seeing. But the figure identified Himself as Jesus. Standing on the roiling water, smack in the middle of the turbulent lake.

At first, Peter did not think that what he was seeing was Jesus (Matt. 14:26). But Peter gained facts and knowledge (v. 27; *recognizing*), and examined them to see if it was really Jesus (v. 28; *realizing*).

Then came The Moment. Peter had a moment of crisis, a point of decision. Jesus had called his bluff, and bid him step out on the water. Peter had only two options. He could continue to rest his weight in the boat, or he literally could put his full weight on Jesus' bare word to him (v. 29; *resting*).

He could not do both.

While Peter remained in the boat, whatever his theories and opinions were, he would not be exercising full faith in Jesus. Full faith would involve embracing His word, and that would become visible only by his stepping out of the boat. Once Peter's second sandal hit the surface of the water, we were seeing full-orbed faith in action . . . however imperfectly and briefly, in Peter's case (v. 30)!

Now we know that Peter's faith did falter. The wind frightened him, and he began to sink. Jesus grabbed Peter and saved him, with the rebuke, "O you of little faith, why did you doubt?" (v. 31).

It was "little faith"—but it was faith enough to get Peter out of the boat on the strength of Jesus' word alone. And so, it serves as a "little" illustration of what faith is. Faith recognizes the facts about its object, it realizes the truth about its object . . . and then it rests upon its object.

In our case, what *justifying faith* specifically means is that we abandon hope of finding meaning or purpose or God apart from Jesus as our Lord. We get out of our boat, whatever it is. We bail out on any fantasies that we are good enough, deserving enough, worthy enough. We stretch police tape across any notion of being self-sufficient, or of finding hope and life and a relationship with God anywhere but through Jesus Christ the crucified and risen master. We cling to Jesus alone, on the strength of His word alone, for hope of eternal life.

So we must know truths about Jesus' person and work, and recognize them for what they are. We must also know that the truths are true that we know about Him, realizing that they correspond to reality, and that this has a potential impact on us. But beyond that, we must abandon ourselves to Him, we must lean on and trust in Him alone for all that He claims to offer: the way, the truth, the life, forgiveness, and God. We must rest all our hopes on Jesus. We bank our present and our eternity on Jesus Christ alone, with no backup plan, no "Plan B." He is *it*.

We must not look to ourselves. We must look away to Christ, to the One who bore our sins and crimes and rebellion, on whom the holy God poured out His wrath. We look to Christ and see the perfect justice of God. We also look to Christ and see our own righteousness, the seamless and flawless purity that God demands. It is *that* vast, immeasurable, flawless righteousness that clothes us before God.

That's living faith, repentant faith, which God enables in us by grace alone, and through which alone He pronounces us 100 percent righteous because of the infinite righteous perfections of Jesus Christ alone.

This brings us to the second towering truth.

Chapter 8

Second Towering Truth—
Born from Above

How God Deals with Our Bad Nature

As we saw, we have two massive dilemmas. Not pollution, taxes, traffic, global warming, or cholesterol. No, our biggest problems are what we do and who we are, our *record* and our *nature*.

I remember very keenly how that truth pressed down on me. It was like an elephant sitting on my chest.

Through my teens, I had been in a "mind science" cult (Religious Science) that taught that deep down inside we were all God expressing Itself. The trouble was, the more honestly I looked deep within myself, the more horrified I was at what I saw, and the less it looked like anything that anyone would call "God."

I'd actually done a good deal of self-improvement, "swept out the house" considerably. I'd been fairly successful. I was a better person than I'd been.

By my standards.

But it didn't really matter. I was still *me*. The problem wasn't simply what I did, but what my heart was like. You can't split the stream from the fountainhead. I did what I did, because I was what I was. I saw that, clearly and inescapably. *I* was the problem.

Yearning for deliverance from that—from that gaping maw of all-consuming selfishness, lusts, brokenness, and idiocies—was a large impetus in sending me running for Jesus Christ, whom I had previously mocked and scorned. I found His solution to the humanly insoluble nightmare: Justification addresses the problem of our record and regeneration addresses the problem of our nature. What Adam's sin made us, God *unmakes* and *remakes*.

Regeneration: What It Is, Why We Need It

Without regeneration, God would just be hosing off the pig and watching it head right back for the muck. With regeneration, the pig is no longer a pig. God does not merely make us clean. He makes us new.

Old Nicodemus was a distinguished teacher and leader in Israel. Perhaps he was a member of the Messianic Claims Investigation Committee. Perhaps not, though. After all, rather than risk being seen bustling down the streets to meet Jesus in broad daylight, Nicodemus pursued an after-hours chat with the Master (John 3).

The great man was all flattery. "Rabbi," he began. I imagine that the apostles elbowed each other and nodded. *Now, this was more like it!* Jesus, a rustic craftsman, had not had any formal advanced education. He had no state-accredited degree. Normally, a man of Nicodemus's standing would not have extended the honorific "Rabbi" to the likes of Jesus. Ah but here, at long last, was a man who recognized His excellence. About time! Sweet!

Nicodemus continued: "We know that you are a teacher come from God, for no one can do these signs that you do unless God is with him" (John 3:2).

The apostles had to think that they were finally getting somewhere. "*We* know," Nicodemus said. So there were others? Could it be that the ruling class in Israel really was coming round to the truth about Jesus, the truth the apostles already knew? Surely Jesus will exploit this opening into the intelligentsia!

If that is what they thought, Jesus' abrupt response must have made them all swallow their gum.

With no answering flatteries or niceties, Jesus replied: "Truly, truly, I say to you, unless one is born again he cannot see the kingdom of God" (v. 3). And in case His point had seemed too general, a moment later He added, "Do not marvel that I said to you [singular], 'You [plural] must be born again'" (v. 7).

What is going on here?

We miss part of it because, long ago, editors put in a chapter break between 2:24 and 3:1. In the original manuscript, the narrative would simply have been an unbroken flow. Read my translation of John 2:23–3:2, emphasizing select words to show John's progression of thought:

> And when He was in Jerusalem during the Passover, at the feast, many *trusted*[1] in His name, as they observed His *signs* which He was doing. But Jesus Himself was not *entrusting* Himself to them, because of the fact that He knew all

---

1. This is the word usually translated "believe," but rendered this way to show the connection with the next verse.

people, and because He had no need that one should testify concerning *man*—for He Himself knew all along what was in *man*.

Now, there was a *man* from the Pharisees, Nicodemus by name, a ruler of the Jews. This one came to Him at night-time, and said to Him, "Rabbi, we know that it is from God that you came, a teacher. For no one is able to do these *signs* which you are doing, unless God be with him!"

Jesus knew what was in man—and Nicodemus was a man. Many men had sign faith, but not saving faith. Jesus did not trust such professions; and Nicodemus made just such a profession of faith, fixed on Jesus' signs.

Jesus saw right past the dazzling duds, the fancy phylacteries, the baronial bearing, and the sycophantic speech. He saw Nicodemus's heart. Nicodemus thought he was paying Jesus a real compliment—but Jesus saw that the darkness within Nicodemus was far deeper than the gloom shrouding the streets without.

So we all know Nicodemus's little joke ("An old man can't climb back into his mama's womb and get born again, can he, heh heh heh?"), and we know Jesus' icy splash of a retort ("You're the teacher of Israel, and you don't know these things?"). But let's focus on Jesus' first response: "Truly, truly, I say to you, unless one is born of water and the Spirit, he cannot enter the kingdom of God. That which is born of the flesh is flesh, and that which is born of the Spirit is spirit" (John 3:5–6). *Water? Spirit? Huh? What is Jesus talking about? Baptism?*

Without duplicating the thousands of words scholars have produced arguing that very question, here's what I'm confident is the answer. The interpretive clue is in Jesus' astonishment that Nicodemus did not know what He was talking about (v. 10)—which rules out baptism, a rite never mentioned in the OT.

Jesus had in mind a prophetic passage Nicodemus should have known, and known well, where Yahweh says:

> "I will take you from the nations and gather you from all the countries and bring you into your own land. I will *sprinkle clean water* on you, and you shall be *clean* from *all your uncleannesses*, and from all your idols I will *cleanse* you. And I will give you a *new heart*, and a *new spirit* I will put within you. And I will *remove the heart of stone* from your flesh and *give you a heart of flesh*. And I will *put my Spirit within you*, and *cause* you to walk in my statutes and be careful to obey my rules." (Ezek. 36:24–27, emphasis added)

In this over six-hundred-year-old prophecy, all the elements from Jesus' words to Nicodemus are there: water, Spirit, new heart.

Can literal water, H_2O, do what Ezekiel depicts? Can it wash away spiritual filth, and rinse away addiction to idolatry? Of course not. "Water" here is a metaphor for spiritual cleansing from spiritual defilement. It translates doctrinally to justification, removal of guilt and impurity, the first towering truth we studied in the previous chapter. The "new heart" and "new spirit" is a prediction of regeneration, of being born anew and from above.[2]

Jesus takes from Ezekiel the elements of water, a new nature, and the Spirit, and puts them together in pointing Nicodemus to his need for regeneration, a birth from above.

How does this happen? Well, don't expect me to be able to explain it fully. After all, Jesus also tells Nicodemus, "The wind

---

2. The adverb Jesus uses can equally mean "again" or "from above." It would be characteristic of John's reporting if both nuances were present. After all, if an adult like Nicodemus (or you, or me) is born *from above*, he is born *again*.

blows where it wishes, and you hear its sound, but you do not know where it comes from or where it goes. So it is with everyone who is born of the Spirit" (John 3:8). There is supernatural mystery to it not reducible to a tidy formula.

But the Scripture does warrant at least these six observations.

Regeneration Is a Sovereign Act of God

Though I realize this knocks heads with a lot of evangelicals' notions (including the view I myself cherished for many years), I do not know any other honest way of handling John 1:12–13: "But to all who did receive him, who believed in his name, he gave the right to become children of God, who were born, not of blood nor of the will of the flesh nor of the will of man, but of God." There we have the certain fact that all who are born again believe in Jesus Christ. But their new birth is expressly traced—*not* to anything they had inherited from their parents, nor to any exercise of their own will or any decision they made, nor to any decision any other mortal had made, *but* to the kingly grace and work of God. They believed savingly in Jesus because God had given them new birth *before* their embrace of Christ.

They received Christ because God had regenerated them, so John writes.

Remember our Lord's talk with Nicodemus. Have you ever noticed that Jesus does not tell Nicodemus how to be born again in John 3? Nicodemus twice asks about the new birth (John 3:4, 9). The second time, in fact, he expressly asks, "How is it possible for these things to happen?" (v. 9 DJP). I think most modern evangelicals, including myself not too many years ago, would have said, "Well, you pray and ask God to make you born again."

We might do that, but Jesus did not. Neither time does Jesus say, "Here's how you do it," or "Here is what God wants you to do to get born again." Rather, our Lord says that being born of the Spirit is a product of the Spirit's mysterious, sovereign working (vv. 5–8), and He expresses amazement that Nicodemus does not already know about regeneration from the OT. But He does not tell him how to get himself born again.

Now, John 3 does go on to emphasize the necessity of believing in Christ. However, nowhere does the chapter say that we get regenerated by believing in Christ. In fact, when the author of that gospel writes about saving faith, he makes it a *result* of regeneration, and not the *cause* of it. Let me show you.

The apostle John, who wrote the fourth gospel, makes faith the result of regeneration. Read 1 John 5:1 very closely: "Everyone who believes that Jesus is the Christ has been born of God." Did you see it? Everyone who *in the present* believes, has *in the past* been regenerated by God. Present faith indicates past regeneration. Faith does not produce regeneration, to John's mind. Regeneration produces faith.

Our Lord's half-brother James sounded the same note when he wrote, "Of his own will he brought us forth by the word of truth, that we should be a kind of firstfruits of his creatures" (James 1:18). God gave us new life as an exercise of His will, not in response to an exercise of our wills. There are the two inseparables yet again: our faith, prompted by God's initiative. God moves first, then we move in response.

Add Peter for a third witness: "Blessed be the God and Father of our Lord Jesus Christ! According to his great mercy, he has caused us to be born again to a living hope through the resurrection of Jesus Christ from the dead" (1 Peter 1:3). It was the Father who caused us to be born again according to His own great mercy, rather than in response to a request from us—a request that never would nor could have come from spiritually dead lips and a heart that hates God and His will.

These apostles surely got the idea from Jesus. Return one more time to John 3, and note that our Lord said that a man must be "begotten again," as the Greek may also be rendered (vv. 3, 5). The verb is in the passive voice. The man does not do it to himself; he doesn't *born-again* himself. He is the recipient of the life-giving action. And so Jesus later says, "You do not believe because you are not part of my flock" (John 10:26). Being in His flock precedes belief, but it is inseparable from it.

So which the chicken, which the egg? Because I see all of Scripture (and these specific passages, among others) giving God all the glory, and tracing regeneration to God's action preceding our faith, it does not shock me to find that the Bible teaches that regeneration precedes and necessarily provokes saving faith. But I would hasten to say that it does so like flicking a light switch precedes filling the dark room with bright light. The relationship is causal, and A precedes B—but not by much!

I wonder whether the analogy of our great-grampa's birth might be helpful. When did Adam become physically alive? When he drew his first breath. But what was that breath? When "the LORD God . . . breathed into his nostrils the breath of life, and the man became a living creature" (Gen. 2:7). So Adam was alive when he drew his first breath . . . but that very breath was God, breathing "into his nostrils the breath of life." Adam began doing what made him alive, when God made him alive.

And so do we, in the spiritual realm. We are alive through faith. But our very exercise of faith is a grace-gift from God, breathed into us through regeneration.

So if you'll pardon my paradiddling this drum for just one more moment, if anyone imagines that *I* imagine a bunch of born-again unbelievers walking around, saved and going to heaven but not believing in Christ—*don't*. I have no such notion. The only sign I have that anyone is born of God is if he believes in Jesus, because that is the sign God Himself gives us (1 John 2:22–23; 4:15; 5:1).

If there's no light shining from the bulb, I conclude that the switch has not been flicked.

God Uses Means

James connects our rebirth with the Word of God, used by the will of God (James 1:18). Peter likewise says we were given new birth by the living and abiding word of God (1 Peter 1:23). Often it is people who bring us this word, and so they become part of God's means (Rom. 10:14; 1 Cor. 4:15; Philem. 10).

This deals death to the common lazy notion that "if that's true, it doesn't matter what we do, and we might as well not tell people about Christ." Disobedience is never wise, nor is unbelief. God tells us to tell others about Christ, so we should. God uses means to accomplish His sovereign will. It isn't our part to guess how He might do what He chooses to do; it is to do what He tells us to do.

Regeneration Makes Us New Men and Women

Most memorably, Paul says, "Therefore, if anyone is in Christ, he is a new creation. The old has passed away; behold, the new has come" (2 Cor. 5:17). He hasn't *turned over* a new leaf; he has *become* a new leaf. Paul tells us to put on the new self (Eph. 4:24; Col. 3:10). Before we come to know Christ, there is no "new" self. There is only the self that hates God and His Word (Rom. 8:7). In Christ, all this changes.

As you see, this is spoken of more than once as an act of *creation*, not just a "makeover." Regeneration is not like some reality show where you get a lift, a tuck, and some spray paint and confetti. God makes us *new* men and women.

Let me hasten to add, however, that God makes *us* new men and women. We are not replaced with new, heavenly pod-selves, bearing no continuity with our old selves.

I remember a non-Christian friend was stunned to learn that I'd come to believe in Jesus. He said, "You don't look different." And I didn't. Yet I was. Before I was a Christian, I liked a rock group named Chicago, fishing, and mayonnaise. I still did. I had a warped sense of humor. I still did ("—and do," the reader adds mentally; *nice*).

But before I was a Christian, I loved to use horrible language. I didn't anymore. I loved to shock people with foul jokes. I didn't anymore. I hated the Bible; now I loved it. I thought Jesus a distant figure; now He was everything. I thought all Christians were idiots. Now I knew *I* was an idiot, and I loved my Christian brothers and sisters.

I was still me. But I was a new me.

As the verses above show, the change is so radical that it is called a new birth and a new creation. At the same time, there is continuity. God saves *us*, He regenerates *us*. He does not take our old sinful selves and annihilate them, replacing them with newly created souls that never sinned (and thus never needed to be saved). God *wanted* there to be a you, with your unique perspective and combination of quirks and intricacies. In regeneration, He does not replace you with something else; He makes you new!

Regeneration Gives Us a New Heart

Remember that our problem was our deceitful, sick heart (Jer. 17:9). Ezekiel says we had a heart of stone—stubborn and stiff before God's word. God removes that heart and gives us a new heart, and puts His own Spirit within us to give us new and different motivations and desires (Ezek. 36:26–27).

That means, then, that the way we think, evaluate, reason, and cherish undergoes a fundamental transformation. As we will see in a moment, it is a lifelong process. But the basic change of heart happens right away at regeneration, the moment God gives life to a dead heart.

Regeneration Issues in Increasing Christ-Likeness

Regeneration starts as an instantaneous transformation. You aren't a little alive any more than you're a little dead, no matter how you feel on Monday mornings. But at the same time, it begins a process, as gradual physical growth follows instantaneous conception. It is proper that we start out as spiritual children, but we are called to grow (Heb. 5:11–14; 2 Peter 3:18). What the whole church has as its goal, each of us as individuals have as our goal: to grow to maturity, to look more and more like Jesus Christ (Eph. 4:12–15). God's goal for us is that we increasingly radiate the character of Christ (Rom. 8:29). Christ is the model, the exemplar, after whom we are being fashioned by life's blessings and bruisings (Heb. 5:8).

In it all there is a grand family resemblance to Jesus Christ (Rom. 8:29; 13:14; 1 Cor. 15:49; Phil. 3:21; 1 John 3:2). Countless myriads of individuals, all distinct from each other, yet all nurtured and fashioned after the likeness of the Lord Jesus.

How? How can one Person be mirrored in so many diverse individuals? Because Jesus Christ is a grand and vast enough person that endless millions of humans can fundamentally reflect His character, and still be genuine individuals.

It is a gradual process. Paul says that our new self is "being renewed [present passive participle in Greek—ongoing activity of which we're the objects] unto full knowledge in accord with the image of the One who created him" (Col. 3:10 DJP). The creation was instantaneous, but the renewal is day by day. We progress from one stage to the next, to the next and onward, as we learn about Jesus and love Him and know Him more intimately (2 Cor. 3:18).

Regeneration's Promise Is Consummated in Christ's Presence

The instantaneous start—like our natural birth—begins a process of living that is daily and detailed. For now, the road of this new life is very rocky and bumpy. We seem to go two steps forward, six back, eight forward, one back . . . It's wearing, and wearying.

But we are going *somewhere.* This new life, now humble and lowly, will burst forth into dazzling splendor one day. We who are in Christ are headed for a definite and assured destination. When Christ returns, when He resurrects dead believers and transforms living believers (1 Thess. 4:16–17), then we will fully bear His image, with no distortions or cracks or scars (1 Cor. 15:49). We will see Him, and that sight will utterly and finally transform us to His likeness (1 John 3:2).

That glorious goal is set and assured the moment we are born again.

Where Do the Two Towering Truths Put Us?

By God's resplendent grace, we who have been declared righteous (justified) and born from above (regenerated) are sitting awfully pretty. We're well positioned to do some serious world-tilting. We have seen that God the Father has addressed our deepest problems, and met our direst needs, in Jesus Christ.

God the Son willingly came in response to the Father's eternal plan, to rescue us from our living nightmare. He was the person we could never be. He lived the life we could never live. And at the pinnacle of the life of God the Son on earth, God the Father took the mass of our offenses and crimes and rebellions and sins, and laid them on the shoulders of Jesus Christ. God the Son bore the agony of the curse due us, suffered the Father's wrath, moaned under His turning away.

And, having fully satisfied the demands of justice, and having overturned the powers of darkness, in His death He dealt Satan a death blow.

Thus, our sins were atoned for. Paid in full. How do we know? We know because on the third day after His death, Jesus Christ strode forth from the tomb, never to die again. Now He sits at the right hand of the Father, one day to rule and reign on earth over all the universe.

And so, because of Him, we are declared perfectly righteous the moment we embrace the Lord Jesus Christ in repentant faith, accepting Him and all He says as true, and relying on Him alone for our salvation.

Our sinful record is fully dealt with when we believe in the Lord Jesus Christ.

And how do we do that?

By a miraculous work of grace, God the Father takes pity on our dead, lost, God-hating selves. He breathes His life into us, bringing sight to blind eyes, life to dead spirits, and the submission of repentant faith to hard, rebellious hearts. He causes us to be born again, and as surely as a newborn babe breaks out in a cry, so our newborn hearts embrace Jesus as Lord, and His gospel as our hope. In Christ, we receive new life.

Our sinful nature is thus also dealt with by the person and work of the Lord Jesus.

So, now that we've been set free, what's the plan? What is our direction? How do we steer, how do we live, what choices do we make and how do we make them?

The Bible says that in Christ we die to sin and live to holiness—in fact, that it is both *impossible and impermissible* for us to go on as we did before (Rom. 6). We will struggle, it is true (Rom. 7:14–25), but the Holy Spirit will lead us in a joyous, hope-filled life that reflects the holy character of God, until He takes us to glory (Rom. 8).

Part Three Summary

How does all this make me a world-tilter and a barrier-buster?

Given the world-tilting truth that our central problem is guilt before God, the world's stabs at solutions involve schemes of evasion on the one hand, or programs of self-improvement on the other. All fall hopelessly short of dealing with the real problem.

The world-tilting truth is that God deals with our sin on His terms in Christ alone. We must abandon our own agendas and programs, and embrace Christ in His truth. We must bow to His lordship. In doing this, we do not realize the world's dim notion of turning over a new leaf. Rather, we can do it only as God makes us new people, with new natures and imputed righteousness.

God's Word shatters this illusion by identifying the source of our discomfort: We have been judged and condemned by His perfect standard.

We also saw how God's Word shatters blurry sentimental notions of faith as a shapeless feeling, or of conversion as something we generate from within ourselves. We had to cast aside as well any delusions of contributing anything to our standing before God, of trying to make ourselves change by ourselves, or of controlling our relationship with God.

Instead, we saw that saving faith is a gift of God, a response of our whole beings to the revealed truths of Christ. We also saw that we only could respond that way by God's transforming grace. Through this saving faith, God counts us eternally and perfectly righteous with Christ's own righteousness. We stand before Him by grace alone, on the firmest of foundations.

What now? Having been transformed, having been forgiven and declared righteous, what do we do? Does the Bible lay out specifics, or are we left to the world or to religious traditions? Let's find out.

Part Four

How Do We Get Going?

Preparing to Launch

Chapter 9

The Struggle of New Life

Growth Is Hard

Where we started together called for hard work. We took an unsparing, truthful look at God's diagnosis of the human race in part 1. It was rough sledding, but it was absolutely necessary. This unhappy knowledge actually prepared us for the wonderful news of part 2, where we learned of God's eternal plan for a dramatic and total rescue operation in Jesus Christ. In part 3, we studied what God accomplished in carrying out His plan, and how we could get in on it.

So now that God has done all these wonderful things for us in Christ, what do we do? Where do we go from here? If part 3 described our conception and birth, what will our life look like?

As we study what the Bible says about the life of faith, I am going to shift my approach a bit. Let me explain how.

In the first three parts we navigated around a lot of reefs together, without my explicitly pointing them out. Even among Christians, there are views of human nature and need, and of God's work of salvation, that do not do the Bible full justice. Rather than name them and wrestle with them and show where I find them faulty, I've done my best to provide a positive corrective for those misconceptions.

But now we must face some more barriers that are sometimes raised by well-meaning but misinformed fellow Christians. These are barriers that can take a man or woman who passionately wants to know, love, and serve Christ, and send him or her off into a dark, dismal ditch.

So let's clear the road ahead. To do that, we must knock down some obstructions together.

The Struggle: Flesh and Spirit

It isn't long before a new Christian begins to realize something: *The Christian life is a struggle.*

It isn't always that way at first. While the instant emotional impact of conversion varies from person to person, many of us find the start of Christian life to be thrilling and joyful. For me, it was a sense of deep relief, of having come home, of finally standing on true truth. For others it is the joy of sins forgiven, the assurance of God's love, hope for the future—any, some, all of those things.

Regardless of our individual experience, something wonderful happens to every believer in Jesus Christ. The Holy Spirit of God comes to live within him permanently.[1] He moves in our heart, producing desires and goals and longings to which we had previously been complete strangers. We want to learn of Christ, to walk

---

1. We will learn more of the work of the Holy Spirit in chapter 13.

close to Him, to serve Him, to make Him look good, to make our lives count for Him, to tell the world about Him.

In pursuit of these new desires, we launch off with enthusiastic prayers and Bible study and church attendance and witnessing. It is thrilling. We may sail steady and hard for a day, a week, a year . . . but then . . .

We always eventually come to find that our new heart and new loves keep tripping over old habits and old desires. Our performance falls far short of the flame of our ardor and aspirations for Christ. Our reach vastly exceeds our grasp.

We sin. We make mistakes. We act foolishly. *Still!* Lame and bad things we used to do in our "BC" days crop back up. It can feel like being slapped in the face with a cold, wet haddock. We thought we were new and improved . . . and here we're still acting old and lame.

It's heart breaking and spirit crushing.

So we pray . . . and foul thoughts or silly distractions still come sidling in to mess up that holy hour with their sniggering wheezes.

We turn to our Bible . . . and it's hard to concentrate, hard to understand, and hard to practice what we do understand.

Our attempts at telling people about Christ aren't all crowned with glorious successes and dramatic conversions. We get stumped or shrugged off. We don't have all the answers. Our marriage isn't instantly transformed, nor are our children. Or, if we're still single, our relationships and desires don't all instantly fall in, like a platoon of Marines.

This is the struggle with the *flesh*,[2] with what the London Baptist Confession of Faith (1689) calls "remaining corruptions"—the unhappy leftovers from what we were before we came to faith in Christ.

---

2. We will discuss "flesh" at length in chapter 12. *Flesh* here is not our physical body, but old drives and habits that struggle against the Holy Spirit (cf. Gal. 5:16–24).

The Imperative: Grow in Holiness

Life starts. When God comes to save us, He finds us as dead, guilty, God-hating rebels. Jesus took our sins upon Himself and fully satisfied God's justice on our behalf. Then in sheer grace, God breathes His life into us. Our eyes open, we gasp in horror at where and what we've been, and we flee to Christ in repentant faith. We are declared righteous, we are reconciled, we are redeemed, we are saved—all by the grace of God alone, through faith alone, in Christ alone, to His glory alone (Eph. 2:1–10).

God does this all *for* us. We receive it. Dead people don't help themselves. God-haters don't seek Him. They don't strive. We do not contribute one copper atom (let alone a penny) to our salvation.

But then, as newborn children of God, we come under a new imperative, a new undeniable drive from within and moral necessity from without. We must grow to be like our Father. To do this, we must be made like our Savior, who is the very image of God the Father (compare Rom. 8:29 with Col. 1:15).

We do not grow to be "like" Him in that we grow to be everywhere-present, or all-knowing, or all-powerful. We do not become timeless. That is not how we become "like" our heavenly Father.

This likeness Scripture speaks of is a moral and a spiritual likeness. We were morally and spiritually unlike Him, walking in trespasses and sins and indulging our fallen nature (Eph. 2:1–3). After we have been born again and declared righteous through faith in Christ, all this begins to change. Specifically, since God is *holy* (chapter 4), we must ourselves grow to share of His holiness to an increasing degree (Heb. 12:10; 1 Peter 1:15–16).

This process of growing in holiness is called *sanctification*. The Bible presents three aspects of sanctification. The first is positional, and refers to what happens to us the moment God saves us. At that moment we are set apart from the world and to God. We become

His possession, set apart for His service (1 Cor. 1:30; 6:11; Heb. 10:10, and every time Christians are called "saints" [e.g., Rom. 1:7; 1 Cor. 1:2, etc.]).

Skipping the second aspect for a moment (bear with me here), the third facet of sanctification is perfect sanctification. One day, we will be freed from every last remnant of the corruptions of our old nature, and fully transformed into the image of Christ (Phil. 3:21; 1 John 3:2). Then we will be fully holy, with never another struggle with temptations, sinful follies, or foul passions from within.

It is the second aspect of sanctification that concerns us now: progressive sanctification. This is the incremental change that begins in us the moment the first spark of new life kindles within us. Regeneration initiates a continuum of growth and maturity that progresses hour by hour, day by day, and is not fully consummated until we see the Lord.

While God acts alone in declaring us righteous (justification), in progressive sanctification we are participants. The concept is framed well in Leviticus 20:7–8, which I translate thus: "Therefore you are to make yourselves holy, and you are to be holy, for I am Yahweh your God. And you are to keep My statutes and do them. I am Yahweh who makes you holy." To "make holy" is the same as to "sanctify." Here, Yahweh says the Israelites should sanctify themselves, because He sanctifies them. In progressive sanctification (unlike justification), both God and the believer work together.

The NT reflects this same concept. In fact, Peter reaches back to the language of Leviticus when he writes, "As obedient children, do not be conformed to the passions of your former ignorance, but as he who called you is holy, you also be holy in all your conduct, since it is written, 'You shall be holy, for I am holy'" (1 Peter 1:14–16).

This process is variously described as growing in grace and knowledge (2 Peter 3:18), putting to death the evil deeds of the body

Justification and Sanctification

It's essential we distinguish between justification and progressive sanctification. We have studied the former at some length, and are about to look at the latter, so I can be brief. It is critical that we distinguish them, but equally critical that we not divorce them.

Justification is instantaneous upon conversion; sanctification begins with conversion and continues until we are in the Lord's presence. Justification is perfect and complete and never grows, improves, or changes—since it is the perfect righteousness of Jesus Christ that is imputed to us; sanctification is imperfect and incomplete, and involves growth and maturing and increasing knowledge and wisdom and conformity to God's Word. Justification is a perfect work wholly accomplished by God, in which we are passive recipients; sanctification is accomplished through God renewing and strengthening and enabling us, so that we must choose and strive and learn and fight and struggle by the power which God gives us. Justification is the ground of our eternal relationship with God; sanctification is the experiential evidence that we have been justified. Justification has absolutely no relation to anything we will do, ever, with or without divine enabling; sanctification is all about what we do by divine enabling. Justification is not in any way based on or caused by sanctification; but sanctification is a necessary result of justification.

I think we can sum up a lot of Scripture in one brief, pointed statement: Justification is the necessary ground of sanctification while sanctification is the necessary confirming fruit of justification. That is, a person who has been justified will necessarily grow in holiness. But that holiness in no way causes or affects his justified standing before God. He is not justified because he grows in holiness; and when his growth has a setback, his justification is completely unaffected. But he will grow in holiness, because he has been justified.

(Rom. 8:13), continuing in His Word and learning freeing truth (John 8:31–32), and heading for maturity (Heb. 5:14). All Christians in Christ's church are to grow in doctrinal maturity in line with the image of Christ—which means, no less, that every individual Christian within that church must be moving in the same direction (Eph. 4:13–16).

While we all are called to grow, and while all genuine believers do grow, it is not a smooth road. It is likened to warfare more than once (Eph. 6:10ff; 1 Peter 2:11). Those remaining corruptions within us oppose the whole direction of the new life.

We want to grow. We are meant to grow, and are called to grow. But we struggle.

Same Problem, Different Answers

All Christians share this struggle. This is a given. The question is, What do we *do* about it?

Unsurprisingly, Christians have thought about how to grow and serve Christ and deal with the flesh since the time the apostle John assumed ambient temperature, if not before. Varying proposals have been made, different models cast up, to give us a grasp on what is happening, and some direction as to what to do.

Other books have discussed more comprehensively the various approaches Christians have taken.[3] I am only going to take out my big broad brush, and paint *three* popular options that I think fall significantly short of the scriptural model. I'll sketch out each, then weigh it by Scripture. Every time we find a way in which the models come short of Scripture, it will help us build a positive, biblical model of what to do now that we've come to know Christ.

The three options we will examine are:

---

3. For instance, Gundry, *Five Views on Sanctification.*

1. Gutless Gracers (chapter 10)
2. Crisis Upgraders (chapter 10)
3. Muzzy Mystics (chapter 11)

Then in the following three chapters, we'll further develop the true world-tilting model of the Christian life.

Gutless Gracers and Crisis Upgraders

Two Misguided Mind-Sets That Are Barriers to Genuine Christian Growth

Hear the wonderful words: "For by grace you have been saved through faith; and that not of yourselves, it is the gift of God" (Eph. 2:8 NASB). Nor is that the only time Paul sounds the "grace alone" note: "To the one who does not work, but believes in Him who justifies the ungodly, his faith is reckoned as righteousness" (Rom. 4:5 NASB). What's more, the Gospel tells us that we are "justified as a gift by His grace through the redemption which is in Christ Jesus" (Rom. 3:24 NASB).

These and many similar verses teach that believers are saved by grace through faith as a gift. Then there is nothing we are to do to add to this salvation, no way we can contribute. The Law and law-works do not enter into our salvation in any manner. Salvation is absolutely free.

In fact, it is *all* of grace. Any hint of works denies grace.

The Impotent Morass of the Gutless Gracers

Gutless Gracers affirm this truth, but they soon go wrong. Their position then isolates "grace alone" and builds on it as if it were the *only* truth, while redefining key words harmfully. For instance, advocates insist that it is out-of-place to call sinners to repent of their sins. Non-Christians can't repent, it is said, and they needn't repent. Calling sinners to repent is like asking them to earn salvation by a good work. In fact, some proponents say that repentance was a Jewish work, appropriate for Israel alone. Gentiles should not even be called to repentance, ever.[1]

What is needed instead (they say) is the preaching of Jesus as God, telling people to believe that Jesus died for their sins, telling them to pray a prayer to ask God for the gift of eternal life. In fact, when a Gentile is called on to believe in Jesus as Lord (Rom. 10:9), it is not a summons to submit to His lordship and authority. Rather, since "Lord" was used in place of God's name "Yahweh" in the Greek translation of the OT, this is a call to believe that Jesus is God. When a person comes round to the opinion that Jesus is God, and just asks for eternal life in a prayer, he is saved. Belief in Jesus as *God* is mandatory. Belief in Him as *Lord* is optional. Thus, Christ's person and work are fragmented.

Now that he is saved, Gutless Gracers teach, his life is all grace (as they define "grace"). He is neither impelled nor compelled to obey,

---

1. Or repentance is redefined as a mere change of opinion about whether Christ is God's Son or not.

to turn from evil works, or to do righteous works. He may do those things, it is preferable—but it isn't any kind of a necessity. Some of them say that, after he asks Jesus to give him eternal life, he could then become a Christian atheist, a Christian Buddhist, a Christian anything. It doesn't matter (to them). They would assure an atheistic ex-Christian that he is still saved and still going to heaven.

To introduce works and obedience as necessary outgrowths of conversion is to deny grace, Gutless Gracers tell us. To call a convert to confess his sins and ask for forgiveness is to deny grace. Holiness is good, but it will just happen. Or not! It's all good. Grace covers everything. Don't worry. Be happy.

Their error would not be subtle if it didn't contain at least some truth. The Christian life is indeed all of grace, every second of it. Our becoming Christians is of grace alone, our remaining Christians is of grace alone. Works that we do, in obedience to any law, have no part whatever in either meriting or keeping our salvation. The sinner is unable to produce anything to help him get saved.

We should preach Christ, not moral reform programs. We should never preach a message that sounds like our hearers need to clean up their acts so that Christ can save them. (If they could do that, why would they need Christ?)

We don't become Christians because we do good works, we don't stay Christians because we do good works, and if we get into heaven, it won't be because we did good works. It will be and can be only by the grace of God alone. This is an absolutely rock-solid biblical truth, and insofar as they affirm these truths, they are formally correct.

There is, however, a world of difference between saying that works of obedience are a necessary *component in* salvation, and insisting that works are a necessary *result of* salvation. The former position is damnable heresy; the latter is biblical truth. Gutless Gracers deny the second in the name of opposing the first.

In other words, Gutless Gracers deny that growth in holiness, obedience to the commands of the Lord Jesus, turning away from sin are necessary fruits of salvation. A man can keep living like hell and still be going to heaven. How can they take what seems like such a mad position? They do it in the name of keeping "works" out of "salvation by grace." Yet as we've already seen, this is a chaotic category-confusion, as nobody is arguing that one must work to be saved. Rather, one will work because he has been saved.

The result of Gutless Gracers' violent distortion of Scripture is disastrous. I am absolutely convinced it has sent many precious souls to hell, clinging to a false and delusive hope. It has patted them on their unconverted, unbelieving, unrepentant, unregenerate heads, and assured them that a quick prayer or a passing thought purchased their eternal fire insurance.

And it's a lie. While the Bible most emphatically does teach that we are saved through *faith*, it never says that we are saved through *claiming* to have faith. And, here's the kicker: Biblical faith *always* produces submission to the lordship of Christ.

On Lord

The gutless-grace view makes utter goop of the foundational Christian confession "Jesus is Lord" (Rom. 10:9; 1 Cor. 12:3b). Probably the most familiar sense of *kurios* ("Lord") in the Greek of NT times was of a master, a slave owner, a person of authority. The plainest reading of these (and many similar) texts is that we enter the Christian life with the conviction that Jesus is *Master*, that He is *The Boss*, that He is the one who has and must have all authority in our lives.

But let's do a little thought experiment. Let's break out a bit of logical karate here, invite our opponent to charge, and see what mayhem we can do.

Suppose for argument's sake that "Jesus is Lord" really does mean "Jesus is God" rather than "Jesus is Master."

So explain this to me: "God" is *less* a title of authority and ultimacy than "Lord"? How does *that* work? What possible sense does that make? "Lord" necessarily means a person with authority—but "God" doesn't? A "Lord" can demand obedience, but "God" can't? "God" is just a philosophical category, with no inherent authority, no real-life impact?

Yikes.

Think about it. It simply does not make sense.

What is more important, the notion of an "unlordly Lord" is not remotely biblical. Jesus clearly and unambiguously used "Lord" as a title of authority. How else can we make any sense of Luke 6:46—"Why do you call me 'Lord, Lord,' and not do what I tell you?" His question makes sense only if Jesus thought "Lord" meant "someone whose words should be obeyed" (John 13:13–14; 14:15; 15:14). A "Lord" is someone who gives commandments, and expects that his commands be obeyed (1 Cor. 14:37).

To confess Jesus as Lord is necessarily to admit that He is the rightful boss, ruler, and authority. It is to acknowledge His right to command.

To confess Jesus as *my* Lord is to admit that He has the right to command *me*.

On Grace

The Gutless Gracers' "grace" is not what God calls "grace." In spite of the PR that Gutless Grace advocates give themselves, the problem with this position is not that it makes too much of grace, and that their critics just hate grace. Rather, the problem is that gutless grace makes *far too little* of grace. It is those who biblically condemn the gutless-grace position who love the true grace of God in Christ.

Listen closely to what God moves Paul to say in Titus 2:11–14:

> For the grace of God that brings salvation to all men has appeared, instructing us that, by renouncing irreverence and worldly desires, we should come to live level-headedly and righteously and reverently in the present age, as we eagerly await the blessed hope and appearance of the glory of our great God and Savior, Jesus Christ, who gave Himself for us, in order that He might redeem us from all lawlessness, and might cleanse for Himself a people for His own possession, zealous for good works. (DJP)

This passage, then, is about grace (v. 11). What's more, it is written by the apostle Paul, whom God assigned a special position of managing the message of His grace (Eph. 3:2). So we must pay close heed if we are to get the "real scoop" about what God means by "grace."

Is grace, in this passage, God's way of making it "okay" that we live on under the authority of sin? Is "grace" how God makes peace with the idea of sin? Does "grace" mean that God accepts our giving no thought to His revealed will, floating along with the currents of our own desires on the waves of the world's trends?

Is grace a passive thing in God, and a "Get-Out-Of-Hell(-But-Still-*Live*-Like-It)-Free" card for us?

Hardly.

If Paul meant anything like that, he should have written that "the grace of God that brings salvation to all men" appeared in order to "instruct" us that we can live crazily, unrighteously, and godlessly, and that we shouldn't give a gnat's toenail about what pleases God.

But Paul wrote nothing of the kind. By contrast, the apostle says that the saving grace of God is a dynamic thing, a transformative, supernatural power. The woman or man touched by the grace

Paul speaks of will never remain the same. That person will be revolutionized, created anew. Focus on Paul's wording:

- Grace *brings* us *salvation*. It effects rescue, deliverance. Grace gives us new life and saving faith. Grace imputes Christ's righteousness. But it doesn't stop there; grace sees to it that we are really delivered, really rescued—saved. If we have been left where we were found, we haven't been saved!
- Grace *instructs* us. The word translated "instructing" is *paideuousa* (pie-DEW-oo-sah), which is a word that carries the idea of "education with a pow." It is discipline, pointed and powerful instruction, training. This verb and the related noun are used in Hebrews 12:5–11, of God the Father's discipline of His children, a discipline that may be like a whipping (v. 6), and which is far from fun to receive (v. 11), but which has the actual effect of bringing us to righteousness of life (v. 11). Paul's uses of the verb have plenty of "pow" as well (1 Cor. 11:32; 2 Cor. 6:9; 1 Tim. 1:20; 2 Tim. 2:25).
- Grace instructs us to *renounce ungodliness*. Renouncing is the "negative" lesson of grace—what it teaches us to put to death. It means "saying 'no' to" these desires, showing them the door (or the shotgun). Not coddling or "gracing over" or shrugging off. This is a necessity for godly living ("*by* renouncing"; that is, "renouncing" is how it is done). It is something that grace instructs us to do, not something that automatically happens to us.
- Grace instructs us to *live levelheadedly and righteously and reverently in the present age*. That means that grace teaches us to live in a way that respects God's lordship, and thus His revealed law-word for us. It describes a life of heartfelt striving to conform to God's Word. That's what God's real,

dynamic grace teaches! A life unconcerned with the Word is a life that hasn't known the touch of this grace.

• Grace *redeems us from all lawlessness.* Paul in Titus 2:14 views "lawlessness" as a slave owner or captor, and Jesus as the one who paid the price to liberate us from that bondage. But "lawlessness" is just what Gutless Gracers end up enabling—a mind-frame that doesn't view itself as obliged to any standard, including God's. With the Gutless Gracer, "to hear" is not "to obey." This has nothing to do with adding works to the Gospel; it has everything to do with the Gospel liberating us to be God's slaves.

• Grace makes us *zealous for good works.* Paul surely cannot be saying "zealous to explain how good works are optional." This zeal is an assured effect of Christ's saving grace, Paul says. "Good works" are behaviors that God's Word identifies as pleasing to Him. According to Paul, then, the person who knows grace will be eager and enthusiastic about finding out what God wants of and for him, and about plunging into it with all he's got.

Put it all together, and what do we have? Grace with *guts*, with transformative power.

This powerful passage is far from the only indicator Paul gives of the real grace of God in the Gospel. It was grace that powered Paul to be such a productive apostle, and caused him to labor all the more abundantly (1 Cor. 15:10). It was grace that sufficed to perfect power in Paul's "thorny" weakness (2 Cor. 12:9). Grace called Paul from death to life, unbelief to faith, hatred to love (Gal. 1:15), gave him a powerful Gospel ministry to the Gentiles (Gal. 2:8–9; Eph. 3:8), and accomplished our salvation (Gal. 2:21).

Grace saved us, with all the never-ending mountains of riches that salvation includes (Eph. 2:5–9). And what does Paul say is the culmination of God's grace? He writes, "For His handiwork are we, having been created in Christ Jesus for good works, which God prepared in advance, that we should walk in them" (Eph. 2:10 DJP). By grace, God *creates* us in Christ for good works, works that serve Him and bring Him glory. By grace He gives us gifts that enable and motivate us for service (Eph. 4:7ff.). Grace motivates all service (1 Peter 4:10–11), and grace is the source of power specifically for the heavy lifting and arduous labor of pastoral ministry (2 Tim. 2:1).

Other biblical writers laud the power of grace as well. Grace helps us in difficult times (Heb. 4:16). The *true* grace of God involves holy, obedient, Gospel-powered and God-centered living even while under terrible suffering (1 Peter 5:12). Grace is a mighty, powerful force.

It is not hard to see why using "grace" as a license and pretext for irreverent and lawless living is a perversion that brings God's wrathful judgment (Jude 4). God's real grace is a gutsy, dynamic, transformative power. No one who receives this grace remains the same. It transforms and motivates.

No transformation = no grace.

If grace has not transformed your life to some degree, then grace has not saved your soul, either.

And so, if we cherish any notion of "grace" that defines it as "God's way of making it okay for me to live as if He didn't exist, wasn't my Master, and hadn't spoken a word of command or prohibition"—we had better *lose* that notion.

Otherwise, there would be no way to make sane sense of the host of *commands* in the NT or of verses such as these (all are my translation):

- "If you love Me, you will keep My commandments." (John 14:15)

- "You are My friends, if you do the things which I am commanding you." (John 15:14)
- "If someone thinks himself to be a prophet, or spiritual, let him acknowledge the things which I write to you—that they are the commandment of the Lord." (1 Cor. 14:37)
- "Finally therefore, brothers, we ask and urge you in the Lord Jesus, that just as you received from us how it is necessary for you to walk and to please God, even just as you do walk, that you abound all the more. For you know what commands we gave to you through the Lord Jesus." (1 Thess. 4:1–2)
- "For this is love for God: that we keep His commandments—and His commandments are not burdensome." (1 John 5:3)[2]

Grace is God's dynamic, free, flowing gift of Himself that delivers us from the guilt and domain of sin (justification), and enables us to live lives that please Him (progressive sanctification). After we become recipients of justifying grace, we become participants in sanctifying grace. If the latter is not happening, then the former never happened.

"Gutless" is the *last* thing God's real grace is.

The Quick-Fix Fails of the Crisis Upgraders

It's a bit sad—and makes my back ache—to realize that many of my readers have never lived in a world without microwave ovens. Perhaps they gather round the fire to hear Grampa Zeke tell of the days of yore when hot dogs would take *ten minutes* to boil on the stove, potatoes would sit in an oven for *an hour*, and the most "instant" way to cook popcorn was Jiffy Pop.

Now it's a matter of pop, slam, beep-beep-beep, whirr, ding! Done!

---

2. See also under the biblical evaluation of the third model, "Muzzy Mysticism."

Can't spirituality be like that?

Those of the Crisis Upgrader mind-set think maybe it can. There are a number of different presentations of this position, with designer theologies to match, and some overlapping. They all amount to this: There is *something* you can do (or get done) that will instantly upgrade you as a Christian. There is some crisis, some way to download a spiritual upgrade, that will take you to Next-Level Christianity.

Some will say you need to seek the baptism with/of/in the Holy Spirit. They will point to Jesus' promise, "But ye shall receive power, after that the Holy Ghost is come upon you: and ye shall be witnesses unto me both in Jerusalem, and in all Judaea, and in Samaria, and unto the uttermost part of the earth" (Acts 1:8 KJV [advocates seem to prefer the KJV of this verse]). Peter was a defeated Christian (Mark 14:71–72) until he received the baptism with the Spirit (Acts 4:19–20). It is the same with us: We will live lives of defeat as Christians until we who have received Jesus as Savior also receive the Spirit.

To be very clear, to these people, this is an experience that comes after salvation. A person can be a genuine Christian, but not have the Spirit. Or, as they often put it, "you might have the Spirit, but the Spirit doesn't have you." There is something more, something vitally important and separate from being saved, that is essential to powerful and victorious Christian living.

Another approach sounds much more exegetical. It focuses on some commands in Romans 6, and calls us to a crisis of consecration or dedication or yielding.[3] Again, the King James Version is often used, though not exclusively. They appeal to Romans 6:13—"Neither yield ye your members as instruments of

---

3. We will examine "yielding" closely, under the biblical evaluation of "Muzzy Mysticism."

unrighteousness unto sin: but yield yourselves unto God, as those that are alive from the dead, and your members as instruments of righteousness unto God" (KJV). Again, in verse 19, "as ye have yielded your members servants to uncleanness and to iniquity unto iniquity; even so now yield your members servants to righteousness unto holiness" (KJV).

If the presenter knows a little Greek (or heard someone who did . . . or who had heard someone who had heard someone who had heard someone who did . . . or once read a book by a guy who—you get the picture), he may observe that the command to "yield" is in the *aorist* tense in Greek, which is true. He will say that the aorist is the "once-for-all" tense. He will call Christians to yield themselves in a once-for-all crisis of decision and dedication.

The *forms* this crisis takes vary. Many seminars and retreats and conferences have been geared to produce this crisis. A certain pattern of preaching is followed, leading to this leap forward in commitment, this "jump to hyperspace" in spirituality.

Perhaps the Crisis Upgrader goes forward and throws a piece of wood on a campfire, symbolizing his all-out commitment to being on fire for the Lord. Maybe he comes up at an invitation, and gets a special prayer offered for him. In some circles, he—a Christian—may have someone "bind" demons in his life, or may himself cast out a demon of lust, of fear, of . . . elevator music, wearing polyester, whatever. Or maybe he "receives the baptism with the Holy Spirit" and speaks in tongues.

After that crisis experience, our Crisis Upgraders will be changed Christians. They will rise to another plane. No longer will they be in the grips of the flesh, trudging along as "carnal Christians." Now they will be "spiritual" Christians, living in victory over sin.

This is spirituality-as-high-jump. And they've jumped.

Now again, we can affirm an element of this teaching biblically.

The baptism with the Spirit absolutely does transform a person. Peter was a different man before and after Pentecost.[4] That reality does provide power for Christian witness and for holy living. There is a definite and utterly distinctive "before" and "after" to this event. All this is true.

Also, Christians should present themselves to God. They should not be wishy-washy about it, or indecisive, or lukewarm. There should be no question in their minds, or in the minds of those who observe them, *whose* they are, and *whom* they serve. An undecided, tepid, wishy-washy Christian is a worthless Christian. This is also true.

But there is so much that is wrong about this approach that even a very thick book would barely get us off the ground.[5] For starters, the glorious Gospel truth is that there is only one kind of Christian. This was inherent in Jeremiah's prophecy of the New Covenant, under which all—without exception—would genuinely know the Lord (Jer. 31:34). And so

> all Christians—without exception—have been blessed with every spiritual blessing in Christ (Eph. 1:3ff.);
>
> all Christians—without exception—have been filled full in Christ (Col. 2:10); and
>
> all Christians—without exception—have been given all the equipment they need for life and godliness in Christ (2 Peter 1:3).

---

4. "Different" (contrast Mark 14:54–72 with Acts 4:7–20; 5:29–33, 40–42)—but far from perfect (Gal. 2:11–14).

5. Andy Naselli provides a superbly helpful study of this teaching in "Keswick Theology: A Survey and Analysis of the Doctrine of Sanctification in the Early Keswick Movement" (*Detroit Baptist Seminary Journal*, 13 [2008]: 17–67). See also his *Let Go and Let God? A Survey and Analysis of Keswick Theology* (Bellingham, WA: Logos Bible Software, 2010).

The Bible knows nothing of a second level to ascend to that distinguishes elite Christians from the benighted rabble who lack that special experience.

Christians grow in Christ (Eph. 4:15–16; 2 Peter 3:18). Growth is ongoing and comprised of many gradations, from one degree of glory to the next (2 Cor. 3:18). But growth is a continuum within the one distinctive of being *in Christ*. There is no biblical warrant for splitting Christians into two kinds, the haves and the have-nots; the plain and the industrial-strength; the regular and the turbo. Within the body of Christ, there are just Christians.

Furthermore, the baptism with the Spirit is definitional of Christianity. That is, it is not a distinctive among Christians, marking off Christian from Christian. Rather, it distinguishes Christians from non-Christians.

This truth is easily established from the Bible, beyond any reasonable doubt. For instance, John the Baptist said, "After me comes he who is mightier than I, the strap of whose sandals I am not worthy to stoop down and untie. I have baptized you with water, but he will baptize you with the Holy Spirit" (Mark 1:7–8).

The two baptisms were definitional of the respective ministries of John and of the Messiah. John was known as "the Baptist" because that is what he did. All of his followers were by definition baptized in water.

And so, John said, baptism with the Holy Spirit would be equally definitional of the ministry of the Messiah. Just as 100 percent of John's followers were baptized with water, so 100 percent of the Messiah's followers would be baptized with the Holy Spirit.

This prediction is fulfilled at Pentecost, which was every bit as much a historical event as was Messiah's birth in Bethlehem. We do not try to reproduce the historical circumstances of the latter; we shouldn't try with the former. That is, if someone wants to trust in Christ as Savior, we do not send him off to the Middle East to imitate the Magi's mission or the shepherds' search in order to get Christ born in their hearts again.

Nor should we attempt the same vis-à-vis Pentecost. Believers simply were in the location to which the Lord directed them. No effort on their part brought the Spirit down, any more than the shepherds caused Christ to be born.

The Spirit came, and we live in the aftermath. Now 100 percent of Christ's followers have already been baptized with the Spirit. You cannot be saved without being in Christ (Rom. 8:1–2), and you cannot be in Christ without having been baptized into His body with the Spirit (1 Cor. 12:13). Scripture does not support trying to invent various kinds of baptism with/of/in the Spirit.

But what of Romans 6 and the aorist tense? That sounded legit. The truth is simply that the aorist tense is not by any stretch of the imagination the "once-for-all" tense. Anyone who says that today might as well wear a T-shirt saying "GREEK NOVICE" (or, more likely, "Greek Faker").

When Jesus tells us in Matthew 6:11 to pray, "Give us this day our daily bread," using the aorist, He isn't suggesting that we ask our Father to do it once for all time, and never to give us bread again. Or when Jesus uses the aorist to ask the Father to "keep" His own in His name (John 17:11), He surely does not mean once for all, that night, and never again. The master in the parable does not tell his servants to "do business" once for all then just sit around until he returns (Luke 19:13), nor should we "honor" everyone once for all then treat them like dirt (1 Peter 2:17), nor "consider" various trials to be pure joy once for all (James 1:2), nor welcome God's Word once for all and then shrug it off (James 1:21).

I don't expect professional grammarians to rewrite their grammars because of the observation I'm about to make. However, in more than 37 years of reading the Greek NT, I've generally come to see the aorist imperative (command) as being used for the "Just do it" form, whereas the present is employed as the "Get on with it" (or "Keep on keeping on") form.

An aorist imperative doesn't concern itself with whether compliance will take a second, a month, a year, or a lifetime. An aorist command just tells you to snap to it and get 'er done. The present (because it is a command) says to get going on it, but is used to suggest the adoption of a habit, the beginning or continuance of a process.

So in Romans 6, Paul is in no way saying that we can pick up a stick, walk over to a camp-meeting bonfire, toss it on the blaze, and say "There! I'm yielded!" Nor can we write, "Dear Diary, on May 23, 2009, I dedicated myself completely to Christ. Woo hoo, victorious living, I'm there!" Scripture never suggests such a thing for a Christian.[6]

In Romans 6:13 and 19, Paul is saying "*Do* it! *Present* yourselves to God as His slaves, body and soul." He certainly is calling us to be decisive and urgent and definite about it. But he neither says nor implies anything about how many times in our lives we will do this. The apostle isn't saying that we won't be doing it again in another context in an hour, when temptation comes from a different angle, or again in a day, or again in a year. Paul is describing a way of life, not a single crisis decision.

Let me break it down still further. Suppose you were to ask Paul, "When should I do this? When should I present myself to the Lord for His service? When should I present the parts of my body as His tools for righteousness? When should I present my body as a living sacrifice?"

I'm quite sure the apostle would say, "Now. Do it now."

But then suppose we met Paul a week later, and asked him the same question.

---

6. For non-Christians, conversion to Christ certainly is a distinct event, and one to which we often may be able to assign a specific date and time.

With a puzzled expression, he'd say, "Now, of course. Now."

Then, if our paths should cross a month later, a year later, ten years later? If we asked the same question?

If he remembered our previous encounters, Paul might look at us as if we were daft, and respond, "Well, let me ask you: When is Christ Lord? When are you his slave? When are the world and the devil your enemy? When are your holy Father's eyes upon you? Your choices, your actions, your inactions—when do they have eternal consequences? When does the flesh strive to overcome you? When is the Holy Spirit in your heart, striving against your flesh, bearing His fruit, empowering you to deal death to the deeds of the body? When is your only opportunity to win glory for your King on the battlefield?"

We'd gulp and whisper, "Now, sir."

To which the apostle might reply curtly, "Thank you," and go find someone less dense to talk to. In fact, everywhere we see that the Christian life is a process. We grow in the grace and knowledge of Christ (2 Peter 3:18), we are being transformed into His image from one degree of glory to another (2 Cor. 3:18), we are in a process of doctrinal growth and maturing into the character of Christ (Eph. 4:11–16). The Christian life is not the checking of a box nor the flicking of a switch. It is a walk (Rom. 6:4; 8:4; 13:13; 2 Cor. 5:7; Eph. 4:1; 5:15). In fact, it is a walk in the Spirit (Gal. 5:16, 25), not a single spiritual leap into victory.

The Christian life is a race that only ends in glory (Heb. 12:1). It is a battle that requires daily preparation and daily effort, and will only be consummated at Christ's return (Eph. 6:11–13). Not only do we not have our best life now, but we are promised that the path to heaven leads through *many* experiences of pressure and trial (Acts 14:22). We look to a hope that is not seen and will not be seen until Christ's return (Rom. 8:24–25). We must get serious, sober up, and make that future hope our single hope (1 Peter 1:13).

Set it down as a fact: Any line of teaching that suggests that you can be exempt from long-term effort, trial, trouble, suffering, and labor, is contradictory to the teaching of Jesus Christ (Luke 9:23–25; John 16:33) and His authorized spokesmen (Rom. 8:18–25; 1 Thess. 3:3–4; 1 Peter 1:6–7; 3:14–17; 4:1, 12–19; 5:8–11).

What we need is not an impatient insistence on quick fixes that don't exist. Rather, we must commit ourselves to a life where faith produces work, and love gives birth to hard labor, and our hope in Christ yields endurance under trials, whether they come from outside of us or from within us (1 Thess. 1:3). We must cultivate endurance, perseverance, stick-to-itiveness (Heb. 10:36). For that, we must look to Jesus, the very model of patient endurance (Heb. 12:1–3).

That is crucial, in the most fundamental sense of the word: We mustn't look for or to experiences of any kind. We must look to Jesus, and we must resolutely and hopefully and joyfully plod on toward Him and His kingdom (Heb. 12:13–15).

While very different from each other, both the Gutless Grace and the Crisis Upgrade positions share a common denominator. Both are born of a failure to grasp the riches of God's provision in Christ. The Gutless Gracer thinks there is only enough in Christ to cause our recategorization, not to effect our transformation. The Crisis Upgrader fails to see that when we encounter Christ, we come to possess all of God's riches and wonders in Him. Both positions end up with folks paralyzed in ignorance and unbelief; and both sets of chains fall off when our eyes are opened to the fullness of God's riches of grace in Jesus Christ.

Chapter 11

The Quagmire of Muzzy Mysticism

Shall We Melt into Christ and Limply "Let" Him Live Through Us?

I will devote more space to the Muzzy Mystics than to the Gutless Gracers or the Crisis Upgraders, both because I'm not aware of other current books devoted to the topic;[1] and because it is the one that messed with my mind in my early Christian days. I think it's still a virulent spiritual neurotoxin in the body of Christ.

Often we encounter this teaching in the form of one-on-one

---

1. Though J. I. Packer does touch on quietism to some degree in *Keep in Step with the Spirit*.

diagnosis. We share our struggles with a Christian friend. Our would-be spiritual doctor listens to our tale of struggles and slips. He (or she) nods sagely. He leans forward. The solution, we can tell, is about to break forth like the blaze of dawn after a black, stormy night.

"Your problem . . ." he begins, then pauses significantly. We lean forward ourselves, holding our breath. The big breakthrough is near, we can feel it.

Yes? My problem . . . ?

"Your problem is that you are trying to live the Christian life."

I— Huh? That's the diagnosis?

Yep. That's it.

"Stop trying to live the Christian life," we are told, "and *let* Jesus live it through you! Let go . . . and let God!"

Oh.

Well, at first blush, that actually makes a lot of sense. What's more, it sounds so deep. We are frail, we are of flesh. Jesus is mighty, pure, and flawless. Who is better qualified to live the Christian life than Jesus Himself? What would glorify God better than just to let Christ live through us? What would get our selves, our egos, our flesh out of the way better than just letting go and letting Christ? After all, He is the vine, right? We're just bendy, clingy little branches with no life in ourselves.

This is the "thinking" that underlies that ever popular (and never biblical) mantra for daily living: "Let go and let God." Charles Trumbull (author of *Victory in Christ*) was the originator of the toxic phrase, but reading Andrew Murray and any of the other "higher life" sorts will freeze you up in the same way. Murray will so terrify you of the thought of acting "in the flesh" or "from the self," that you'll collapse into shuddery goo. You will want to be a pliant glove on Jesus' hand, moving only when He moves, dissolving into nothing, so that He may be all in all. Until then, you won't dare think a thought or make a move.

To get a taste of what I mean, hear a few excerpts from Murray's classic *Abide in Christ*:

> What [the believer] can do of himself is altogether sinful. He must therefore cease entirely from his own doing, and wait for the working of God in him. . . . just in proportion as he yields himself a truly passive instrument in the hand of God, will he be wielded of God as the active instrument of His almighty power. . . .
>
> You have but to bow in the confession of your own ignorance and impotence; the Father will delight to give you the teaching of the Holy Spirit. If but your ear be open, and your thoughts brought into subjection, and your heart prepared in silence to wait upon God, to hear what He speaks, He will reveal to you His secrets. And one of the first secrets will be the deeper insight into the truth, that as you sink low before Him in nothingness and helplessness, in a silence and a stillness of soul that seeks to catch the faintest whisper of His love, teachings will come to you which you had never heard before for the rush and noise of your own thoughts and efforts. . . .
>
> The heart occupied with its own plans and efforts for doing God's will, and securing the blessing of abiding in Jesus, must fail continually. God's work is hindered by our interference. He can do His work perfectly only when the soul ceases from its work.[2]

Scores and scores of Christians have read such teaching—perhaps from one of Murray's two-hundred-forty-plus publications!—and been convinced that this is the call to the deeper life. There

---

2. Murray, *Abide in Christ*, 105, 106, 107; emphasis in original.

are secrets they won't learn from their Bibles, that study (no matter how devout and prayerful) and attendance on the preached Word (no matter how Christ-centered and Spirit-blessed) will not provide. They have to strive to stop striving—to stop, cease, go limp and passive, to seek a state of vaporous resignation. To be nothing.

Longing for a solution, for relief from the misery of spiritual warfare, earnest souls eagerly lap up writings like this. They are convinced. They set out on their quest . . . , and the imprisoning bonds start wrapping themselves tighter and tighter than Jacob Marley's spectral chains, until eventually these poor folks can't move at all.

As Andrew Murray shows, this teaching is always clothed with gloriously spiritual and mystical language. It sounds absolutely wonderful, deep, appealing. I mean—who wouldn't want that? What Christian wouldn't like to quit striving and struggling and battling and sweating and groaning . . . and failing? What Christian wouldn't want this glorious, blessed, precious intimacy with Christ, where He bends over and whisper-whisper-whispers secrets that nobody else can hear? What Christian wouldn't like to be so mastered by Jesus that he lives and breathes and emanates Jesus, so that he no longer fails, so that Jesus lives through Him in the sense of replacing the individual Christian's will and responsibility? Who thinks the world needs more us? Doesn't it need more Jesus?

Yikes, I'm almost convincing myself!

But not quite. Been there, did that, *never* going back. But the reason so many, including myself, have been allured by this thinking is again because of the grain of truth it contains. Christians should and do want to be intimate with God. Jesus does bid us to abide in Him (John 15), and John echoes the call (1 John 2:28). There is no purer life than God's life, no better will than God's will. Our flesh is a malignant force that would pull us in entirely the wrong direction (Rom. 7:14–25; 8:5–8), and we mustn't yield to it.

But even as I affirm these things, I am in fact standing in the road in front of you, waving my arms for all I'm worth and shouting, "Turn around, bridge out ahead!" This is dangerous and paralyzing teaching. For starters: How does "Let go and let God" measure up against Scripture? Remember, the test isn't what sounds deep, what sounds holy, or even what makes sense to us. For the Christian, the test is Scripture.

One passage springs immediately to my mind. "Strive to enter through the narrow door," says Jesus. "For many, I tell you, will seek to enter and will not be able" (Luke 13:24).

The Greek word translated "strive" is *agōnizesthe* (ah-goh-NEEDS-ess-theh), from which we get our word "agonize." In Jesus' day, the sense was to work hard, to struggle, like an athlete in a contest. It is used to describe the hard, self-disciplined competition of a runner in a stadium (1 Cor. 9:25), or of revolutionaries battling for military supremacy (John 18:36). The apostle Paul employs it to describe his tireless, extreme labors (Col. 1:29; 2 Tim. 4:7), and to depict Epaphras as struggling in prayer (Col. 4:12). In fact, the related noun *agōn* (ah-GŌNE) characterizes the entire Christian life as a race to be run (Heb. 12:1)—it is a struggle, a match that requires that we strain every nerve.

What specifically does He mean? How do we enter into life? We've got to hear the Word of Christ. But it is not enough merely to hear the Word (Luke 8:5, 12). Nor is it enough to receive it with an initial response of joy (Luke 8:6, 13). Nor are we helped if we take it in and file it somewhere with things we *really* care about (Luke 8:7, 14).

No: When we hear the Word, we must receive it with joy, take it in, grab onto it, and hold it fast in a good and honest heart (Luke 8:8, 15). We must be moved by that Word to repent (Matt. 4:17; Luke 13:3, 5; 16:30; Acts 17:30). We must be moved by that Word to believe in the Lord Jesus (Acts 16:31), to come to Him and no other (Matt. 11:28–30; John 6:35), to come to the Father through Him alone (John 14:6), to call on His name alone for salvation (Acts

4:12). It is a narrow door. If we want to live, we must strive to enter through that door, and only that door (John 10:9).

Note that *we* are called on to do all these things: hear, hold fast, repent, believe, come, enter. Our Lord does not say, "Yield, be nothing, collapse into holy quietness, wait passively for God to carry you into the narrow way." No. What Jesus says is, struggle. He says make every effort; He says labor hard, strain every muscle to enter the narrow way. He tells *us* to do that.

But wait . . . weren't we *dead*? Given what we saw in part 1, we know that we lack the native ability to do this. We are dead in sin, union with Adam in his rebellion against God has corrupted every part of our makeup, we are hopelessly distant from God, we are unable to lift a finger to help ourselves. We can't repent. We can't believe. We can't hear, listen, keep, heed, come. The only effort we naturally expend is to flee from the narrow gate at all costs.

Yet this is the precise form the Gospel always takes: God calls on dead people to hear and believe, and then He gives them life so that they can (as we saw in chapter 8). Just think about Jesus' friend Lazarus, who had been dead for four days (John 11:39). Jesus stands a few feet away from his dead, rotting, stinking, stiffening corpse. He tells that corpse to do precisely what it cannot do: walk out of the tomb.

But it can't. Tell a corpse to leave its tomb? Why not tell down to be up, or circle to be square, or politicians to spend less of other people's money? It is an absurd command! Ridiculous!

And yet, with that command, the Lord, who is the resurrection and the life, sovereignly grants Lazarus life. Jesus bestows on Lazarus the ability to hear and respond, and Lazarus comes forth in answer to his Lord's call (John 11:43–44).

Jesus orders Lazarus to do what he cannot do, then enables him to do it. He gives an impossible command, then makes it impossible to resist that command—Why would a living man stay in a tomb?

Linger just a moment longer with me here, and consider this: Jesus does not tell Lazarus, "Be sure that you do nothing, Lazarus! You are impotent and powerless! Wait on Me, until I move you to respond. Wait, Lazarus! Wait! Be nothing, Lazarus! Melt!" How absurd.

Don't you see?

If dead Lazarus could hear Jesus' call, it was time to obey.

How much more is this the case in our situation? When we were spiritually dead, the Lord called us to believe, and He gave us life. Now that He has given us life, now that we died to sin and rose to newness of life with Christ (Rom. 6:1–5), how much more can He call to us, direct us, command us?

We are alive in Jesus Christ, united to Him who is our life (Col. 3:1–4). The Lord bids us do what we could not have done but now can do. The Holy Spirit lives in us to produce righteousness that pleases God (Rom. 8:4–10). And how does He do that? By enabling us to put to death the sinful deeds of the body (v. 10). By working in us that we would will and do that which pleases God (Phil. 2:13).

We hear the voice of God in His Word only because He has given us ears to hear (Deut. 29:4; Prov. 20:12; John 6:44–45, 65; Rom. 10:17). Our very hearing is an obligation to respond—not to tempt God and insult Him by waiting for something further.

And it is us whom He addresses, and it is we who must respond. Jesus does not say—(I speak as a fool)—"Father, I command You to give them the ability to struggle to enter the narrow gate; and Holy Spirit, I command You to cause their limp, unresponsive, passive carcasses to struggle to enter the narrow gate; and I command them to do nothing but wait, silent and passive."

No, the command is addressed to *us*; we are the ones of whom Jesus demands a response.

And with the command, He enables us to respond.

But is that a just-in-the-Gospels thing? Did matters change after Pentecost? What did the Holy Spirit lead the apostles to lay out as the tenor of Christian living? Was Jesus talking only about the beginning of the kingdom life—after that, we "let go"?

Before I answer those questions, let me pose a question of my own: Wouldn't a shift like that be odd? Wouldn't it be strange for Jesus to tell dead people to do something, and then tell the living ones to do nothing?

But I digress.

The verses we just looked at create the strong impression that Christians are called—commanded!—to act, to do, to respond. Here is another array of apostolic marching orders from various portions of the NT:

- "Bless those who persecute you; bless and do not curse them. Rejoice with those who rejoice, weep with those who weep. . . . Beloved, never avenge yourselves, but leave it to the wrath of God, for it is written, 'Vengeance is mine, I will repay, says the Lord.' To the contrary, 'if your enemy is hungry, feed him; if he is thirsty, give him something to drink; for by so doing you will heap burning coals on his head.' Do not be overcome by evil, but overcome evil with good." (Rom. 12:14–15, 19–21)
- "But put on the Lord Jesus Christ, and make no provision for the flesh, to gratify its desires." (Rom. 13:14)
- "Flee from sexual immorality." (1 Cor. 6:18a)
- "So, whether you eat or drink, or whatever you do, do all to the glory of God." (1 Cor. 10:31)
- "Therefore, my beloved brothers, be [or possibly *become*; Greek *ginesthe*] steadfast, immovable, always abounding in the work of the Lord, knowing that in the Lord your labor is not in vain." (1 Cor. 15:58)
- "Therefore go out from their midst, and be separate from them, says the Lord, and touch no unclean thing; then I will welcome you." (2 Cor. 6:17)

- "For you were called to freedom, brothers. Only do not use your freedom as an opportunity for the flesh, but through love serve one another." (Gal. 5:13)
- "Husbands, love your wives, as Christ loved the church and gave himself up for her." (Eph. 5:25)
- "Therefore, my beloved, as you have always obeyed, so now, not only as in my presence but much more in my absence, work out your own salvation with fear and trembling, for it is God who works in you, both to will and to work for his good pleasure." (Phil. 2:12–13)
- "Train yourself for godliness." (1 Tim. 4:7b)
- "Having purified your souls by your obedience to the truth for a sincere brotherly love, love one another earnestly [or *strenuously*] from a pure heart." (1 Peter 1:22)
- "But you, beloved, building yourselves up in your most holy faith and praying in the Holy Spirit, keep yourselves in the love of God, waiting for the mercy of our Lord Jesus Christ that leads to eternal life." (Jude 1:20–21)
- "Only hold fast what you have until I come." (Rev. 2:25)

That is a mere representative smattering from scores and scores of such NT passages. But think of it: *bless* those who curse you, *serve* one another, *go out* from the unclean, *love* your wives, *love* one another strenuously, *flee* immorality, *work out* your salvation, *train yourself* for godliness, *keep yourselves* in God's love, *hold fast* what you have . . .

Does any of that sound like "Let go and let God"?

Doesn't it sound more like "Hang on tight and get moving"?

Let me summarize my argument by two pointed observations about *every* such passage in the NT:

1. *Not one* of these commands is addressed to the Holy Spirit.
2. *Every one* of these commands is addressed to the believer.

Does "Let Go" Even Make Sense?

Not only is the "Let go" thinking not biblical, it isn't even logical. It simply does not make sense.

Think it through with me. The problem (we're told) is us, right? We need to stop doing things, stop trying to be Christians. We must let go and let God. How does that address the supposed problem? "Let go and let God" only moves the obstacle, the hindrance. It doesn't *re*move it.

How so? The idea is that I stop getting my grubby hands all over everything, right? I must let Jesus control everything. I must stop trying to do things right. I must let Jesus do it.

If that is the reality, then we must ask, Why isn't He already doing it? If He needs to control everything directly, then who's stopping Him? Since I am the problem and I just need to be out of the picture, how can He possibly wait for my permission? I *am* the problem, but I must also *solve* the problem? Isn't that a sure prescription for an eternal stalemate?

In this system, I am stopping Jesus because I haven't let Him be in control, not in the right way. I haven't yielded right, I haven't surrendered right. I haven't adopted the right resting, silent, passive, yielding attitude.

Do you see it now? It's still all on me! I still have to do something right! I have to yield right. My will is sovereign over Jesus. We have moved the focus from a born-again, Spirit-indwelt child of God believingly *obeying* in a God-pleasing way by grace (which is an explicitly biblical focus)—to my mystically *yielding* right (which is not biblical).

This teaching does not truly call me to look away from myself to Christ and His Word. Instead, it calls me to look within myself for Christ, apart from His Word, so I can hear His holy whispers in the stillness. I'm not seeking above, where Christ is seated at God's right hand (Col. 3:1). I'm not enjoying fellowship with God through the apostles' teaching (1 John 1:1–3). I'm not abiding in Christ's love as the Son remained in the Father's love, by faith-driven obedience to His word (John 15:9–10). Instead, I am seeking a mystical plane of being, within myself, rather than a Christ-centered spiritual life of believing and doing.

And I still fail! But now it's even worse. Now I can't put my finger on it because it's not about God's black words on white pages. I can't apply a biblical diagnosis or prescription. I can't say, "Argh, I lied, when God says not to lie [Eph. 4:25]. I showed disrespect for my husband, when the Bible says I must subordinate myself [5:22]. I was motivated by fear of man, rather than trusting God [Prov. 29:25]. I snapped back nastily, when God calls me to return a blessing instead [Rom. 12:14]." And so on. With this bewildering, paralyzing doctrine, I'm out of the arena where apostolic teaching moves and breathes and shines God's light on my path (Ps. 119:105). I've no biblical landmarks to give me my bearings. I've drifted into a hazy, foggy, incense-beclouded room where I bump about helplessly into beanbag chairs and bead curtains, unable to make anything out clearly.

So you see, in this doctrine it isn't about truths Jesus actually utters, such as John 14:15 ("If you love me, you will keep my commandments") or 15:10a ("If you keep my commandments, you will abide in my love") or 15:14 ("You are my friends if you do what I command you"). It isn't about any clear, specific, major line of biblical truth.

Now I must achieve the right mystical attitude, I must somehow shift into "J" for Jesus-life, through some elusive, para-biblical, unattainable process. If I'm not there, there's something more for me to do. *Yield* better, *let* better, *surrender* better, *be nothing* better. Get God going for me by bringing the right technique into play.

But it's still me doing something—and not doing what God's Word expressly calls me to do. I still control the relationship.

Doing nothing is doing something. It's doing the wrong thing.

So you see, even apart from being unbiblical—which it is!—it's nonsensical. It collapses on itself. The "deeper life" teaching isn't really deep. It just looks deep because it's so muddy you can't see any bottom.

But there is even a more critical problem with this Muzzy Mystical, quietistic approach to Christian living.

It effectively leaves out the cross.

Missing the Centrality of the Cross

The key to sanity in the Christian life is to understand what the cross is, and what it is to us.

Paul abominates the very suggestion that he would boast in anything "except in the cross of our Lord Jesus Christ, by which the world *has been* crucified to me, and I to the world" (Gal. 6:14, emphasis added). The apostle views this crucifixion as a past event, an abiding reality, a *fait accompli*. It isn't a mystical experience to which Paul yearns to attain, or a plane of exalted Christian living to which he aspires. It is a historical event, on the settled basis of which he lives by faith.

Beyond that, the cross is the dividing line in the Christian's life. Before it, I was alive to sin and dead to God; after encountering the cross, I have died to sin and live for God (Rom. 6:2, 10–11, 18). On that cross, the believer died with Christ, to the guilt and power of sin. Now he may not and he cannot continue to live under sin's dominion.

Yes, the believer struggles (Rom. 7:14–25; more on that in the next chapter), but he lives to God in Christ because of the cross. The cross is everything to the Christian: It is God's saving power to us (1 Cor. 1:18), it is how we were reconciled to God (Eph. 2:16), it is how our sins were forgiven and done away with (Col. 2:14; 1 Peter 2:24); it is why we are free from sin's bondage.

Our present appropriation of the benefits of the cross is not an actualization, but a matter of faith. We don't *make* the cross work. It *worked*. The triune God succeeded. God accomplished everything He set out to accomplish by means of the cross. Our response is to believe it, and live on the basis of it.

That is, I am called on to reckon, calculate, or consider myself as dead to sin because of the cross (Rom. 6:11). I do not do so to make the cross-work of Christ true and actual, but *because* it is true and actual.

It isn't *mystical*, it's *pistical*, if I may coin a word—that is, it's a matter of *faith* (*pistis* in Greek). And so we take up our cross daily as a matter of a faith that rests on an assured fact (Luke 9:23). That fact became our reality on conversion: "And those who belong to Christ Jesus crucified the flesh"—not "need to try to crucify," but *crucified*, at conversion—"with its passions and desires" (Gal. 5:24 DJP).

We are not helping God. We are believing Him and resting on what He has already done.

Every aspect of the Christian life, then, is *cruciform*, it is cross-shaped. By the cross of Christ, we die to our old identities and lives as spiritually dead rebels (Matt. 16:24). By the cross of Christ we break finally and definitively from living for sin, from being alive to the power of Satan and the world, and from living with ourselves as our final reference point.

By the cross of Christ, we are dead to all of that—and in the resurrection of Christ, we come alive to God (Rom. 6). We are alive to His person and His will (2 Cor. 5:15). We are no longer our own, we have been bought with a price of inestimable value—therefore *we* are commanded to glorify God with our bodies (1 Cor. 6:19–20).

So we do not attempt to rise to mystic heights by seeking experiences of passivity, yieldedness, or absolute surrender. We were dead! You can't get much more passive than dead!

But now in Christ we are alive. We are not called to "play dead" to God any more. There is no call here to "yield" limply and passively to a force that wells up from within.

What does "yield" mean, anyway? Where did the Muzzy Mystics' call to "yield" come from in the first place? It is a reference to "yield" in the King James Version of Romans 6:13, 16, and 19. The English word brings to the mind of many the idea of surrendering, of giving over, of going limp and passive and giving up control.

That wasn't what Paul had in mind at all.

Paul uses a form of the Greek word *paristanō* (parr-iss-TAH-no). So far from any notion of passivity, this verb connotes actively bringing something up to someone else, and presenting it to him. The verb says, "Here, this is for you." When it has an object, *paristanō* is used of placing something at someone's disposal, providing something for someone, presenting someone or something to someone or something, for some use. It is used of:

- The Father *placing* twelve legions of angels *at Jesus' disposal* to serve and protect Him (Matt. 26:53).
- Jesus *presenting* Himself after His resurrection, to be seen by the apostles (Acts 1:3).
- Soldiers *providing* Paul with horses to ride (Acts 23:24).
- The soldiers *making* Paul *stand before* the governor (Acts 23:33).
- Paul's accusers' failure to *present* or *provide* evidence against him (Acts 24:13).
- Christians *presenting* their bodies to God as a living sacrifice (Rom. 12:1).
- *Presenting* the church to Christ as His bride (2 Cor. 11:2; cf. Eph. 5:27).

Paul's exhortation in Romans 6, then, is that we place ourselves at God's disposal, for His service and use. We are to bring ourselves—our hearts and souls, and our hands and feet—and place them before God, reaffirming our allegiance, reaffirming that we are His to command. Picture a soldier presenting himself before his commanding officer and snapping a sharp salute, ready to take and execute orders. We are being called to report for duty, ready to obey, not to dissolve into a limp heap, yearning to be possessed. We are there to receive and carry out our master's commands.

Now, I can envision a Christianoid mystic bestirring himself to say, "Ah yes, finally you have it. We stand before God, as Andrew Murray said, waiting in silence to hear Him whisper secret revelations directly to us, for our ears alone."

"Wait"? Nonsense. Paul had no such notion in mind. Nowhere in Paul's letters do we find that the tenor of Christian living is individual Christians "waiting" for God to "whisper" secrets meant for them alone. Listen up, and listen well:

> But thanks be to God, that you who were once slaves of sin have become obedient from the heart to the standard of teaching to which you were committed, and, having been set free from sin, have become slaves of righteousness. I am speaking in human terms, because of your natural limitations. For just as you once presented your members as slaves to impurity and to lawlessness leading to more lawlessness, so now present your members as slaves to righteousness leading to sanctification. (Rom. 6:17–19)

Here Paul describes conversion to Christ as a matter of submitting ourselves to a standard of teaching, a pattern of doctrine—the doctrine of Christ's apostles. These are instructions, explanations, and marching orders. The apostle is not speaking of inner, mystical revelation, but of external, objective, public, apostolic teaching, such as we have in Scripture alone. When God saves us, He delivers us over to that teaching.

And this is what Paul means by "righteousness" in this passage: conformity from the heart to the Word of God through the apostles.

The apostle uses *paristanō* in verse 19, and says we present ourselves body and soul to God, providing them for His use. To what end? To the carrying out of the Word of God, as shown in holy living.

So you see, we can't really separate yielding from obedience. We are not to allow sin to reign in our bodies so that we obey, or submit to, its strong desires (Rom. 6:12). Rather, we are to present ourselves to God as slaves to righteousness, which leads to holy living (v. 19). And what do slaves do? They submit. They obey. They take orders.

That is what vibrant, living, biblical faith does. Faith submits. Faith obeys. Faith takes orders (Gal. 5:6; 1 Thess. 1:3; James 2:14, 18, 26).

My friend Chris Anderson, pastor of Tri-County Bible Church in Madison, Ohio, shared this illustration with me:

> Yielding is essentially doing what you're told. If I tell my daughter to clean her room and she instead falls at my feet telling me how worthless she is, waiting for me to do something, that's not yielding. It's disobedience. Pious rebellion, but disobedience nonetheless. And I'll not be impressed with her yieldedness. To yield her will to my own will mean that she [does what I say, and] cleans her room. She obeys me. Nothing mystical about it.[3]

We have work to do: Obeying God's orders is a primary way for us to show we believe Him and love Him.

---

3. From a personal correspondence (August 2009).

We are to cleanse ourselves, and bring holiness to consummation in the fear of God (2 Cor. 7:1). We do that, because God tells us to. We do not dare to insult God by demanding that He do in our stead what He commanded us to do. As old John Owen well said, the Holy Spirit of God "works in us and with us, not against us or [outside of] us."[4]

Objectively, this teaching is fairly plain and obvious in the NT. But not all Christians have caught it. Many fall under the influence of Muzzy Mysticism with its call to something more, other, and supposedly deeper than the teaching of Christ's apostles.

Leaving What?

Each of these three models lacks some biblical truth we need for the Gospel-centered living that will turn the world upside down. Each time we held the thought to Scripture, we learned more about what God really does have to say to us about our lives in Christ.

In the next two chapters, we will more closely focus on the flesh, and then on the role of the Holy Spirit. After that, we will put it all together.

---

4. Owen, Kapic, and Taylor, *Overcoming Sin and Temptation*, 62.

Chapter 12

What About the Flesh?

Christians' Biggest Problem Isn't External

You may not have realized this, but the preceding chapters in this section of the book have been dealing with something the Bible calls "the flesh." The Gutless Gracers, Crisis Upgraders, and Muzzy Mystics have each invented different ways of dealing with the flesh. Let us briefly look at what Scripture actually teaches on the subject. We will learn also how that teaching is perverted into a sort of "tranquilizer dart," and we will uncover the biblical corrective.

Biblical usage of the term is sometimes simply literal. When Exodus 29:32 says that "Aaron and his sons shall eat the flesh of the ram and the bread that is in the basket," nobody needs a PhD in Semitic languages to explain that "flesh" means "meat," as in "Nom-nom-nom, *meat!*"

When applied to humans, the same word refers to our bodily makeup, our flesh. When our resurrected Lord tells His apostles, "See my hands and my feet, that it is I myself. Touch me, and see. For a spirit does not have flesh and bones as you see that I have" (Luke 24:39), His words are very significant, but not opaque at all. "Flesh" is what covers the bones.

In other passages, however, it is clear that something else is at work. Paul says, "While we were living in the flesh, our sinful passions . . . were at work" (Rom. 7:5). Huh? "Were"? Wasn't he dictating this to his scribe from a mouth? Wasn't that mouth in a head? Wasn't that head on a body? Wasn't it all made out of flesh? How can "flesh" be spoken of in the past tense?

And again, Paul writes "that nothing good dwells in me, that is, in my flesh" (Rom. 7:18). What is that about? Didn't God create our flesh, call it good, and make arrangements to resurrect it (cf. Gen. 1:31 and 1 Cor. 15:44)?

Finally, when the apostle John writes that "the desires of the flesh" are "not from the Father" (1 John 2:16), what is he saying? Being hungry is sinful? Pleasurable marital relations are sinful? Enjoying sleep is sinful? Doesn't that totally clash with the rest of the Bible and its affirmation of the goodness of material creation as it came from God's hands?

Finally, given that the "flesh" is the source of problems and heartaches for the Christian, what are we to do about it? Hide off in a monastery? Beat ourselves bloody? Live on tofu and vitamins? Chant? Hold our breaths twice an hour? What?

You see, understanding "the flesh" really is an issue, and we really do need to sort it out. Without pretending to be exhaustive, I've singled out *four* senses for the Hebrew or Greek words for "flesh." Usually it is wise to begin with the literal sense of a word, in order to grasp the more metaphorical uses, so let's start there.

Literal Flesh

As mentioned already, many biblical uses of "flesh" are just like the first occurrence of the word, which is in Genesis 2:21—"So the LORD God caused a deep sleep to fall upon the man, and while he slept took one of his ribs and closed up its place with flesh."

"Flesh" here simply refers to what covers a creature's bones, the body's physical flesh. Sometimes it is human flesh, sometimes animal flesh. This is true very frequently of the OT Hebrew word *bāsār* (bah-SAR; Gen. 2:21, 23; 41:2–4, etc.), and of the NT Greek word *sarx* (Luke 24:39; 1 Cor. 15:39; Col. 2:13; Rev. 19:18, 21).

There is no hint in these passages that the flesh is *bad* in any way. Remember, God created flesh along with the rest of the material universe; and He called it all "very good" (Gen. 1:31). The Bible isn't opposed to physical matter, contrary to what we find in Platonic or Gnostic philosophy, as well as in worldviews influenced by Eastern mysticism.

Body or Human Nature

"Flesh" also is used to denote human nature, though I'd say specifically corporeal human nature, embodied human nature. This application focuses on the whole man as possessing a body of flesh. Again, this is true both in the OT, where it can mean human nature (Num. 16:22), and in many verses in the NT (e.g., Matt. 24:22 [Greek]; Luke 3:6; John 1:14; 17:2; Acts 2:17; Rom. 1:3; Heb. 5:7; 1 John 4:2; 2 John 7).

When David asks, "What can flesh do to me?" (Ps. 56:4), he isn't asking if it would hurt to be hit with frozen meat chub. "Flesh" means "a human being made of flesh." Again, when David sings, "O you who hear prayer, to you shall all flesh come" (Ps. 65:2), we aren't meant to picture hundreds of T-bones making their way across the desert. David means human beings. Isaiah's grand vision that "all flesh shall see" the glory of Yahweh together (Isa. 40:5) again refers to people, humans of all kinds. Paul means that no human being can earn righteousness in God's eyes, when he says that "by the works of the Law no flesh will be justified in His sight" (Rom. 3:20 NASB).

This use is an example of the figure of speech known to pointy-heads as *synecdoche*. With this subdivision of that figure of speech, one singles out one part of a larger whole, and uses it to stand in for the whole. We do that when we say, "Keep an eye on my iPhone while I go to the restroom." We aren't asking our friend simply to point his eyeball to the device, but to use his brain (which stands behind his eyeball) to watch over it. Again, when we refer to "Washington," we mean America's federal government, which meets in Washington, DC.

Again, there is no negative connotation in this use.

Human Nature as Morally, Spiritually, or Physically Weak

Here I think we start seeing the effects of the Fall, as sin extends its baleful contagion through all of human nature. This use is subtler than the two before it, and the one to follow. Some would lump it in with one of the other senses. The idea here is not simply flesh as flesh; nor is it flesh as evil. It presents us with human nature, flesh, as weakened by the Fall, and as frail.

We observe this use very early in the OT, where Yahweh sees that "all flesh" had "corrupted" its way on the earth in Noah's days (Gen. 6:12). Also in Psalm 78:39: "He remembered that they were but flesh, a wind that passes and comes not again." Another well-known example is found in Isaiah 40—

> A voice says, "Cry!"
> And I said, "What shall I cry?"

All flesh is grass,
> and all its beauty is like the flower of the field.
The grass withers, the flower fades
> when the breath of the LORD blows on it;
> surely the people are grass.
The grass withers, the flower fades,
> but the word of our God will stand forever. (vv. 6–8)

New Testament examples would include Matthew 26:41 ("The spirit indeed is willing, but the flesh is weak") and John 6:63a ("It is the Spirit who gives life; the flesh is no help at all").

This sense of "flesh" is what forms the seedbed for the fourth use.

Human Nature as Corrupted by Sin

Perhaps launching off of Genesis 6:12, the next usage we discuss is found in the NT, and particularly in Paul's letters. We'll devote this next section to Paul, but here let's note that Jesus used the word "flesh" as the opposite of the word "Spirit," saying that what is born of the flesh alone can neither see nor enter the kingdom of God (John 3:6). In this usage, there is something wrong with "flesh." It is inadequate for spiritual, kingdom realities.

So when Jesus speaks of judging "according to the flesh," He means it as the opposite of giving true, godly judgment (John 8:15). Peter uses it of corrupt nature in 2 Peter 2:10 and 18, as does John in 1 John 2:16, and Jude in verse 23.

Note carefully: This use is distinct from the first use we discussed—literal flesh. When Scripture describes *sinful* flesh, it's talking about our spiritual condition, not our physical condition.

As I mentioned at the outset, we must carefully note context and usage to determine which sense of "flesh" is being employed. If we read that Jesus "became flesh" in John 1:14, and plug in "sinful nature"—we're heading for a stone wall at light speed. That interpretation would clash with the rest of the NT, and produce damnably false teaching. We need to get it right.

It is the apostle Paul who uses this last definition of "flesh" in the most significant way,[1] when it comes to understanding the Christian life and struggle.

Flesh in Paul's Letters

Though Paul uses "flesh" in the same senses as the other writers in some passages, he most notably uses "flesh" to describe *human nature as corrupted by sin*. To feel the force of Paul's teaching, it's important we dig in here to get a *tactical* understanding of how the Gospel is to be lived out this side of Christ's coming kingdom, while we practice our faith in these plainly unglorified bodies.

So I will lay out a brief and pointed survey. Here are *nine truths about the flesh* from Paul's writings.

1. The Flesh Is What We Are Outside of Christ

Paul refers to preconversion time as "while we were living in the flesh" (Rom. 7:5). This is a simple affirmation of Jesus' words in John 3:3—all natural-born men are born of the flesh, and so that defines their nature. So we all did the whims and passions of the flesh, Paul says, "among whom also we all once conducted ourselves in the lusts of our flesh, fulfilling the desires of the flesh and of the mind, and were by nature children of wrath, just as the others" (Eph. 2:3 NKJV).

So, unsurprisingly . . .

---

1. And most frequently, with 91 uses of *sarx* ("flesh"). John comes in a distant second with 23 uses (Naselli, *Let Go and Let God?* 321).

2. The Flesh (in This Sense) Is Evil

Remember, Paul is not talking about our body, which is weak, but not inherently evil. Rather, he is using the word as shorthand for corrupted human nature. So Paul can say that "nothing good dwells in" his flesh (Rom. 7:18), in this sense.

Nor is this a passive evil. In fact . . .

3. Specifically, the Flesh Hates God and His Law

The attitude or mind-set produced by the flesh is the polar opposite of the mind-set produced by the Holy Spirit (Rom. 8:4–6; Gal. 5:17–21). The flesh is not dull or numb or neutral to God and His will. No, it positively *hates* God's law (Rom. 8:7). That is why the myth of the "objective" unbeliever is just that: a myth. Outside of Christ, we are under the overt power of the flesh (Rom. 7:5), and the flesh hates both God and His law.

That being the case . . .

4. The Flesh Cannot Be Redeemed

The flesh is not redeemable. It cannot be tamed to true holiness, nor taught genuine, heartfelt godliness. Note this very well: The man who is "in the flesh," who is outside of Christ and under the flesh's control, *cannot submit to the law of God* (Rom. 8:7). What is more, the man "in the flesh" *cannot please God* (Rom. 8:8). Paul's Greek is emphatic, in both cases: *not able*, he says. They lack the ability. It is not in his power to take God's word to heart, nor to produce anything that will please God.

So it is futile to try to persuade anyone by reason alone to submit to any expression of God's will as such, including the Gospel. Man, enslaved to his flesh, instinctively rejects and rebels against God's

truth (Rom. 1:18ff.). He can no more make himself do otherwise—
by reason, by free will, by effort—than he can sprout wings and fly
to the moon.

The flesh cannot be rectified. It must be crucified (Gal. 5:24).
That is why . . .

5. Only an Act of God Can Free Us from the Domination of the Flesh

Since we *are* flesh, and flesh is the problem, the answer *cannot*
come from us. You cannot hover four feet (nor four millimeters) off
the ground by bending over and pulling up, really, really hard, on
your Birkenstocks.

Nor can the flesh free the flesh from the flesh. "That which is
born of flesh, is flesh" said Jesus (John 3:6; cf. 1:13). So Paul never
tries to convert his flesh or anyone else's. He does not try to tame
his flesh per se—rather, he cries to be *delivered* from it (Rom. 7:24).

When we are regenerated and justified through faith in Jesus
Christ, our flesh is neither renewed nor removed. What, then?
Read on . . .

6. God's Sovereign Work of Salvation in Christ Frees Us from the Flesh's Dominion

Here is where many Christians go wrong. They speak of doing
this and that "in the flesh." They speak of "carnal Christians," as if
there are two optional and absolute modes of existence (i.e., carnal Christians and spiritual Christians). They talk about these two
supposed levels of Christianity as you might talk about your head-
lights: low beam or high beam. And so in the Christian life, many
imagine that it is possible to shift back and forth from being "in the
flesh" to being "in the spirit."

Note well: Paul says the exact opposite. I think if he heard the way some Christians talk in church meetings, the apostle might take a page from his Lord's book—knocking over some tables and throwing a chair or two to be sure to get attention.

Hear the apostle of Christ very carefully: "For when we were in the flesh, the passions of sins which were through the Law were at work in our parts, so as to bear fruit for death" (Rom. 7:5 DJP). Did you get that? "When we *were* in the flesh." That means we are no longer "in the flesh" in that same sense. Plainly, Paul views being "in the flesh" as a *past* reality, not a present dynamic or option for Christians.

Even more pointedly, ". . . in order that the righteous requirement of the law might be fulfilled in us, who walk not according to the flesh but according to the Spirit" (Rom. 8:4). In the context, it is clear that "who walk not according to the flesh" does not describe a subset of Christians. Paul does not entertain the possibility that there are Christians who do walk according to the flesh, and other Christians who do not so walk.

These words are a description of the Christian *as* a Christian— any Christian, every Christian, no exceptions. It is as if one were to speak of "the fish who swim in the water." We are not suggesting two kinds of fish, those that swim in the water, and those that ride Harleys. We are simply using a phrase that describes fish, period. Fish swim. That's what they do.

Similarly, what Christians do is walk not according to the flesh, but according to the Spirit. That's what Christians do. Anyone who does walk according to the flesh, in the apostle's terms, is simply not a Christian.

"And those who are in the flesh are not able to please God. But you are not in the flesh, but in the Spirit—if indeed the Spirit of God dwells in you. But if one does not have the Spirit of Christ, this one is not His" (Rom. 8:8–9 DJP). You see once again, to the inspired apostle, speaking on Christ's behalf, there are only two kinds of people: those in the flesh (not the Spirit), who lack the ability to please God and do not belong to Jesus Christ; and those in the Spirit (not the flesh), who are able to please God and do belong to Jesus.

I can't imagine language being much clearer. These are two mutually exclusive humanities, described in mutually exclusive terms. Are you "in the flesh"? Then you are not in the Spirit, and you do not belong to Christ. Do you belong to Christ? Then you are in the Spirit, and not in the flesh. It may not fit some popular books, but it does fit this one book that we call the NT rather spiffily.

To Paul, to be "in the flesh" is to be outside of Christ. It is to be unsaved, to be a non-Christian—*not* to be a "carnal Christian."

7. Though Free from the Flesh's Dominion, We Still Struggle with the Flesh All Our Lives

Reality can stinketh. Oh boy, do I wish statement 7 were not true. Do I wish I had a formula for you that could get you past this reality. Believe me, I'd take a hefty dose of the cure myself, then start passing it out by the truckload. I long as ardently as anyone else for a way around this. I have often said that the thing I will miss least in eternity is me, Dan Phillips, as I now am—and when I say that, this is what I mean.

Because, as the sage said, "Everywhere you go, there you are." What's worse, everywhere we go, there our *flesh* is.

And, in this life, there isn't a way around it. The classical passage that dwells on this struggle is Romans 7:14–25. Academics and writing pastors have tussled with the section since Tertius, Paul's scribe, first stuck the postage stamp on the epistle and dropped it in the mailbox.

Let's try to get a grip on this crucial passage. I'd like to offer *three* guiding observations.

First, our struggle with the flesh is not a "stage" of the Christian life. Some see Romans 5–8 as a progression. In Romans 5, Paul finds justification and its blessings. This is where the Christian life starts. Then in Romans 6, Paul moves on from experiencing justification to experiencing sanctification, which is to say growing in holiness. This is seen as the second phase of the Christian life.

Romans 7 is taken as the next phase, a period where Paul struggled with the flesh, experiencing defeat and discouragement in his Christian life. He cried out for deliverance in verse 24. And he got it! Accordingly, in Romans 8 Paul is seen as finding deliverance from this struggle, by his discovery of the joy and freedom of life in the Spirit.

Nice, tidy, appealing. But wrong.

Paul *never* teaches that justification, sanctification, struggle, and life in the Spirit form separate, detached "stages" of the Christian life. That is, we do not become justified, and then just remain inert, while progressive sanctification dangles "out there" somewhere as an elective option rather than an imperative. Nor do we begin to grow in holiness and experience a struggle for a while, and then discover the wonderful "secret" of the Spirit-filled life—ever after living in cloudless victory, never to revisit the "struggle" phase again.

Nothing in Romans points to such an interpretation of the progression of Paul's thought, let alone his experience. Look at the *start* of chapters 5, 6, 7, and 8. Do you see any progression signals, any sequential tags such as "Next," or "Then," or "After that"? Not at all.

What is more, notice how each chapter *ends* with something about our salvation in Jesus Christ:

- ". . . so that, as sin reigned in death, grace also might reign through righteousness leading to eternal life through Jesus Christ our Lord." (5:21)

- "For the wages of sin is death, but the free gift of God is eternal life in Christ Jesus our Lord." (6:23)
- "Wretched man that I am! Who will deliver me from this body of death? Thanks be to God through Jesus Christ our Lord! So then, I myself serve the law of God with my mind, but with my flesh I serve the law of sin." (7:24–25)
- "For I am sure that neither death nor life, nor angels nor rulers, nor things present nor things to come, nor powers, nor height nor depth, nor anything else in all creation, will be able to separate us from the love of God in Christ Jesus our Lord." (8:38–39)[2]

So you see, it is better to see these chapters as *four simultaneous facets of the Christian's life.* The Christian is a justified man, a man counted righteous in and because of Christ and thus at peace with God (Rom. 5). This justified man needs to embrace the truth that he has died to his sin, and has come alive to God in Christ (Rom. 6). He has also died to the law, yet continues to struggle with the flesh (Rom. 7). Nonetheless, in all this he is more than a conqueror in Christ, and knows the Spirit's life-giving, sanctifying, hope-inspiring, and joyous ministry (Rom. 8)—not as erasing his struggle with the flesh, but as strengthening and encouraging him in the midst of that ongoing battle.

All these things are true of *every* Christian at *all* times.

One of those four simultaneous facets is our struggle with the flesh. This is true of the newest believer, and it is equally true of the most seasoned saint. In fact, a low view of the corruptions of the flesh is not a mark of Christian maturity or growth in holiness.

---

2. Indeed, when one observes the flow of Paul's thought from Romans 7 to Romans 8, one discerns that Romans 8 was written to encourage and give hope to the Christian who struggles with sin.

The better one knows Christ, the more aware he is of those baneful passions within, and the more conscious he is of his need of Christ's grace and strength, and his own need to keep a vigilant watch on himself.

The struggle continues until we go to be with the Lord through death, or He catches us away to be with Him, whichever comes first.

Second, Paul casts this passage very emphatically in the present tense. If you could study Romans 7 in Greek, you would see a striking consistency. Paul uses one past tense or another of himself in verses 5, 6, 7, 8, 9, 10, 11, and 13. Then he switches to the first person singular present active indicative in verse 14, and continues it *unbroken* in verses 15, 16, 17, 18, 19, 20, 21, 22, 23, and 25. Paul's only departure is in verse 24, where he uses the future tense—to speak of when he will be delivered from this struggle!

Simply put: Paul paints this struggle as a "now" thing, not a "used to be" thing. It is a "live feed," not an archive photo.

Though very fine pastors and commentators have found ways to argue that this is not a picture of Paul's ongoing struggle, one main question prevents me from following them. It is this: If Paul had wanted to depict his battle with the flesh as personal and ongoing, how could he have said it more clearly? I can't think of any reasonable way. In fact, Paul is a pretty poor writer, I think, if he does not mean us to interpret "I do not do what I want, but I do the very thing I hate" (Rom. 7:15) as depicting his present reality.

Another major roadblock is verse 25b. If verses 14–25a depict a past struggle, which is no longer Paul's present reality, what is up with Paul saying in sum, "Wherefore accordingly on the one hand I myself, with my mind, am a slave to the law of God; but, on the other, in my flesh, to the law of sin" (DJP)? This surely reads as Paul's summary of the section. Paul is telling us the way things are now,

right now, where we live as justified Christians. I find it both difficult and unnatural to cast this clear summary statement back into
the apostle's unregenerate past.

*Third and finally, viewing Romans 7:14–25 as the Christian's
ongoing struggle with the flesh fits what Paul says elsewhere.* Though
Romans 6 is full of Paul's teaching that we died to sin in Christ and
must reckon ourselves so, we mustn't miss his allusions to what life
is for us. When Paul tells us to keep not "letting" sin reign (present
tense) in our mortal bodies (v. 1), does he not suggest that it will
keep trying to reign, but we mustn't allow it to do so? When he says
that sin will not lord it over us (v. 14), does he not hint that it will
attempt to overpower us, but we must resist it?

And in the glorious Romans 8, which some see as a higher level
of Christian living, are there not several references to this ongoing
struggle? Think these questions through:

- When Paul says we must continually be mortifying the practices of the body by the Holy Spirit's enabling (v. 13), what
  can that mean but that we continually find more and more in
  us that needs to be put to death?
- If we must "suffer with" Christ now (vv. 17–18), aren't part of
  the sufferings our ongoing cry for deliverance from the flesh-
  ridden body of death (7:24)?
- When Paul says that we now groan (v. 23) right along with
  creation (v. 22), is not the cry of 7:25 part of that groan?
- Is not the longing for the redemption of our body (v. 23) a
  longing to be delivered from the daily battle with the flesh?
- If we must hope for this redemption as future (vv. 24–25),
  does that not necessarily mean we aren't freed from it yet?
- What is the "weakness" in which we need the Holy Spirit's
  help (v. 26), if not the weakness caused by our battles with
  the flesh?

When we were born again, our flesh did not move out or move on. Would that it had! The flesh has not been replaced, but it has been displaced by a superior power. This powerful influence assures that the sinful passions of the flesh will never again rule us as our lord.

What is that power?

8. *The Only Counter to the Flesh Is the Holy Spirit*

We are new people in Christ. But we are not like cordless drills that can get a charge and then go off and work independently all day.[3] The whole point of being a new person (as we will see in chapter 13) is being indwelt and led by the Holy Spirit, who ushers us into God's presence and glorifies Christ to, and in, and through us.

Let us be specific. What counters the flesh is not willpower. It isn't more religious rules. It isn't medication. It isn't psychotherapy. It isn't a rigorous course of diet and discipline.

In fact, the Greek text of Colossians 2:23 suggests that these things actually *satisfy* the flesh, rather than *mortifying* it.[4] Coming up with our own systems for sanctity and wonderfulness, trying to bypass the struggle the Bible says we will all have, simply bloats us with pride in our superior wisdom, godliness, and accomplishments. And pride, in case we need a reminder, is a fleshly, ungodly trait (2 Tim. 3:2).

While we're at it, let's be even more specific. You can't run away from the flesh by joining a monastery. Ask Martin Luther. Why not? Because no matter how far or how fast we run, our flesh comes with us.

Social reform won't reform the flesh. I am not necessarily op-

---

3. Analogy adapted from Mahaney, "Cultivate Humility," 131.
4. "These sorts of things lead—though indeed having a reputation for wisdom in self-made worship and humiliation and harsh treatment of the body (not with any value)—to the gratification of the flesh" (DJP; cf. the translations of Goodspeed and Moffatt, and J. B. Phillips's paraphrase).

posed to social reform, as readers of my blog well know, but let's harbor no illusions. We could shut down every salacious media outlet, turn off every TV, cancel every magazine subscription, and we'd still have the same restless problem within.

I remember too vividly one of my most miserable, disheartening battles with my own flesh. It took place beside a lovely Sierra lake, miles away from a TV, a movie screen, or a magazine. Only one person was there: your faithful correspondent, me. And with me was . . . ? My flesh. That was enough. Idyllic externals cannot silence the flesh.

Nor can parents produce flesh-conquering children by the implementation of precise techniques. I've been chagrined to see the implication in otherwise sound teaching that, if parents just apply a particular pedagogy to a "T," they will produce godly children, like so many cookies on a factory conveyor belt. Sometimes homeschoolers—and I speak as a rabid homeschooling proponent—seem to imagine that, if we can just isolate our little cherubs from the riffraff, they'll turn out to be holy little plaster saints.

Our children's worst enemy is not the government education camps, or their nasty little friends. Their worst enemy is within. They were born with it. They got it from Mom and Dad, who got it from Great-grampa Adam.

The flesh can't be regulated out, dieted out, disciplined out, isolated out, techniqued out, cast out, nor willed out. It's as true as it is sad: As long as we're absent from the Lord, we're present in the body (2 Cor. 5:6) and struggling with the flesh. Human efforts alone can neither counter the flesh nor produce godliness.

The only remedy for the flesh is the Gospel, and all the blessings it brings. One of the choicest blessings (as we will see in the next chapter) is the indwelling of the Holy Spirit of God. It is *the Spirit* who produces in us a life that pleases God (and thus is not dominated by the flesh; Rom. 8:2, 4). It is *by the Spirit* that we put to death the deeds of the body (Rom. 8:13b). If we *walk in the Spirit* we will not fulfill the flesh's desires (Gal. 5:16). It is *the Spirit* who battles the flesh in us (Gal. 5:17).

And He does all this by applying the cross to the flesh (Gal. 5:24), and producing His fruit in us (Gal. 5:22–23).

Do not lose heart in the struggle. It is actually a wonderfully good thing that you struggle. I know that is counterintuitive. I realize I may be saying this to souls locked in mortal battle with passions that would reduce many grown men to tears.

Let me explain myself with an image.

In your mind's eye, picture a rapidly flowing mountain stream, hundreds of gallons of crystal clear water rushing by every minute. You creep up quietly to the bank to sneak a closer look. What do you see in the water? A few slim, olive shapes, in constant motion. These are some Brook Trout. Their life is an unceasing struggle, every moment fighting a current that would pull them downstream. They can never rest, never stop swimming. Struggle, shimmy, swim; dart here to grab a nymph, there to leap for a mosquito. Flee for the cover of a submerged boulder when a menacing presence crunches along the stones of the stream's bank. Struggle.

Ah, but there you see another fish. What you see is not olive, however. It is a clammy white. It is a trout's belly.

This trout is different from all the others. He is not struggling, not at all. He isn't fighting the current, chasing food, fleeing enemies. He looks perfectly relaxed, perfectly at ease, perfectly at peace with the stream's current as he languidly passes down, downstream, and out of sight.

Why was that trout so peaceful and relaxed?

Because he was *dead.*

Why do you struggle?

Because you're *alive!*

Paul experienced the exact same exasperating, exhausting, disheartening fight as we, Christian friend (Rom. 7:14–25). These battles against fleshly enticements to sin mean that the Holy Spirit is within us, transforming our heart and mind into the image of Christ degree by degree (2 Cor. 3:18). It is He who causes us to loathe the old passions from within, who makes us sigh with frustration over our fleshly failings, bids us run to the cross, leads us to repent, braces us to get up and get at it again in the Lord's strength, fills us with yearning for the presence of Christ and for final deliverance from sin's every stain and blemish (Rom. 7:24).

So we mustn't lose heart. This is not the last act. The final act will be *glorious*, and will transform every one of our present struggles into lasting splendor (Rom. 8:18; 2 Cor. 4:16–18).

9. Only Glorification in Christ's Presence Will End the Battle

Paul groans for deliverance (Rom. 7:24), and reveals that it will come when Christ transforms all creation and glorifies our bodies (Rom. 8:19–25). In Philippians 3:20–21 he says that Christ will use his power to transform our bodies into the likeness of His own glorious body—which means the eradication of the remaining corruptions of sin that daily plague us.

John speaks similarly, when he writes, "Beloved, now we are children of God; and it has not yet appeared what we will be. But we know that when He appears, we will be like Him, because we will see Him just as He is" (1 John 3:2 djp). This dazzling vision will glorify us. Then the struggle will be over, the strife with the flesh will be a fading memory, and eternal joy will overtake us as we live forever in Christ's glorious presence.

Then all creation will be transformed. This will be new heavens and a new earth, in which righteousness is at home (2 Peter 3:13). God will make all things new (Rev. 21:5). The curse will be reversed (Rev. 22:3 nasb; cf. Isa. 11).

And we ourselves will be at last and finally freed from every last vestige of sin's dark and ruinous touch (Rev. 21:4).

Including the battle with our own remaining corruptions.

Lord, bring that day quickly.

Dealing with the Flesh

We have seen the enemy, and he is us. Or at least the enemy is our flesh. Now, what to do about this indwelling anchor?

As I see it, there are three basic approaches to the flesh: denial, defeat, deal. We have already seen two of them.

Denial shows itself in the crisis upgrade myth, where I can get catapulted out of a carnal Christian life and into a spiritual Christian life, untroubled by the flesh. We talked about some of those bogus models in chapters 10 and 11. In this case, *denial* is way more than just a river in Egypt.

Defeat shows itself in the errors of gutless grace teaching. By refusing to deal honestly with the biblical teaching that a holy, obedient life is a necessary product of saving grace, this teaching leads to a yielding to the flesh. Grace, to them, does not empower us to battle the flesh (as Paul says it does in Titus 2:12). So we end up simply giving up the battle, rationalizing sin as inevitable, insinuating that God's commands are either mere suggestions or cruel tricks to be avoided, and painting "grace" over a life given over to the flesh.

A more biblical approach is to deal. That is, we see the flesh is a potent and ever-present hazard and handicap. In a way, it is like having a bad knee. I speak from experience, having injured my knee in karate. My bum knee is just there. I can't wish it away, physical therapy did not fix it, and there is no good surgery for it. It keeps tripping me up.

Yet I haven't let it stop me altogether. I suppose that I could sit down and never walk again, using my knee as an excuse. But that would be just too pathetic to bear. Or again I could pretend I don't have it, put myself in situations that will certainly trigger it, and make it far worse.

Or I could do what I do: keep aware of it, and push back as much as I can, trying to regain ground.

It's an imperfect analogy, but the flesh is similar. Scripture won't let me pretend that the flesh is my "note from God," excusing me from the work of growing in holiness, and of seeking the Spirit's enabling to keep Christ's commands. But if I pretend it isn't real, and put myself in tempting situations that I know will exacerbate my particular fleshly weaknesses, I'm foolishly putting myself at hazard and asking for some serious humiliation.

So I battle.

But let's pause and look closely at one way Christians fail to do serious battle, in the name of doing serious battle.

The Flesh-o-phobia Dodge

Do you remember the muzzy mystics we dealt with back in chapter 11? We're going to pay them one more visit . . . because I used to be in their number, and I know what a trap this mind-set is. I don't want any of you to be stuck where I was.

Some Christians so fear obeying God "in the power of the flesh" that they'd rather do *nothing*, than do something carnal.

It's sad, but it's true. Whatever their holy-sounding theory, these folks' practice can be summed up in this motto: better to disobey God outright, than obey Him in the flesh. Or, better to do nothing piously for God's glory, than do something fleshly for God's glory.

The result is not merely paralysis, but a pungently sanctimonious form of paralysis that is particularly repugnant. It has its own aroma, but it isn't the fragrance of Christ, who said, "I have come to do Your will, O God" (Heb. 10:7). It smells more like the son who, called to work for his father, chirped, "Sure, Dad, you bet!"—then sat still (in holy meditation and "yieldedness"? [Matt. 21:30]).

You dare not confront these brothers or sisters for their sin in disobeying God. If you even try, no matter how lovingly and biblically, you mark yourself as shallow and, well, carnal! Because clearly, you don't understand: When they disobey God, it's really because they love God so much. It's because they just want Jesus to be all, and God to be all; they long to be nothing, like little lead soldiers melted down into the big molten vat of goddishness. (I speak as a fool.)

I was touched with the mysticizing doctrine early in my Christian life.

As I mentioned in chapter 8, before my conversion I was a member of a non-Christian cult called the Science of Mind, or Religious Science. This sect taught we were all part of God, all God's self-expressions. We only needed to "manifest" the God-life. We were neither sinners needing atonement through Jesus' blood, nor guilty souls yearning for His imputed righteousness. There was no external law of God that judged and condemned us. We simply needed to affirm the God-consciousness within us all, and manifest this life in all its peace and joy and wonderfulness.

So daily living, for the Religious Scientist, was not a matter of believe and do. There was no call to respond to any authority outside of ourselves (particularly not the Bible). The thing was to know, and to realize, and to affirm. Guidance came from within, not from without.

When I encountered the mystical Christianoid "let go" teaching, then,[5] it was eerily familiar. Its advocates were Christians who talked about Jesus, unlike the mysticized redefinitions of Religious Science. Still, like Religious Scientists, they called to yield, be silent, passive, spiritually open to receive direct impressions and guidance.

---

5. Described more fully in chapter 11.

So, after my conversion, teaching such as Andrew Murray's caught me. I tried and tried. That is, I tried *not* to try. I tried to melt— er, that is, to *let* myself be melted. (But wait, if I'm doing the not-doing . . . if it takes me to not take me to . . . whoa, as I said, this gets really confusing!) It made me pretty miserable.

My circle of Christian friends was also infected. We all had the same fear: acting "in the flesh." We were afraid of going to church *in the flesh*, witnessing for Christ *in the flesh*, praying *in the flesh*, studying the Word *in the flesh*, obeying the Word *in the flesh*, serving God *in the flesh*. So, for fear of doing any of those things *in the flesh*, we'd stop doing them altogether. Better not to do at all, we reasoned, than to do *in the flesh!*

There was also a nasty little side effect. Some of us could be pretty smug about our abstinence from doing things in the flesh. We could look down on others who were very energetically involved in church, witnessing, and holy living—because we were pretty sure that they were doing all this in the flesh. Their examples did not spur or convict us. Who wanted to be fleshly? Not us.

It came to a head for me in my first round of pastoral training. It's a long story in itself, but the bottom line is that the Lord had brought me from being a lazy, undisciplined student before my conversion, to committing myself to become immersed in Greek so as to gain a firm grasp of the NT.

But many of my fellow students wouldn't do that. They wouldn't study too hard. They wouldn't get into it too deeply. Why? Why ever not?

You've already guessed, haven't you? All that studying was *in the flesh.*

I was headed for disaster. When you are naturally prone to over-introspection (as I am), this teaching multiplies that tendency by a factor of a bazillion.

The effect of all this was that I was constantly taking my spiritual pulse, constantly checking within, freezing up, paralyzed, spiraling down into deeper and deeper morbid introspection and depression. In the name of "looking to Jesus" (revealed in His Word) I was constantly looking to myself, within myself.

What should I do? Should I leave off the hard, sweaty, grueling work of study? Should I close the books and "let God," for fear of studying in the flesh?

Somewhere around that time I began to realize how comparatively simple, straightforward, and in-broad-daylight NT Christianity was, and God set me free.

Never once in the NT do you see an apostle or any other Christian caught in a whirlpool of fearful introspection and navel-gazing. Never once did they shrink back from serving God by Spirit-enabled, faith-motivated, grace-empowered obedience to Gospel commands because it might be *in the flesh.* The book of Acts contains not one tale of an apostle yanking a Christian to a stop because that Christian was serving God biblically and by-grace-through-faith in the flesh. Nor did we ever read of an apostle issuing a series of directives in Christ's name, then immediately cautioning his readers against obeying them in the flesh.

In fact, you can divide many NT apostolic letters into two simple parts summed up in six words:

1. Here's Some Truth.
2. So Do This.

Nor was the concept of flesh introduced by Paul to make Christian living more complicated and tangled. True, Paul vividly depicted how the flesh complicates Christian living (Rom. 7:14–25). But the apostle never compounds the issue by reeling off horror stories of grace-saved, born-again, Spirit-indwelt Christians living for God's glory in the flesh—as if it were some sort of indefinable mystical state of being, more powerful than the Holy Spirit and the new nature.

Now, the apostles did speak of the flesh. They warned against pride, arrogance, lust, covetousness, divisiveness, bitterness, and such things; and, these are indeed works of the flesh (Gal. 5:19–21). But Paul says those works are *phanera*, which means obvious, apparent, plainly evident (Gal. 5:19). Never would Paul have interrupted an aglow, on-fire, God-centered, Christ-loving Christian from telling the Gospel, and told him to go to his closet and stop witnessing and serving and doing until he was sure he wasn't doing it in the flesh.

So I came to a decision that affected studying Greek and a great many other things. I decided that I would heed Solomon's counsel: "Whatever your hand finds to do, do it with your might" (Eccl. 9:10a). I would seek to do as Paul the apostle—who, after all, knew about flesh—said: "Whether you eat or drink, or whatever you do, do all to the glory of God" (1 Cor. 10:31). I would give it everything God gave me to give, out of love for Christ, and to be of use to His church. Pedal to the metal.

What if my studying made me proud and arrogant? Here's the sad truth: It did! But that's not all. Not studying would have had the same effect. I still would have been proud, but I'd have been ignorant and ill-equipped to boot. In fact, I have learned this pathetic truth about pride: It can live and thrive on nothing. My pride is the ultimate "air plant." Swerve to avoid some good thing for fear of pride, and your avoidance will blow you up like a blimp. Avoiding activities that might make me proud is a prescription for avoiding anything, period, because anything and nothing can make me proud.

Such a dilemma. What to do?

We have already seen the answer. Pride calls for the same prescription as any sin: *Take it to the cross.* Then, by repentant faith, get on with keeping Christ's commands.

I saw, then, that pious inactivity had nothing to do with love for God. Scripture shows us what love for God is: "For this is the love of God, that we keep his commandments. And his commandments are not burdensome" (1 John 5:3). And it shows us what people who love Jesus do: "You are my friends if you do what I command you" (John 15:14).

Do you see how straightforward both Christ and His apostles are? We know that the greatest thing in all the universe is to love God with all our heart, soul, mind, and strength (Mark 12:30). And what does such love look like? It looks like a man who does what Jesus says to do, who keeps God's commandments. It looks like believing obedience.

And so I had no excuse to avoid all-out living for God's glory, through grace, by the Spirit's power, in obedience to the commands of God. In fact, it was my great joy to shake off flesh-o-phobic paralysis, and throw myself into the love of my life.

Chapter 13

What About the Holy Spirit?

Demystifying the Mysterious Person of the Trinity—a Little!

Jesus told Nicodemus that one must be born of water and the Spirit to enter the kingdom of God (John 3:3). Then He described such a person as one "born of the Spirit" (John 3:8). As we saw in chapter 8, Nicodemus should not have been shocked to hear Jesus say this, because this work of the Holy Spirit had been prophesied centuries earlier by Ezekiel (Ezek. 36:27; 39:29).

A Bible student might feel a twinge of sympathy for Nicodemus, however. The presence of the Holy Spirit in the OT is not always as clear as it is in the NT. Even a close reading does not find the Spirit depicted performing all of the ministries that He does in the NT.

There is a reason for that, and it lurks behind words that we might have just brushed past: "Old Testament," "New Testament." Of course we all know those two terms as designations of the two major parts of the Bible: The first 39 books are the Old Testament, and the last 27 are the New Testament.

What we need to remember is that the word *testament* is another way of translating the Hebrew and Greek words more usually rendered as *covenant*. That word is a big, big concept in all of the Bible, from start to finish. A *covenant* is a regulated relationship, a relationship that has been formalized and defined and put into words (and, usually in the Bible, writing).

We get the wording "new" and "old" covenant from the Bible itself. In what we call the "Old," there is a prophecy of the "New": "Behold, the days are coming, declares the LORD, when I will make a new covenant with the house of Israel and the house of Judah" (Jer. 31:31). The prophet contrasts that covenant with "the covenant that I made with their fathers on the day when I took them by the hand to bring them out of the land of Egypt" (v. 32), which is to say the covenant of Moses, made at Mount Sinai. That covenant, by implication, is the old covenant.

This phrase "new covenant" is echoed by the Lord Jesus, when He refers to the cup of wine at the last supper as representing "the new covenant in my blood" (Luke 22:20). And so the book of Hebrews reflects on Jeremiah's words and mentions both covenants: "In speaking of a new covenant, he makes the first one obsolete. And what is becoming obsolete and growing old is ready to vanish away" (Heb. 8:13).

I introduce that massive topic (too briefly!) to say this: The Bible depicts a particular, special ministry of the Holy Spirit under the terms of the New Covenant. Believers in Jesus Christ today enjoy and benefit from works of the Holy Spirit to which the great men and women of OT times were strangers. Not even Abraham, Moses,

David, Ruth, Esther, or Daniel knew the fullness of what God has given us in Christ.

We will see that the New Covenant believer knows an intimacy and permanency of the operations and presence of the Holy Spirit that none before him ever experienced. Nor is this the birthright of a select, elite, favored few. We will see that the Lord Jesus made specific provisions equally for every last single believer, throughout this entire age.

Understanding the New Covenant ministry of the Holy Spirit will help us grasp how richly God has blessed us and equipped us for our life in Christ. There has been a lot of unhelpful and misleading teaching about the person and work of the Holy Spirit. I will stick with my general approach in this book: Rather than name and refute, we will focus on positive exposition and application of Scripture, and leave it to you to make the connections as to which false doctrines are swept away by Scripture.

The Holy Spirit as a Gospel Gift

What do you think of when you reflect on the wonderful accomplishments of Christ on the cross? What did He do for His people, what did He secure for them? You may think of forgiveness, justification, reconciliation, redemption. All that is gloriously true. We might go on to list adoption, eternal life, assurance of hope, constitution as a kingdom of priests to God His Father. Again, wonderful truths, all of them.

But know this as well: The gift of the Holy Spirit is a particularly glorious reality that our Lord secured for us by His suffering on the cross. The presence of the Spirit in us, marking us as God's children and doing His work within us, is a New Covenant reality. It is a blessing not shared in the same way by our great forefathers in faith, not even Abraham, Moses, and David.

The fact that these ministries of the Holy Spirit are uniquely New Covenant blessings is not an obscure, uncertain inference from the white spaces between a hazy text or two. It's *in* the text.

First, note the words of Jesus' forerunner, John the Baptist: "After me comes he who is mightier than I, the strap of whose sandals I am not worthy to stoop down and untie. I have baptized you with water, but he will baptize you with the Holy Spirit" (Mark 1:7–8). We'll return to these words in a moment. For now, simply note: The baptism with the Holy Spirit was a future event to John. Great a prophet as he was—and the Lord Jesus said none was greater (Matt. 11:11)—John had no part in this particular activity of the Holy Spirit.

The Lord Jesus Himself later sounded the same idea in so many words, and the apostles affirmed the same truth. Well before His crucifixion, at the Feast of Tabernacles, Jesus went up to Jerusalem,

> stood up and shouted out, "If anyone is thirsty, let him come to me, and let the one who believes in me drink. Just as the scripture says, 'From within him will flow rivers of living water.'" (John 7:37–38 DJP)[1]

What was He talking about? Thankfully, the apostle John explains for us: "Now this he said about the Spirit, whom those who believed in him were to receive, for as yet the Spirit had not been given, because Jesus was not yet glorified" (v. 39). The gift of the Holy Spirit was then a future event, and was dependent on Jesus being "glorified." This is John's rich way of referring to Christ's death, burial, resurrection, and ascension as one complex concept. And

---

1. I am persuaded that this rendering and punctuation gives the sense of Jesus' words as John records them better than the familiar punctuation seen in versions such as the ESV and NASB. (Though cf. NRSV, as well as the margin of the ESV, NIV, and TNIV.)

all these events must be accomplished *before* the Holy Spirit could be given to believers.

Jesus sounds the same note later in John 15:26, when He refers to the Holy Spirit as the Helper, "whom I will send to you from the Father." Even now, on the last evening of His earthly life, Jesus spoke of the sending of the Spirit as a future event.

With even greater explicitness, the Lord says very solemnly, "I tell you the truth: it is to your advantage that I go away, for if I do not go away, the Helper will not come to you. But if I go, I will send him to you" (John 16:7). Once again, the Spirit's coming is contingent on Jesus going away by means of His atoning death on the cross. There is a necessary sequence in the Father's eternal plan of redemption. Event A must precede Event B, as history plays out. Jesus must "go away" through His death on the cross, or the Spirit will not come. If He goes, Jesus will send the Spirit.

What a momentous event this must be. Think about it: Jesus actually says that it is *better* for Him to leave, so that the Spirit may come. Doesn't that strike you as awfully counterintuitive? Wouldn't you have said, "Um, tell You what . . . why don't You just stay?" I think I would have.

Good thing it wasn't up to us. In vast wisdom, the entire Trinity had planned this out before time began. In the counsels of God, His children's greatest blessing would come through Jesus going to Calvary, rising from the dead, ascending to the Father's right hand, and pouring out the person of the Holy Spirit on His people.

Jesus must "go away," that the Holy Spirit might "come" to us.

The Cross and the Spirit

Why is the cross—if you'll pardon a sober pun—so *crucial* to this new ministry and gift of the Spirit? It is because the cross inaugurates the New Covenant, and the Holy Spirit is one of the wonderful blessings that is granted to believers by the terms of that covenant. At the last supper, Jesus says of the cup, "This cup that is poured out for you is the new covenant in My blood" (Luke 22:20). The blood He sheds on the cross, then, establishes the New Covenant. And the Spirit is expressly prophesied as one of the gracious grants under that covenant (Ezek. 36:27; see further below).

After His resurrection, Jesus underscored this truth yet again. Twice Jesus stresses the necessity of His death on the cross. The first time, Jesus calls them "foolish" (Luke 24:25) for not knowing that it was "necessary that the Christ should suffer these things and enter into his glory" (v. 26). Again, when He meets with the apostles, Jesus says that "everything written about me in the Law of Moses and the Prophets and the Psalms must be fulfilled" (v. 44). Both times, Jesus says that His death was a necessity. God's eternal plan had a certain necessary succession of events. Before the Spirit could be given, Christ must die a bloody death for His people's sins on the cross, and must rise bodily from the grave.

Only after these redemptive events could forgiveness of sins be proclaimed globally (Luke 24:44–47). Furthermore, Jesus said, "Behold, I am sending the promise of my Father upon you. But stay in the city until you are clothed with power from on high" (v. 49). They had to wait in the city of Jerusalem.

This is repeated again in Acts 1:4, where we read that He "ordered them not to depart from Jerusalem, but to wait for the promise of the Father." That *promise* is explained to be the baptism with the Holy Spirit that John had predicted (v. 5). One more time in that chapter, Jesus puts this in the future, saying "you will receive power when the Holy Spirit has come upon you, and you will be my witnesses in Jerusalem and in all Judea and Samaria, and to the end of the earth" (v. 8)

Nearly two months later it came to pass, just as the prophet John and the Lord Jesus had both predicted.

In the church's inaugural sermon on the day of Pentecost, Peter preached that Jesus had to be raised from the dead—and indeed He was (Acts 2:22–32). Then Peter concluded: "Being therefore exalted at the right hand of God, and having received from the Father the promise of the Holy Spirit, he has poured out this that you yourselves are seeing and hearing" (Acts 2:33). Observe the sequence yet again: Jesus dies, rises from the dead, is exalted to God's right hand, receives the promise of the Spirit that had been pledged under the terms of the New Covenant, and then imparts Him to the church.

To appreciate more fully why this is such a huge, epoch-making event, let us back up to the very beginning, and take a whirlwind survey of the sweep of biblical teaching about the Spirit up until Pentecost.

Please strap on your seatbelts, and keep your arms and legs inside the car at all times. Ready? Here goes.

The Holy Spirit in the Old Testament

It is fair to say that the Spirit of God is an enigmatic figure in the OT.[2] However I do believe we find Him there. Though revelation is unfolding and progressive (Heb. 1:1–2), all revelation is revelation of the same body of truth. To adapt a figure from nineteenth-century theologian B. B. Warfield,[3] the room may be dimmer in the OT before the full light of Christ shines, but all the furniture is there. Since the Trinity is an eternal reality, I am not surprised to find that truth at least foreshadowed from the start.

---

2. Bible-believing Christians differ very widely on how much is revealed about the Spirit in the Old Testament. A full treatment of all the evidence and all the views would fill a massive book indeed. This is simply a very brief positive presentation of the highlights of my understanding of the Torah's teaching.

3. Warfield, "Trinity," 3014.

The truth is, the work of the Spirit in the OT is selective and sporadic. Though He has a role in creation and providence (Gen. 1:2; Job 33:4; Pss. 104:30; 139:7), He is not expressly said to have an ongoing work inside of all believers at large, or a permanent ministry of indwelling.[4]

What we do read is of the Spirit rushing on various judges (Judg. 3:10; 6:34; 11:29; 13:25; 14:6, 19; 15:14), empowering and motivating them for specific actions related to God's purposes for the nation of Israel. The Spirit also comes upon prophets (1 Sam. 10:6, 10; 11:6; 19:20, 23; Num. 24:2; Ezek. 11:24), granting them the ability to hear and relay God's word to Israel without error. We also find Him having an occasional, special ministry to kings (1 Sam. 16:13), and even equipping artisans to do intricate work in the construction of the tabernacle (Exod. 31:3; 35:31).

Numbers 11 is a particularly revealing passage. In the context, God has taken some of the ministry of the Holy Spirit in Moses, and extended that work to seventy elders, who are then also enabled to speak the word of God (vv. 16–17, 25). Two who did not go where they were supposed to go nonetheless receive this ministry of the Spirit (v. 26), and Joshua objects (v. 28). In reply, Moses says, "Would that all the LORD's people were prophets, that the LORD would put his Spirit on them!" (v. 29b). Moses' implication is clear enough: The Spirit has not been put on all the people—and not even all believing Israelites. While the Spirit did special works related to the kingdom of Israel, "garden variety" saints were not objects of His regular working.

But God has a plan. This will change.

Some bold prophecies connect the Holy Spirit to the coming King from David's line, the Messiah. Isaiah particularly sounds this note. Of Messiah, Isaiah proclaims that

---

4. For an extended study of this issue, see Hamilton, *God's Indwelling Presence*.

The Spirit of the LORD will rest on him,
  The spirit of wisdom and understanding,
  The spirit of counsel and might,
  The spirit of knowledge and the fear of the LORD. (Isa. 11:2)

The Spirit *rests* on Messiah. He does not rush, then depart, as with judges and kings.[5] Yahweh rests His Spirit on Messiah, permanently, so that Messiah brings forth justice for the nations (42:1). In fact, it is the Spirit who makes Messiah *Messiah*. In decades of serving in various church settings, I find that most English readers cannot define or explain the words "Christ" and "Messiah." Surely these are words we should know.

The simple truth is that "Messiah" and "Christ" mean the same thing. They are both transliterations of Hebrew and Greek words, respectively, and both words mean "anointed one." The allusion is to the fact that prophets (1 Kings 19:16; Ps. 105:15), priests (Exod. 28:41), and kings (1 Sam. 10:1; 16:13) had *oil* poured on them to inaugurate them into office. The Messiah is so-called because He will be the perfect Prophet (Deut. 18:15–19), Priest (Ps. 110:4), and King (Ps. 2), all in one splendorous Person.

Like prophets and priests and kings of old, Messiah would be anointed as His inauguration for office. However, Messiah would not have mere physical oil for His anointing, no matter how fragrant. His anointing will be personal and divine. The Holy Spirit Himself would anoint[6] Messiah for His ministry of healing and restoration (Isa. 61:1). And, as prophesied, this anointing of the Holy Spirit indeed was granted to the Lord Jesus before His public ministry (Luke 4:18; Acts 10:38).

---

5. For instance, compare Judges 14:6, 19; 15:14 with 16:20; and compare 1 Samuel 11:6 with 16:14.
6. The Hebrew verb is *māšaḥ*, mah-SHACK, "anoint"—from which comes "Messiah" (*māšîaḥ*, mah-SHEE-ack), anointed one.

Since the presence and work of the Holy Spirit so characterizes the Messiah, it isn't surprising that He is also associated with
Messiah's ministry to His people.

In fact, the pouring out of the Spirit on *all* of Messiah's people—
and not merely selected judges, prophets, and kings—would mark
the Messianic age (Isa. 44:3; Ezek. 39:29; Joel 2:28–29; Zech. 12:10).
What is more, the Spirit's presence and work would mark the New
Covenant specifically. After his prophecy of the new birth (Ezek.
36:26), Ezekiel quotes Yahweh as promising, "I will put my Spirit
within you, and cause you to walk in my statutes and be careful to
obey my rules" (v. 27). This is echoed again in 37:14a—"And I will
put my Spirit within you, and you shall live."

Do you see it? What Moses could only wish for, would become
a reality under Messiah and His New Covenant. What was selective and sporadic under the old covenant would be universal and
all-inclusive among the people of the Messiah. The Spirit would be
poured out on all of them, and would indwell all of them.

The Coming of the Spirit in the New Testament

From the opening pages of the Gospels we find that Messiah Jesus
is indeed visibly and repeatedly blessed with the Spirit's presence and
ministry, just as prophesied. The Lord Jesus' conception is an act of
the Holy Spirit (Matt. 1:18, 20); His baptism marked by the Spirit
descending and "resting" upon Him (Matt. 3:16); His ministry marked
by the Spirit guiding and empowering Him (Matt. 4:1; Luke 10:21;
cf. Acts 10:38). The Father gives the Son the Spirit without measure
(John 3:34). Jesus' entire person, life, and ministry are marked by the
fullness and abundant operations of the Holy Spirit (cf. Matt. 12:28).

On the night of His betrayal and arrest, Jesus promised the apostles a special ministry of the Spirit, guiding them to the inerrant
communication of further truth (John 14:26; 15:26–27; 16:13–15).

The Spirit would glorify Jesus by this process of revelation, unveiling truths from God that they could not have figured out with any certainty or authority on their own (John 16:14). We hold the realization of these promises in our hands when we open our New Testaments.

But the Spirit would minister far beyond the apostles' circle. As to the world, the Spirit would focus the world's attention on the implications of Jesus (John 16:8–11). As to believers, John the Baptist predicted that Messiah will immerse every one of His followers with the Holy Spirit (Mark 1:8). Jesus predicts the same (Luke 24:49). Toward that end, He tells them to go to Jerusalem and wait there, for this event would occur on Pentecost (Acts 1:4–5).

And so it happened when the Spirit came in Acts 2, ushering in the promised age of the Spirit under the New Covenant. Now, as promised, all believers without exception are baptized with the Spirit (1 Cor. 12:13), indwelt by the Spirit (John 14:17; Rom. 8:9), and sealed with the Spirit (Eph. 4:30).

Remember, these are not marks of a *subset* of Christians. They are *definitional* of being a Christian. Before you find me a Christian who has not been baptized with, indwelt by, and sealed with the Holy Spirit, you're going to have to find me a lake full of water that isn't wet.

If it isn't wet, it simply isn't water.

And if one hasn't been baptized with the Spirit, he's simply not a Christian.

In Adam, we're bereft of the Spirit. We're dead, and far from the God we hate (Eph. 2:12). We are defiled and impure (Titus 1:15). We are sinners (Rom. 3:23). We are, in short, the polar opposite of holy—and there is a reason why the third Person is called the *Holy* Spirit. There can be no murky mingling of the unholy with the Holy. For that reason, it isn't only false teachers who are devoid of the Holy Spirit (Jude 19).

But then the Spirit comes to God's chosen ones in connection with the Gospel. He convicts us of our sin, so that we don't look so pretty to ourselves anymore, and so that God and His Christ are no longer distant and boring and irrelevant (John 16:8–11). We start to worry about what hadn't really concerned us before—realities such as God and eternity and judgment—and to be attracted to what had repelled us.

Perhaps we'd heard the Gospel before, and it had been forgotten moments later (cf. Matt. 13:5, 19). But now we hear the Gospel, and everything seems different. The Holy Spirit so moves that the words are now powerful, arresting, compelling in a very personal way (1 Thess. 1:5). This Gospel, this Jesus, is not just out there anymore; this is the news we need to hear, and the Savior we need to embrace. And so we do (1 Cor. 2:4, 14), with a joy the Holy Spirit gives (1 Thess. 1:6).

The reason for this change in us is not the result of any philosophizing or reasoning or even searching on our part—though all of those activities may have taken place to an exhausting degree in us. No, the cause of the change is the Holy Spirit! We have been given new birth by Him (John 3:3–8). By a sovereign act of God alone in grace alone, the Holy Spirit has washed us clean and given us new life (Titus 3:5).

Though we may not feel it, at conversion we were immersed ("baptized") with the Holy Spirit into the spiritual body of Christ (1 Cor. 12:13), a baptism that involves no water. We are "in Christ," by that ministry of the Spirit, sealed forever in Christ—not with wax or glue or duct tape, but with the majestic and all-powerful Person of God, the Holy Spirit (Eph. 4:30). The Holy Spirit permanently dwells within us, bringing God's very presence to our hearts and thus transforming our bodies into sanctuaries (1 Cor. 6:19). He has been poured out in every Christian's heart to communicate God's love to us (Rom. 5:5), and He has freed us from the law of sin and death (Rom. 8:2).

Now the Holy Spirit produces God's righteousness in us (Rom. 8:4) by enabling us to put to death the sinful deeds of the body (Rom. 8:13) and by leading us in obeying God's Word from the heart (Rom. 8:14). He places His very desires in us, desires that are contrary to the desires of the flesh—and so, a battle rages (Gal. 5:17). God calls us to walk in His power, so that the flesh's desires are not realized in us (Gal. 5:16). As we so walk, the Spirit unerringly builds in us the character of Christ, which is marked by love, joy, peace, and a bouquet of other lovely, God-exalting graces (Gal. 5:22–23).

What's more, the Holy Spirit has graced each Christian with at least one motivating ability ("gift") to serve God and others within the church (1 Cor. 12:4, 7). He moves us to worship and serve in a God-pleasing way (Phil. 3:3), inspires us to loving toil (Col. 1:8), and produces fellowship with our Christian church family (2 Cor. 13:14). The Christian's life should be characterized by being filled with the Spirit (Eph. 5:18), which will produce heartfelt, God-centered, grateful, loving worship filled with rich doctrinal content (Eph. 5:19–20), as well as producing respect for the authorities God has placed in our lives (Eph. 5:21–6:8).

The Holy Spirit prays unerringly for (not in, with, or through) us (Rom. 8:26). We are always to pray in Him (Eph. 6:18; Jude 20), as He ushers us into the Father's presence through Christ (Eph. 2:18). We receive His ministry as we receive the Word of God, which He inspired (1 Cor. 2:13; 1 Peter 1:11–12; 2 Peter 1:21). The Holy Spirit continues to speak to us, through the words of the OT (Heb. 3:7ff.), and through the writings of the apostles (John 16:12–14; 1 Cor. 14:37; 2 Peter 3:2). That Word is the only weapon God gives us, and it is forged by the Spirit for the battle in which we are all engaged (Eph. 6:17). As we walk with Christ and suffer for Him, the Spirit of grace and glory rests on us (1 Peter 4:14).

Individual Believers and the Spirit

Now that we've sketched the doctrinal outlines, let's color between the lines, on a more personal level. On the basis of these truths, what should we do and expect? I suggest that we should *thank, trust, target,* and *toil.*

First, we must thank God for the sweeping and extraordinary work of the Spirit in us. Were you once a despiser and a mocker, as I was? Or were you indifferent and ignorant? Were you a spiritual sleepwalker? Have you now come to embrace the Gospel of Christ? Do you look to Jesus with reverence and love, yearn to know Him better, strive to be more effective for Him? Does His word have an impact on how you think, and live, and make decisions? Do you strive to shrink from sin and cleave to what pleases God? Do you cherish the Word? Do you judge a church by whether Christ is preached and exalted, rather than entertainment value, trendiness, and décor?

If *any* of those changes are true in your life, you have God the Holy Spirit to thank! These are His works. These are the fruits of His labors. These are marks of His presence. The Spirit brings the life of God to us, exalts Christ to us, convicts us of our sin, opens our eyes to the Gospel and our hearts to the Word, transforms our orientation.

Too many lines of teaching about the Spirit have left Christians feeling like paupers living in pre-Pentecost times. Too many have urged Christians to seek ministries of the Spirit that are already theirs by birthright. Such preaching and thinking is an insult, however unintended, to the Holy Spirit.

The Spirit of God has done marvelous things for us, to us, and in us. Jesus accomplished and secured all the riches of our salvation, and the Holy Spirit brings us into the possession and enjoyment of those treasures. The proper response is to thank God for the Spirit's person and work.

Second, we should trust—not seek—what God has given us in the Spirit. And we should not wander about, forlorn and pathetic, holding up a "Will Work for Spiritual Buzz" sign. The former insults God; the latter tests Him . . . and insults Him. They're both really massively bad ideas.

You have been baptized with the Spirit, you have been given the Spirit, you are indwelt with the Spirit, you have been sealed with the Spirit, the Spirit does intercede for you, the Spirit is working in you to produce Christ's character.

Either all that is true, or you are not a Christian, in which case, seek the Lord Jesus Christ—not the Spirit (Acts 2:33).

So get up in the morning and thank God for the Spirit's indwelling and ministry in you. Trust God that the Spirit will work in you through the day. Open the Word, trusting God that the Spirit will speak to you through it.

Now, am I saying that all of the Spirit's ministries are automatic? There is nothing mechanical about the Holy Spirit. The bad habit some Christians have of calling Him "It" is a nasty vice, and we should drop it like a wormy apple. I am, however, saying that too many Christians think that "spooky" is a synonym for "Spirit" (perhaps a holdover of the King James Version's rendering "Holy *Ghost*"?). Many look for bizarre experiences, as if the Spirit were still in the relative shadows of the OT. Instead, we should be rejoicing in what He has already done for us in the bright daylight of the NT.

Nor does it help that hucksters, showmen, phonies, frauds, and outright heretics have capitalized on the ignorance of professed Christians. Nature may abhor a vacuum, but the Devil is nuts about it, because he loves nothing better than to come in and fill empty little heads with his lies and deceptions. So in the absence of solid, systematic, passionate, deep, God-honoring, expository teaching of the Word of God, the Father of Lies has deployed angels of light with counterfeits and distractions.

So we have the shameful spectacle of professed Christians barking, mooing, and acting like raving loons in the name of the Spirit. All this in spite of the fact that the life lived under the Spirit's fullness is expressly contrasted with wild, excessive behavior (Eph. 5:18). This glorifies the frauds, abuses the saints, and disgraces the name of Christ.

The only solution for the morass of the enemy's lies is the truth of God's Word lived out by Spirit-filled, joyous, holy, Christ-centered men and women.

Apostolic commands do point us to seek certain realities in relation to the Spirit—but not nearly as many as some teaching implies! Most of the statements about the Spirit are in the indicative mood (i.e., things He has done or is doing), rather than the imperative (i.e., things we are to seek or do).

For instance, Paul says, "And stop getting drunk with wine, in which is debauchery; but instead, keep getting filled with the Spirit" (Eph. 5:18 DJP). That is something I am to do . . . yet not. It is an odd word-beast, a passive imperative. In other words, *I* have to *do* something (imperative), but what I have to do is *get* something done *to* me (passive). I need to seek God that He fill me with His Spirit.

Now, "fill" is not "baptize" or "give," both of which happened at conversion and are definitional of being a Christian (1 Cor. 6:19; 12:13). Never is any Christian commanded to seek baptism with the Spirit. That would make nonsense of the Bible, as we saw.

Nor is being "filled" an absolute term, as if I am always either chock-full or bone-dry empty. If I am a Christian, I have the Spirit, period (Rom. 8:9). What I need is to be "under the influence" of the Holy Spirit. To get filled with the Spirit means that He is the dominant influence in my thoughts and affections, so that His effects spill over in what I love and do (see the aftermath Paul himself sketches out in Ephesians 5:19 and following: a God-centered, other-involved life of singing, speaking, teaching, subordinating myself).

That, too, is what I think Paul means when he says to stay in step with the Spirit (Gal. 5:25): being dominated by Him. This always, necessarily, and inevitably means a close and closer heartfelt conformity to the Holy Spirit's *magnum opus*, the written Word of God (Rom. 8:13–14; 1 Cor. 14:37; Col. 3:16; Heb. 3:7ff.).

That modern Christianoid notion of "spirituality" that is all about experiences and feelings, and little or nothing about solid growth in biblical knowledge, wisdom, and holiness, has no connection with what the Lord or the apostles taught or envisioned. It is not the work of the Spirit.

Third, we must target the glory of Christ, not the Spirit Himself. This is consistent with the fact that the Spirit targets the glory of Christ, not Himself. One of the modern affectations of Christians that must be most offensive to the Holy Spirit, however unintentionally, is the descending-dove insignia.

Why? *Because the focus of the Holy Spirit is not and never has been the Holy Spirit!* Noting the emphasis in the verses below, check out what God's Word plainly says:

- "I will pour out on the house of David and on the inhabitants of Jerusalem, the *Spirit* of grace and of supplication, so *that they will look on Me* whom they have pierced; and they will mourn for Him, as one mourns for an only son, and they will weep bitterly over Him like the bitter weeping over a firstborn." (Zech. 12:10 NASB)
- "When the Helper comes, whom I will send to you from the Father, the Spirit of truth, who proceeds from the Father, he will *bear witness about me*." (John 15:26) • "And when [the Holy Spirit] comes, he will convict the world concerning sin and righteousness and judgment: concerning sin, because they do not believe in me; concerning *righteousness*, because *I* go to the Father, and you will see me no longer; concerning

judgment, because the ruler of this world is judged." (John 16:8–11)

- "[The Holy Spirit] will *glorify me*, for he will *take* what is *mine* and declare it to you. All that the Father has is mine; therefore I said that he will *take* what is *mine* and *declare* it to you." (John 16:14–15)
- "No one speaking in the Spirit of God ever says "Jesus is accursed!" and no one can say *"Jesus is Lord"* except in the *Holy Spirit."* (1 Cor. 12:3)
- "Concerning this salvation, the prophets who prophesied about the grace that was to be yours searched and inquired carefully, inquiring what person or time the *Spirit of Christ* in them was indicating when he *predicted* the *sufferings* of *Christ* and the subsequent *glories."* (1 Peter 1:10–11)

The great love, focus, and fascination of the Holy Spirit is the Lord Jesus Christ. This has been an eternal love. The Spirit moved the prophets to write of Jesus. The Spirit moved the apostles to write of Jesus. The Spirit works in our hearts to lead us to believe in and love and exalt Jesus.

The Holy Spirit of God loves to make sure that everything is all about Jesus Christ.

On that basis, I will say this categorically and emphatically, and only just barely resist the temptation to say it twice:

Show me a person *obsessed* with the Holy Spirit and His gifts (real or imagined), and I will show you a person *not* filled with the Holy Spirit.

Show me a person focused on the person and work of Jesus Christ—never tiring of learning about Him, thinking about Him, boasting of Him, speaking about and for and to Him, thrilled and entranced with His perfections and beauty, finding ways to serve and exalt Him, tirelessly exploring ways to spend and be spent for Him, growing in character to be more and more like Him—and I will show you a person who *is* filled with the Holy Spirit.

We should learn what the Bible says about the Holy Spirit. We should teach what the Bible says about the Holy Spirit. We should seek God to live lives full of the biblically defined ministry of the Holy Spirit.

But we should never lose sight of this: To the degree that we are filled with the Holy Spirit, we will be targeted on, focused on, the person of the Lord Jesus Christ.

Fourthly, we need to toil in the Spirit's power. The Spirit has given us much, and continues to give us much. We must *do* something with it.

Holiness of life is an obvious priority here (cf. Gal. 5:22–25). But I think we need to remember that this relates to the previous: focusing on Christ.

After all, what is practical holiness, if not saying "No" to the works of the Christ-hating flesh and world, and saying "Yes" to the lordship of Christ as exercised in His Word? What is it if not likeness to Christ, the Holy One of God? And where does the ability to do or be any of that come from? It is "by the Spirit" that we put to death the deeds of the body (Rom. 8:13). It is "the fruit of the Spirit" in us (Gal. 5:22–23) that counter the deeds of the flesh (vv. 19–21). It is the Holy Spirit who produces righteousness that pleases God (Rom. 8:4), and sanctification (1 Peter 1:2).

Consider very closely these momentous words: "We all, with unveiled face, beholding the glory of the Lord, are being transformed into the same image from one degree of glory to another. For this comes from the Lord who is the Spirit" (2 Cor. 3:18). We must never imagine that Christian growth is simply a matter of self-effort and discipline. Those factors alone will produce nothing but proud, loveless, lifeless, Christ-eclipsing legalists.

Rather, true Christian growth is an effect of the ministry of the Holy Spirit transforming us. How? Paul tells us. He focuses our attention on the glory of the Lord Jesus Christ, which we find unveiled in the Word of God. And in that beholding, a supernatural work takes place. It involves hearing and studying and learning the Word; it involves discipline and denial. But what is happening is a miracle of transformation, inch by inch, degree by degree, into the image of Jesus Christ.

How? By the Holy Spirit.

All these are realities that adorn our testimony as living signs pointing the way to Jesus Christ.

But do not miss the fact that *the work of the Spirit* and *hard work on our part* are not mutually exclusive. One of the most brilliantly compressed verses in Scripture is Romans 8:13—"For if you are living according to the flesh, you are certain to die; but if by the Spirit you are putting to death the practices of the body, you will live" (DJP).

Note well:

- Christians themselves must put to death the practices of the body.
- Christians themselves cannot put to death the practices of the body unaided.
- Christians themselves must put to death the practices of the body by the Spirit.

John Owen brought out Paul's sense brilliantly, hundreds of years ago: "Do you mortify; do you make it your daily work; be always at it whilst you live; cease not a day from this work; be killing sin or it

274

will be killing you."[7] But, I would add, you and I can only do that by the Spirit's enabling. Otherwise, it's just flesh vs. flesh, with a result that is predictable, lamentable, and inevitable. In fact, hear Owen again: "Mortification from a self-strength, carried on by ways of self-invention, unto the end of a self-righteousness, is the soul and substance of all false religion in the world."[8]

But how do you do any of this? I have to do it. But I can't. But I must.

I can only do it by the Spirit.

How?

The answer is in putting it all together (which is actually the subtitle of the final chapter). But in this connection, let me just say that I mean we must put together all four of these points. To wit:

1. *Thank God* for the vast storehouse of riches He has given us when He poured out His Spirit on us; and
2. *Trust God* that this God the Holy Spirit will not fail us, but will delight to do His work in and through us; and
3. *Target* the glory of the splendors of the Lord Jesus Christ in all we do, by the single-minded focus of faith; so as to
4. *Toil* with everything the Holy Spirit gives us toward that end—thanking God as He does, trusting Him to continue to do so, targeting Christ, and toiling yet more and more!

---

7. Owen, Kapic, and Taylor, *Overcoming Sin and Temptation*, 47.
8. Ibid.

Chapter 14

Culmination

Putting It All Together

Now, don't tune out yet! This chapter is "culmination," not "conclusion." In many books, by the time you get to the conclusion, the author is done. He's fired his last bullet, drowned his last worm, lit his last firework. Now he's just summing up.

This is not that.

This is our all-out run toward home plate. We are about to synthesize all that we've seen together from a different angle, put it together, and distill the essence of how the biblical Gospel worldview we've learned positions us to be world-tilters and barrier-busters.

The primary aim of this book has been to gain strategic intelligence. That is, we have focused on "What?" and "How?" and "Why?" Our discussion has been about truths, about ideas, about how we see and approach our world.

Humans aren't dogs or cart horses. It isn't enough that we know what to do. We need a rationale, we need understanding. That is why so many of the letters in the NT begin with an extended doctrinal section, and only then turn to focus on practical implications (e.g., most famously Eph. 1–3, compared with 4–6).

Ideas do have consequences, however. There isn't that much of a gap between the truths we've learned together and the application of those truths. In this concluding full chapter, I'd at least like to suggest for you nine ramifications of the Gospel. These ramifications move us beyond traditional, world-flirting Christianoid barriers, and into serious, world-tilting engagement with the Gospel.

#1 Over Everything, God

Back in chapter 2 we saw the creation of the universe out of nothing, in exquisite order and beauty. In that chapter and in chapter 4, we met the Creator, the infinite-personal God. We learned that every object that you and I can see, touch, or imagine, is contingent; everything depends on something. Ultimately the very existence of the cosmos depended on the creative act of God. Even now, its existence as cosmos rather than chaos depends on Jesus Christ's continued sustaining power (Col. 1:17; Heb. 1:3).

Let's break down this whole concept of contingency and see how it relates to God. Picture a piece of paper with writing on it. The writing is divided into two columns.

The left column is labeled "Contingent." Under it is a list of everything that depends on something else for its existence. It is a very long column. It goes on for miles. That column lists every created thing, visible or invisible. It contains everything that the world lives for: jewels, sex, power, money, cars, technology, fame, beauty, popularity.

Everything in that column is not ultimate. Money did not create the universe. Hollywood does not hold atoms together. Gravity is not the result of an opinion poll. All these things add up to a breath, a vapor, a quickly fading dream.

It's all like spam e-mail in your Inbox: there for a second, then *click! Blink!* Gone.

The right column is labeled "Noncontingent." In it we put everything that is self-existent, everything that depends on absolutely nothing for its origin or its continuation.

What goes in that column? Well, it is a very short column. It only has one item: God.

Only the One who spoke the universe into existence, upholds it, and guides it can fit into that column. Only He is noncontingent, only He depends on nothing for His existence and meaning and happiness; and only His will is ultimate.

The horizontal—the created universe—is contingent and temporary. The vertical—God—is eternal and ultimate.

> Of old you laid the foundation of the earth,
>   and the heavens are the work of your hands.
> They will perish, but you will remain;
>   they will all wear out like a garment.
> You will change them like a robe, and they will pass away,
>   but you are the same, and your years have no end.
>
> (Ps. 102:25–27)

. . . because by [Christ] were all things created, in the heavens and on the earth, the visible and the invisible, whether thrones, whether lordships, whether rulers, whether authorities: all things have been created through Him and for His sake, and He Himself is before all things, and all things cohere in Him. (Col. 1:16–17 DJP)

Jesus Christ is the same yesterday and today and forever. (Heb. 13:8)

How is this a world-tilting truth? The first lie humanity bought into (as we saw in chapter 2) was that *we* could be ultimate, if only we would simply cast off God. Further, we were told that we could use a created thing (the fruit) to become ultimate. Eve's eyes fell from her Creator to her own inner desires and notions, and the fruit, as the key to everything.

Completely duped, she exalted these above the Most High God.

Adam was not duped. He rebelled against God deliberately. In an act of compliant defiance, he crossed the line God had drawn.

In that moment there was a colossal and all-encompassing shift. All our weight as creatures relocated from the vertical to the horizontal. Life had been about God and His will. He had created us, He sustained us, He commanded us, He was God.

But when Adam ate that fruit, he committed us all to a path that was 180 degrees off-kilter. He made everything about the horizontal. Life was about what pleased Adam, not what pleased God. God was no longer the arbiter of right and wrong; Adam and Eve would make their own decisions. Delight in God's nearness would not be the thrill and passion of their souls. They doomed themselves to the hopeless pursuit of fulfillment in created things, far from God. Fear of God's judgment would not be a motivator, nor His word a binding instructor. All would be about self. All would be horizontal.

That is where the world is right now. Religion bubbles from within—if and insofar as religion serves one's interests. Values are poll-driven. The highest criteria are good feelings, happiness, self-realization, self-fulfillment. "Truth" is in the gland of the fabricator. Man is the measure of all things; man is ultimate, and God is a servant at best.

So man imagines.

The truth of God's absolute centrality is a wrecking ball to all that. It dismantles the façade, and proclaims the Godhood of God. It reminds us all of what we know deep down inside (Rom. 1:18): We are creatures, we are not gods. We are not ultimate. This truth reminds us that God is God.

It lays out the fact that the most vital consideration in life is not finding out how to please and relate to ourselves. Life is about finding out how to please and relate to God. This is a world-tilting truth.

How is this also a barrier-busting truth? Too much of the professing church—I'll call them "Evanjellybeans"[1]—has come to take its cue from the world. This chunk of the church is like the homely kid in high school, longing to go to the dance. Evanjellybeans want so desperately to be liked that they repackage their message to appeal to the world on the world's terms. They tacitly accept the premise that the horizontal is ultimate. They try to reshape and repackage the Gospel to serve that goal, to serve the world's goal.

This truth smashes that barrier. In God's name, we remind all Christians that we of all people must think and live and operate as if the centrality of God were the single dominant factor in every department of our lives—including how we "do" church. The kingdom of God is at hand, and that makes a difference. If we don't believe that particular bit of good news, we're at loggerheads with Jesus. Which is a really bad place for a "Christian" to be.

We don't serve the world by joining it in its lie. We serve it by bringing it the truth of God. "The things that are seen are transient," we tell ourselves and the world; "but the things that are unseen are eternal" (2 Cor. 4:18). "Do not fear those who kill the body but cannot kill the soul," we tell them. "Rather fear him who can destroy both soul and body in hell" (Matt. 10:28).

---

1. Thanks to British blogger Kay Stokes (http://englishmusings.blogspot.com) for this marvelous term, which I tweak a bit for our use.

"The time is fulfilled, and the kingdom of God is at hand," we tell it. "Repent and believe in the gospel" (Mark 1:15).

God is ultimate. Not creation. And not man.

In everything, the primary dimension is the vertical. We must tell the world *this truth* that God delivered to us for that very purpose.

#2 Sin Is a Massive, Universal, Nightmare Factor

Chapter 1 set both a challenge and a dilemma. We must know ourselves, yet our "knower"—our means of thinking and valuing and deciding—is irreparably broken (Jer. 17:9). Our heart is deceptive and incurably sick. Since every bit of information we process, every conclusion we draw, every delicacy we cherish is filtered through our sick, deceptive heart, we have a major problem.

Why is our heart so out-of-whack?

The cause is a universal factor that looms over all of the world's misery and tragedy. That factor is the nightmare of *sin*.

We saw in chapters 2 and 3 that sin came into mankind through Adam's lawbreaking, his attempted deicide. We saw that, as a result, we're all born with a disposition against God's person and law, a hostility that must be described as hatred. We saw that this affects and infects every area of our lives: our relationships (horizontal and vertical), our values, our self-image, even the way we process information.

We saw that sin brings death—physical, spiritual, mental, and eternal. We saw that it puts us at an infinite distance from God. We receive kindness from Him now, but we can anticipate only judgment and justice from Him in eternity. Sin is not a bad habit, not a minor peccadillo that can be shrugged off or ignored. It is a massive and virulent cancer that invades everything.

Further, sin is sin as God defines it. Given the primacy of God, as established above, when God pronounces an attitude or thought or action to be bad, that pronouncement is ultimate and final. We can't maneuver around it, rationalize it away, or overcome it on our own. Sin is a disaster on every level, a catastrophe that both transcends and underlies disease, war, famine, and every other natural and man-made calamity.

Sin is the great destroyer and our great enemy—yet we are powerless to part ourselves from it.

How is this a world-tilting truth? Men naturally minimize sin insofar as it relates to God. If they could, they would make the concept disappear.

Some postmoderns deny sin altogether. Or they try. Still, they have to have some way of expressing their distaste for certain kinds of violence and trendy wrongs such as not being "green" enough.

But postmoderns shrug off the concept of sin as culturally determined, or simply defined by each individual. Sin is what *you* think sin is, because (see #1) you are God. This is where the world starts.

So "sin" is either deleted from the vocabulary, or redefined in relative terms. It may be embraced as an alternative lifestyle or a necessary expression of freedom. It may be flaunted in its most outrageous forms, to show how "free" they are from "god" (the lowercase "g" is very important to them).

Or it may be treated as an unproductive habit, for which there is some man-generated program or medication or book or exercise or other horizontal cure. Man-made religions spring up with their own alternative remedies, though always keeping man in the center.

This truth about sin puts sin back where it belongs: directly between the God of the Bible and our guilty selves. Sin is defined by God, and embraced by us to our own ruin.

It also corrects our trivialization of sin. Sin is not minor. It is not incidental. It is at the very center of every woe and nightmare.

It equally destroys individuals and nations. Left unaddressed in a heart, sin brings a nightmare that is literally without end.

Without a "cure" for sin, we are without hope. And we are helpless to "cure" ourselves. This is a world-tilting truth.

How is this also a barrier-busting truth? Evanjellybeans know that the world hates hearing what God says about sin. So, driven either by a perverse desire to be more popular, or by a mistaken notion of being more winsome (and maybe sneak in the truth later), they muzzle themselves, and sin becomes "the s-word." Or they knock the more popular sins off the list. Or they tone down sin's horrors so much that one wonders why anyone would make such a fuss. The cross becomes (literally) pointless overkill.

This truth reminds all Christians that *God* says sin is our central problem. It reminds us that our Lord was called "Jesus" because He came to save us from our sins (Matt. 1:21), that He came to save sinners (1 Tim. 1:15), that the Gospel is all about how God saves us from sin (1 Cor. 15:1–3; Gal. 1:3–4). It reminds us all that Christ died to secure us pardon for our sins (Eph. 1:7), and to free us from the dominion of sin (Rom. 6).

It also points us to our proper stance with respect to the world. This truth teaches us that the ultimate cause of all the world's miseries is sin. Therefore, the ultimate solution for all the world's miseries is the Gospel.

So while we show practical love in feeding, clothing, and materially caring, we do not lose the focus Christ ordered us to keep (Matt. 28:18–20). We do not forget that man's greatest problem is neither poverty nor pollution. It is sin, and the wrath of God against those who cling to it. We must love people too much to send them off to face the wrath of God hopeless but well fed. We point them to the cross of Christ with that world-tilting, sin-crushing treasure that Christians alone possess: the Gospel of Christ.

Sin is a massive, universal nightmare factor. We must tell the world this truth that God delivered to us for that very purpose.

#3 The World Is Not Self-Defining

The world did not create itself. Matter is neither eternal nor self-causing. Therefore, no object defines its own meaning or significance. This is true for two reasons:

1. An infinite-personal God of limitless wisdom created all objects.
2. In *creating* all, God *defined* all.

We are born into a creation that already exists, whose meaning as a whole and in all individual parts was defined long before our births. Put another way, in reality, things are what God made them to be. There are no "brute" facts, as theologian Cornelius van Til often said; only created facts.

How is this a world-tilting truth? The world is fond of the fantasy that life, the universe, and all that are a blank slate, waiting for us to assign meaning. Life is what we make it, we are told. Celebrities and politicians are not the only ones who reinvent themselves at will, when convenient. Countless movies, plays, and TV episodes turn on the proposition that nothing has inherent meaning, until we assign meaning by our own decisions.

I Googled "life is what we make of it" and got 116,000 hits. Months later, I Googled it again and got 123,000 hits. Then after the passage of several more months, I got 241,000 hits. The concept is not dying out.

The truth, however, is that reality is not what we make of it. Reality is what God already made of it. This is why the mere suggestion of "intelligent design" drives so many supposed scientists barking mad. If everything is designed, they don't get to be God.

The reality is that everything is designed, overseen, and judged. Including us. This is a world-tilting truth.

How is this also a barrier-busting truth? Evanjellybeans too often bow before practitioners of philosophies hostile to God's self-revelation. They start and end with meanings declared by people who themselves are on the run from God, accepting goals and methods set by (say) psychologists who deny God and His truth, or sociologists who are ruled by the statistical norm, or marketers who think that numerical success is self-vindicating.

Evanjellybeans take those meanings, and scramble for ways to paste God onto the whole anti-God jumble. They preach psychological sermons. They survey neighborhoods and build churches to mirror what is already there. They repackage and sell the Gospel like fast-talking, glitzy infomercial hucksters.

Biblically faithful Christians have something radically different to offer. This alone justifies our place on the public stage, and our claim to be Christ-ians rather than Just-like-everyone-else-ians. We do not bring a word that rises up from within creation, but one that crashes down upon creation, from without and from above. This truth tells us that the God who created all is Lord of all, and that to understand anything we must turn to the Creator, not to the creation.

If people want to know the true and ultimate meaning of anything, they will not and cannot find it by searching the things themselves. They must turn to God, the Creator.

The world is not self-defining. We must tell the world this truth that God delivered to us for that very purpose.

#4 Meaning and Fulfillment Cannot Be Found Within the World

Since the event of the Fall, sin has affected both the material universe (Gen. 3:17–18; Rom. 8:20–22) and our intellectual/spiritual universe (Rom. 3:11, 18 [contrast Prov. 1:7; 9:10]). We learned about this in chapters 2 and 3.

There's irony to spare in this fact. Think about it. How did the world get so messed up? By being moved to the center, where it never belonged. That is, everything literally was fruit and cream until Eve decided that a particular fruit was everything, and thus (pardon me) "creamed" her relationship to God. Adam followed her lead, and the whole went into the toilet.

Sin's advent into creation changed both the nature of the world and the way we relate to it.

How is this a world-tilting truth? The world strives manfully to find fulfillment here and now. Things are sold as giving meaning and fulfillment. Or if it wants to pose as nonmaterialistic, the world will hold forth intangible (but still horizontal and self-selected) goals—such as feelings of achievement, worth, significance—as means of ultimate fulfillment.

This truth tells the world that it cannot itself bring meaning, and it cannot fulfill. Living for a paycheck, or a raise, or a promotion . . . or great sex, great health, great popularity, great power . . . none of these will give us meaning or fulfillment.

The futility of the sheerly horizontal forms the premise of the intense, challenging book of Ecclesiastes. Twenty-nine times the Hebrew text has the phrase translated "under the sun." It might help if we thought of "under the sun" as meaning "on the horizontal," that is, life considered without God in the center of the picture. Solomon is subjecting the man-centered, hedonistic life to a searching X-ray examination.

What does the philosopher-king find? What are his results? You know the book's refrain:

> Vanity of vanities, says the Preacher,
> vanity of vanities! All is vanity.

> What does man gain by all the toil
> at which he toils under the sun? (Eccl. 1:2–3)

The Hebrew word translated "vanity" means a breath, a vapor. It connotes what is insubstantial, transient, and illusory. The phrase "vanity of vanities" literally renders the Hebrew way of expressing a superlative. The meaning is "sheer vanity, utter vanity, absolute vanity."

Solomon is saying that the "you shall be as God" project is an utter failure. Life in this fallen world, with no real relationship with God, is futile and illusory. Nothing lasts, nothing satisfies.

Solomon was in a position to try it all, and that he did (1:16–18). Everything our world so longs for, he discovered to be empty. Wealth? Hedonism? Possessions? Power? Success? Sex? Whatever. Solomon had it all (2:1–10).

But then the sage asked himself, What happens next?

What happens next is that you die, and it all goes to some idiot (2:18–19).

The entire book of Ecclesiastes is a *tour de force* expanding on that reality: Meaning and fulfillment cannot be located within the horizontal plane, within creation, apart from the Creator. This world was never created to be ultimate. It is the Creator who is ultimate.

Thus Solomon lays down the conclusion blunt and strong in the last chapter: "The end of the matter; all has been heard. Fear God and keep his commandments, for this is the whole duty of man. For God will bring every deed into judgment, with every secret thing, whether good or evil" (Eccl. 12:13–14). For real meaning and eternal purpose, and lasting joy, we must look away from the world and beyond the world. We must look to the Judge before whom all our life will be paraded, and by whom it (and we) will be judged. We must look to the King of the kingdom that cannot be shaken, that will survive this first creation (Heb. 12:25–29). This is a world-tilting truth.

How is this also a barrier-busting truth? Again, Evanjellybeans tacitly accept the world's value hierarchy. Without saying so, they agree that the "best life" consists of such things as the world seeks.

Rather than bringing God's truth to bear on those false goals, Evanjellybeans twist the Gospel to make God the delivery service. They depict a God who lives to give the world its best life right here and right now.

The cross of Jesus Christ is the deathblow to the notion of finding fulfillment in this world and on its terms. Jesus said that it is only he who hates his life in this world who will gain real life (John 12:25). He calls us to take up our cross to follow Him (Matt. 16:24), and to do it daily (Luke 9:23).

What do you do on a cross? You die.

To what must we die on the cross? To the world (Gal. 6:14).

It is not the call of the church to lead seminars in how to find meaning within the world. The Gospel calls us to turn our backs on the world, and find joy and life and truth and significance and meaning in a relationship with the triune God—though it *costs* us the friendship of the world (James 4:4; all this is discussed in chapters 7–9, 12).

Meaning and fulfillment cannot be found within the world. We must tell the world this truth that God delivered to us for that very purpose.

#5 We Mustn't Reason from "Is" to "Should"

This truth grows out of all that has preceded. What is now is not what ought to be. We are not seeing a world that is as God created it. All is out-of-whack, off-kilter. Diseases and disasters are not the way God made the world to be, they reflect how sin has re-made the world. It is only worse when we look to the world of men. Brokenness, hatred, and all the resultant ideologies and actions (and legislations) are not reflective of God's creation, which was "very good" (Gen. 1:31). They reflect sin's devastating effects, which are very bad (chapters 2 and 3).

How is this a world-tilting truth? The world defines "healthy" as "normal." It defines "normal" by statistics, polls, studies of what people do. The assumption is that if most people do it (other things being equal), it's normal. If it's normal, it's healthy.

"Is" equals "should."

The fundamental flaw is the premise. What is "normal" is "healthy" only if people are—and the world is—as they should be.

But we aren't, and it isn't!

Coming up with norms and standards of behavior by observing human society is like drawing up a motor vehicle handbook by filming a drunk driver, or concluding that the average weight is the ideal weight. What is, in this world, is not usually what should be.

The Bible alone shows the truth of the matter. A pristine universe flowed from the vast mind of the perfect God by the power of His word. All was beauty and harmony, and God was at the center. Then sin entered, and chaos erupted on every plane except the divine. The world as we see it is marred by sin. Normal human behavior is broken human behavior, abnormal behavior, when judged by the standard of God's original intent and stated norms.

God's unchanging, transcendent moral and spiritual absolutes shatter the world's echo chamber of self-serving back-patting. This is a world-tilting truth.

How is this also a barrier-busting truth? The world is so tangible, immediate, loud, and insistent. Evanjellybeans find it and its "I'm okay/you're okay" message distracting and, too often, convincing.

If we do not guard our hearts carefully (Prov. 4:23; James 1:27), and if we do not cultivate a love for the one true God that flows over into keeping our minds full of His Word (Deut. 6:4–6), and if we are careless in our company (Prov. 13:20; 14:7; 1 Cor. 15:33), and if we do not keep putting sin to death (Rom. 8:13), then we will find that the world's norms sound normal to us.

We must never forget: Our task as Christians is never to echo, much less to embrace, the world's broken value system. Our calling is to be caught up in God and His revolutionary truth, which sets us at loggerheads with the world (John 7:7; 15:18–20; Eph. 5:11; James 4:4; 1 John 2:15–17; 3:3; chapters 6–8, 12).

We mustn't reason from "is" to "should." We must tell the world this truth that God delivered to us for that very purpose.

#6 We Must Reason from "Designed," "Commanded," and "Re-Created" to "Intended"

We cannot glean man's purpose from what he is now. However, we find our answer in a long, hard look at what we were when we originally came from the hand of God. This is the focus of chapter 2. God created the first man and woman as finite reflections of Himself, image bearers formed with the high calling of filling and subduing and ruling the planet in His name.

While sin ruined that likeness, Christ restores it in His new creation (2 Cor. 5:17). In chapter 8, we learned that in Christ we are born anew to repentant faith and submission to God's Word. In Christ, the last Adam, we become what men and women were meant to be. We bear God's image, we are renewed into that likeness stage by stage (2 Cor. 3:18). This is a continuous renewal, and involves restoration to accurate knowledge based on God's own revealed wisdom (Col. 3:10). We will one day come to bear that image perfectly (1 John 3:2) and eternally (1 Cor. 15:49–54).

That commandment of God, that new spiritual reality, and that ultimate destiny must direct our daily living. We must become in practice what we are in Christ (1 Peter 1:14–16). This is the high, world-tilting call of God in Christ.

How is this a world-tilting truth? The world has no "should" against which to measure itself. Its horizon is low and shifting: itself. It has no clue what a human being should be. It stares fixedly in a mirror and shrugs. It measures itself by itself. It has no authority, no basis, for any other standard, call, or pattern.

This truth pulls the cover off and reveals that God created man for a high and distinctive purpose, in which His own person and Word are central. This truth points to Christ as the model of what a man should be. It calls us to Jesus Christ, the head of a new humanity, for forgiveness and reconciliation—but also for re-creation and rededication to God's intended design.

This truth declares that man is not a highly evolved animal; he is a far-fallen bearer of God's image. And it calls him to be made what he should be by the sovereign grace of God in Jesus Christ. This is a world-tilting truth.

How is this also a barrier-busting truth? Motivated by compassion (at best), Evanjellybeans often sigh, "Nobody's perfect," and focus preaching and writing on making people feel fine as they are, where they are. They blur the line between holy and unholy, between righteous and unrighteous—and between saved and unsaved.

It is not compassionate, however, to lie to people. The Christian serves a Lord who called His students to "be perfect, as your heavenly Father is perfect" (Matt. 5:48), and who moved his apostles to urge believers not to sin (1 John 2:1). We are to bring holiness to perfection in the fear of God (2 Cor. 7:1). There is a high standard, and God urges us all to press on toward it (Phil. 3:14; Heb. 12:14).

We learned in chapters 4 through 6 that God conceived, launched, and completed a plan to rescue men and women from the insane asylum of sin. God sent His own Son into the world to live that perfect, as-intended, righteous, whole, unbroken life that no human had achieved. Christ lived the life we should live, fulfilling all God's requirements of righteousness in our behalf. Then God the Son Himself took our sins, our ruin, our guilt onto Himself, and accepted God's just judgment in our behalf.

This was not a lowering of His standard to meet our norms. It was God Himself meeting His own perfect standard in our behalf.

And then we learned in chapter 7 that God, by sheer grace, credits the righteousness of Christ to us. We do not stand on our bankrupt record, but on Christ's perfections. What's more, in chapter 8 we saw that God gives us a new nature that is patterned after Christ Himself, so that we are being daily restored from sin's norm to God's glorious holiness. Further, we learned that one day we will embody that purity, when we see Christ as He is.

Until then, we must not pattern our lives (nor call others to pattern theirs) after the "is" of this fallen world. Anyone who embraces that abnormal norm will perish under God's wrath.

Anyone who trusts Christ will be called to a different norm, a norm not of this world, a norm from above. In Christ, he will fulfill the destiny Adam failed to fulfill. Indeed, his is a yet loftier destiny, as he will not only subdue the world under God, but will rule and reign with Jesus Christ (Rev. 5:10; 20:6)—a truth that should make a difference even now (1 Cor. 6:3).

We must reason from "designed" and "re-created" to "intended." We must tell the world this truth that God delivered to us for that very purpose.

#7 Jesus Christ Is the Most Important Person, Event, and Figure in All of History

My, doesn't that sound like a lovely bit of sanctimonious frippery? I say, "Jesus Christ is the most important person ever," and everyone nods piously. Then we move on to the more important stuff that we really wanted to talk about, now that I've checked the box.

Yet I assure you just as earnestly as I can—envision me leaning over into your "space," my eyes fixed on yours—that I mean this in the most literal sense.

It doesn't matter whether we're talking metaphysically, spiritually, historically, ontologically, or any other "-ally" you care to list off. In any plane, on any level, Jesus comes first. He is top, bottom, beginning and end. He is alpha and omega (Rev. 22:13).

We saw as much in chapter 7. Jesus is the cause of creation, the agent of creation, the focus of creation, the aim of creation. He is the king and sustainer and controller of creation. He is spectator and participant, author and conductor, lawgiver and judge. He is savior and condemner. The atoms that winked into existence did so at His word. The atoms that are you will stand before Him for final judgment. The atoms that were you, along with the spirit they house, will either spend eternity suffering His wrath or delighting in His love.

Does it get any more important than that?

If we want to know who we are, we must deal with Jesus. If we want to know who God is, we must deal with Jesus. If we want to get from here (where we are) to there (where God is), we must deal with Jesus.

God has dealt with our horrid rap sheet of crimes against Himself—in Jesus (chapter 6). God has secured for all His people the perfect righteousness they will need to stand before Him—in Jesus (chapter 7). God has provided a new life and a new nature and a new animating principle for all His people—in Jesus (chapter 8).

God may be known. God wants to be known. God bids all to come, know Him. But we may and must know Him only in, through, and because of Jesus Christ (Matt. 11:25–30; John 14:6).

How is this a world-tilting truth? The world has tried to do all sorts of things with Jesus.

It has tried hard to ignore Him. Eighteenth-century radicals tried to make Him a mythical figure, until the spade of the archaeologist rendered that endeavor intellectually absurd. (That news hasn't reached the somnolent chambers of the Jesus Seminar, which thrives on the ignorance of the public at large, and the shallowness of the pulpit.) Even now a hard push is underway to sweep the calendar notes of AD and BC aside in preference for CE and BCE—though the dividing point of Christ's birth remains.

Failing all that, the world has repeatedly tried to mash Him into its image for its own endeavors—as political/social revolutionary, hippie, sage, philosopher, champion of ____ rights, antiestablishment iconoclast, eco-warrior. It tries to tame Him, control Him, cage Him.

The world needs to hear the truth about the Jesus who won't be ignored, tamed, lassoed, or co-opted. It needs to hear about Him in all His raw, rude, gate-crashing, table-bashing power. It needs to hear about His nature, His cross, His resurrection, His crown, His warnings, His demands, His offer.

If Jesus is real, all the world's values and plans and tidy little sand castles are doomed.

And He is.

And they are.

This is a world-tilting truth.

How is this also a barrier-busting truth? Evanjellybeans think they need to hide Jesus, or make Him "behave." So they emphasize music and entertainment, offering the world . . . well, what the world already has. But with a nice frosty "Jesusy glaze" on top.

They don't talk about His lordship, the sin from which He saves us, His call to repentance and discipleship, His cross, His crown.

In so doing, in trying not to scare the world away, they withhold the very thing the world needs to hear from us. Christianity is about Jesus. Christian living is about Jesus. It's that whole "Christ" part of "*Christ*-ianity."

What is the center of Christian life? Jesus Christ. What is the center of Christian thought? Jesus Christ. What is the center of Christian worship? Jesus Christ. What is the center of the Christian message? Jesus Christ.

And so it is the worst kind of faithlessness, treachery, and folly to hold back the truth about Jesus. It's hateful toward God, and it's hateful toward our neighbor.

This truth reminds us of that fact, and leaves piles of shattered barriers in its wake.

We must tell the world this truth that God delivered to us for that very purpose.

#8 In Christ and Through the Cross, We Have Been Given All We Need for Godly Living

God's wisdom is vast beyond all imagination or tracking or tracing (chapter 4). From that limitless reserve, God's knowledge and understanding of the depth of our need and the direness of our dilemma is literally inexhaustible.

It only stands to reason, therefore, that if God is going to do anything actually to address the catastrophic morass we've gotten into, it must be comprehensive. It must address every aspect of every doleful facet of our devastation.

And so it does. God leaves nothing to us, in and of ourselves. All we contribute to the whole is the sin, slavery, misery, and folly, from which we need saving.

God made the plan to rescue and redeem us before we even existed (Eph. 1:4, 9, 10; 3:11). God announced and imposed every aspect of it, leaving nothing to human unraveling or discovery (chapter 5). God worked it out Himself and in person, not only despite human sin and folly, but making full use of the same (chapter 6). God amasses spiritual riches for us by His own doing, and

He applies those riches to us by sheer and sovereign grace. Even our ability to respond in repentant faith is a gift, gained for us by Christ at the cross (chapters 7 and 8).

God set His love on us in eternity past (Eph. 1:4), and granted us to Christ, for Him to save us (John 17:2, 6, 19, 23). In our lifetimes, God the Holy Spirit convinces us of our guilt and of the truth of the Gospel (John 16:8–11; 1 Thess. 1:4–5; cf. chapter 13 of this book). God grants us repentance and saving faith (Acts 11:18; Phil. 1:29; 2 Tim. 2:25; cf. chapter 8 of this book), regenerates us (chapter 8), and declares us righteous (chapter 7). He comes to live within us Himself, by means of the person of the Holy Spirit (chapter 13), empowering us to live life on a plane we would not have imagined outside of Christ.

It is literally true, then, that God in sovereign grace has given us everything we need in Christ for life and godly living (Eph. 1:3ff.; 2 Peter 1:3ff.).

How is this a world-tilting truth? The world is all about pulling itself up by its bootstraps. It has programs, rules, principles, tips, disciplines, and a thousand other things that promise perfection . . . or at least marked improvement. And happiness. And fulfillment. And meaning.

If all that doesn't work, it just redefines "up" down, and doesn't move.

Our message to the world is both profoundly pessimistic, and gloriously optimistic. The world's gloomiest funeral dirges aren't nearly dark enough. We are incapable of that godward self-improvement without which everything else is a passing sham (chapter 3). It is only by the sheerest grace of God alone that we can be restored to everything God had in mind when He had the idea called "man" (chapters 4–13).

This truth reveals that no program or set of rules will perfect man nor even improve him. This truth points to the treasure trove that can only be found in the Perfect Man, Christ Jesus, in whom all the treasures of wisdom and knowledge are hidden away (Col. 2:3), and in whom alone we can be filled full (Col. 2:10). In that way, it is the most glorious of hopeful messages. Despair of self can give way to glorying in Christ. This is a world-tilting truth.

How is this also a barrier-busting truth? Many Evanjellybeans notice that the world will not naturally embrace the despair that must come before conversion (cf. Luke 9:23–25). So they tone down the message, and come up with ways to massage and comfort the world, hoping it will come to feel better about God and Christ (and them!) as a result.

However, to preach a message that offers hope anywhere but in Jesus Christ is to damn the world. It is to hold back the one truly distinctive gift we have to give, the one truth that they most desperately need to hear.

And so churches premised on the notion that they mustn't offend unbelievers with the straight-up, hardcore truth of Christ must repent. They must get back on-message. And they must do it soon, or Christ will not even regard them as among His churches (cf. Rev. 2:5; 3:15–19).

We must tell the world this truth that God delivered to us for that very purpose.

#9 The Vast Bounty of God's Provisions for Us in Christ Enables and Obliges Us to Get on with It to His Glory

A man joins the military. They give him a uniform, extensive training, commanding officers, and equipment.

Then what?

Does he rent an apartment somewhere, hook up a satellite dish, buy a twelve-pack or two, and sit down to watch TV and work at becoming a human oval? Hardly. All the training and equipment has an aim, a purpose.

God made each of us as factors in a strategy that has been unfolding for thousands of years, which has a definite aim in mind. He spared no expense to make us His own and to equip us (Rom. 8:32). He has opened the very storehouse of heaven to us (Eph. 1:3ff.; Col. 2:10), disclosed His heart to us (cf. John 15:15; Eph. 3:3–11; Col. 1:24–27). He has enlisted us and made us participants, and He has given us a comprehensive set of orders (2 Tim. 3:15–17). He has provided for our training (Matt. 28:18–20; Eph. 4:11–14; Heb. 13:7, 17), and He has put His own Spirit in our hearts to enable us (cf. chapter 13).

And so you see that God commands and God provides. By the New Covenant established with Christ's blood (Matt. 26:28), God writes His law on our hearts (Jer. 31:33). He puts His own Spirit within us to move and enable us to fulfill the law (Ezek. 36:27). The Holy Spirit pours out God's love in our hearts (Rom. 5:5), provoking an answering love for God from us (1 John 4:19). The shape that love takes is keeping His commandments (John 14:15; 15:14; 1 John 5:3). We find these commandments all over His Word, and every one is addressed to us—not the Holy Spirit.

They are addressed to us because He has crucified our old man, we have died to the law and to sin, we have been born again, we've risen to new life in Christ, we're indwelt and enabled by the Holy Spirit—we have been given everything we need in order to be able to snap a smart salute, acknowledge our orders, and get on with it.

Which is precisely what He means us to do: Get on with it.

How is this a world-tilting truth? The world is opposed to Christians getting on with it. At heart, it hates our Lord, and therefore it hates us (John 15:18–19). It hates light, hates anything that exposes its hobbies as sins, and its glitz and glamour as nothing more than a fake movie set (John 3:19–20). To the degree that we walk with Jesus, we reflect His light (Matt. 5:14; John 8:12; Eph. 5:8–14), which the world finds repulsive (2 Cor. 2:14–16).

The world, then, has a vested interest in our *not* walking with Jesus. At least not where they can see us. So they don't want our distinctively Christian views—not in public!—and they particularly don't want our insistence on the Gospel.

Because the Gospel turns the world upside down. It is the ultimate world-tilting truth.

How is this also a barrier-busting truth? I'm nearing my fifth decade under the grace of God in Christ, since the Lord saved me in 1973. In those years, I've had loads of surprises, of which too many have been unpleasant.

But the most unpleasant surprise of all continues to shock me as if I were encountering it for the first time.

The surprise: the degree of energy and ingenuity professed Christians put into getting around some of the plainest and most potent truths of Scripture. Here I have particularly in mind the Gospel and its implications. We fudge on the holiness of God, the inexcusable heinousness of sin, and the raging fire of God's wrath against sin. As a consequence, we are unprepared for the slack-jawed astonishment of God's rescue plan in Christ, haven't a clue about the centrality of the cross, and thus haven't the categories to process the real sheer grace with which God applies His salvation to lost sinners.

But wait. There's more. I wish there weren't, but there is.

Having downsized the entire scope and meaning of sin and salvation, we tame and trivialize Christian living into something that doesn't end up making us very different from the world. We glorify the flesh and minimize the Spirit; we transform imperatives into indicatives; we bypass the inerrant word of God in Scripture for some imaginary holy mumble in the ether. We find diabolically ingenious ways of making simple "do this!" commands hopelessly complex, and painting over the straightforward concept of Gospel obedience.

You'd think that Paul had written that part of Christ's design in the atonement was "that . . . He might purify for Himself a special people, *repelled by the very thought of* good works," rather than "*enthusiastic for* good works" (Titus 2:14 DJP).

We're a mess.

What we need to do is rub the sleep-dust out of our eyes, pull the plugs out of our ears, get out of our recliners, and hit the Book. We need to expose our hearts to the true, howling darkness of our sin, and the blinding blaze of God's holiness. We need to rivet our attention on the overflowing majesty of the person of Jesus Christ, then direct our gaze to the humbling of that majesty in the miserable death of the cross.

Thence we need to trace the path to the empty tomb, and upward to the occupied throne at the Father's right hand. We need to see the glorified Lord pouring forth the Holy Spirit on all His children in extravagance. We need to take cheer at the endless catalog of graces and blessings that have been secured for us by Christ, and made ours in Him.

We need to take that message to heart.

We need to thank God for giving us absolutely everything we need in Christ, through the Gospel.

We need to get on with living it.

We need to get on with telling it.

In the name of God, we need to get on with it: Take that Gospel—that mighty, robust, saving, whole-Bible Gospel—bust barriers, and turn the world upside down again.

- "For this is the love of God: that we keep his commandments. And his commandments do not weigh us down, because everyone who has been fathered by God conquers the world. This is the conquering power that has conquered the world: our faith. Now who is the person who has conquered the world except the one who believes that Jesus is the Son of God?" (1 John 5:3–5 DJP)

- "But God forbid that I should boast except in the cross of our Lord Jesus Christ, by whom the world has been crucified to me, and I to the world." (Gal. 6:14 NKJV)
- "These men who have turned the world upside down have come here also." (Acts 17:6b)

Say . . . What Did You Just Do?

Surprise!

Before we part, I have one last little surprise to leave with you. Though I have scarcely alluded to it in so many words in the text of the book, our whole study has been framed by one particular passage. Call it a Mystery Passage.

What is it? It is 1 Corinthians 15:1–11. Here is my translation of that passage (with the italicized words added for a smooth reading):

Now, I make known to you, brothers, the good news, which I announced as good news to you, which also you received, in which also you stand, through which also you are being saved, in which word I announced the good news to you, assuming that[1] you are holding it fast—unless you believed arbitrarily.[2] For I delivered to you first and foremost that which I also received: that Christ died for our sins in accord with the Scriptures; and that He was buried; and that He has been raised, on the third day, in accord with the Scriptures; and that He was seen by Cephas, then by the Twelve; thereafter He was seen by over five hundred brothers at one time, of whose *numbers* the most remain until now, but some fell asleep; thereafter He was seen by James, then by all the apostles—and last of all, as it were to the one abnormally born, He was seen also by me! For I, I am the least of the apostles, I who am not adequate to be called an apostle, because I persecuted the church of God. But, by the grace of God, I am what I am; and His grace which was *extended* unto me did not turn out to be empty, but *instead* I labored more abundantly than all of them; yet not I, but *rather* the grace of God which was with me. Therefore, whether *it is* I, or whether it is others, thus we proclaim, and thus you believed.

Here the apostle Paul outlines the essential facts of the Gospel he preaches. As you read that portion of Scripture, can you see that my entire book has served to frame that passage, to give the necessary worldview, the indispensable array of underlying convictions and certainties, without which that passage cannot be understood?

You see, I've encountered two kinds of professed evangelical Christians who concern me deeply. Both think the Gospel is important in some way, and both think they know the Gospel. But there is a crucial difference between the two.

---

1. Literally "if," but phrased in Greek to assume the reality.
2. That is, without due consideration, haphazardly; or, without cause.

The first are those who, if you asked them to locate and define the Gospel biblically, could not do so to save their lives. I say *biblically*. They might know the Four Spiritual Laws, or they might be able to murmur some sort of traditional formulation. But as far as finding it in the Bible, defining it in expressly whole-biblical terms? No way.

You could literally hold a gun to their heads (but don't), and they could not come up with one passage that defines the Gospel. Maybe a few could point vaguely to John 3:16. That is a wonderful verse. But John 3:16 says nothing expressly about the "Gospel," and when taken in isolation begs a great many central and crucial questions. Yet that verse would be about the best these folks could do, and it would be far from adequate.

To such folks, simply putting their hands on 1 Corinthians 15 is a start. But it isn't enough.

Because there is the second set of professed Christians who do know this passage. They could isolate the elements: Christ died for our sins, was buried, raised, and witnessed; we believe and are saved. You could say that they have the street address of the Gospel, and that is also a good thing.

What they do, though, is isolate these elements: died for sins, raised, believe, saved. They tell moderns those individual elements. They bid them to agree to those elements. If they agree with them— sign the card, or check the "Yes" box next to each one—and pray a prayer sincerely, they tell them that they are for-sure Christians.

Am I saying that is bad? It may not be a bad start, but what I am saying is that it is not enough. I am saying that our culture's mindset is (at best) ignorant and (at worst) diametrically opposed to the background meaning and worldview that make those words have any saving import. Note this well: The world has its own definitions for died, sin, raised, believe, and saved. It has its own thoughts about God and man. So we use the words, and the worldling filters those words and nods—and nothing redemptive has occurred.

Because the worldling's filter is in direct conflict with what God means by the words.

What's left out? Paul says it twice: *in accord with the Scriptures, in accord with the Scriptures.* What is missing is the whole-biblical worldview that assigns specific meaning to the words that express the Gospel.

The modern sees every element in the Gospel dead wrong. He has dead wrong notions about who he is. He has dead wrong notions about who God is. He has dead wrong notions about who Christ is. He has dead wrong notions about what sin is. He has dead wrong notions about what he really needs God to do for him. He has dead wrong notions about why Christ came and what Christ did. He has dead wrong notions about what faith is. He has dead wrong notions about what grace is.

So, subtract the truth about humanity, God, Christ, sin, man's real and deepest need, why Christ came and what Christ did, faith, and grace—and where does that leave the Gospel? Meaningless, incomprehensible, empty, plastic, and powerless.

That is what this book was about.

Read Paul's words over one more time, and it is my dear hope that you will see that this entire book labored to give meaning to every element in that passage, without framing itself as an exposition of the passage.

We talked about mankind's creation and fall, about God and His world, about sin and redemption, about Christ's person and mission, about His death for sin, His burial, His bodily resurrection, the meaning of saving faith, the meaning of grace, and how grace powerfully works in the life of the believer. We talked about what we need to be saved from, what we need to be saved to, and how salvation happens. We engaged the Scriptures that explain all these things.

Everything we talked about biblically frames 1 Corinthians 15:1–11.

And that, my dear friend, is the Gospel. That is the message by which you and I must be saved. That is what must define us as individuals and as churches.

That Gospel—not programs or tricks or gimmicks—is what will still turn the world upside down, as surely as it did in the first century. But first, it must turn *our* world upside down.

Two Parting Questions

First, let me ask just before I leave you: Has this Gospel turned your world upside down? Have you yourself embraced this Christ as your only hope in life and death? Have you accepted what Christ says, and who Christ is, as wholly true? Have you seen that He is what you need, to meet your deepest needs before God? Have you leaned your whole weight on Jesus Christ—crucified, buried, risen, and ascended—as Savior and Lord, leaving yourself no escape routes and no Plan B?

If not, that is your greatest priority in life. Seek God's grace in Jesus Christ. Make peace with God on God's terms, in Christ alone.

Second, let me ask if this is the Gospel you have been telling others. Whether you're a pastor, a leader, a teacher, or "just" a (so-called) garden-variety Christian: Is *this* Gospel *your* Gospel? Is it what others hear from you? Or have they heard something watered-down, sweetened up, edited, decaffeinated, defanged, de-edged, and thus de-Gospeled?

If so, I urge you to repent. Drop that false, compromised message like something soft, wet, and squishy you grabbed in the dark. Embrace the Gospel of God for yourself, and use every opportunity God gives you to tell it to others.

It is that Gospel, and not our methods or programs, that is the saving power of God for everyone who believes (Rom. 1:16). It is the best you have to give anyone.

Grasp it firmly.

Live it robustly.

Give it profligately, in Christ's name.

And just watch things start to shake and shift.

Because, you see, this Gospel answers the need I highlighted in chapter 1: We need "a relationship with God that is real, dynamic, and going somewhere." The Gospel of Jesus Christ, as understood in terms of the whole-Bible worldview, is the foundation, the frame, and the definition of that relationship.

This Gospel-created relationship is *real* in that it is the plan the triune God designed in eternity past and carried out in history, for the rescue and redemption of lost men and women for God's glory.

This Gospel-created relationship is *dynamic* in that it is the very power of God resulting in the salvation of every person who believes in Christ through it (Rom. 1:16).

And finally, this Gospel-created relationship is *going somewhere* in that it results in a blood-purchased, grace-given, Christ-centered life of freedom and joy and God-glorifying purpose that begins now and is consummated throughout the endless ages of eternity future.

Amen.

Bibliography

Ankerberg, John, John Weldon, and Walter C. Kaiser Jr. *The Case for Jesus the Messiah: Incredible Prophecies That Prove God Exists.* Eugene, OR: Harvest House, 1989.

Berkhof, Louis. *Systematic Theology.* Grand Rapids: Eerdmans, 1941.

Busenitz, Nathan. *Reasons We Believe: Fifty Lines of Evidence That Confirm the Christian Faith.* Wheaton, IL: Crossway, 2008.

Calvin, John. *Institutes of the Christian Religion.* Edited by John T. McNeill; translated by Ford Lewis Battles. Philadelphia: Westminster, 1960.

Charnock, Stephen. *The Existence and Attributes of God.* 1682. Reprint, Grand Rapids: Baker, 1996.

Combs, William W. "Does the Believer Have One Nature or Two?" *Detroit Baptist Seminary Journal* 2 (1997): 81–103.

Frame, John M. *The Doctrine of God: A Theology of Lordship.* Phillipsburg, NJ: P&R Publishing, 2002; Logos Bible Software, 3.x.

Greidanus, Sidney. "Preaching Christ from the Cain and Abel Narrative," *Bibliotheca Sacra* 161, no. 644 (2004): 387–97 (Galaxie Software).

Gundry, Stanley N., ed. *Five Views on Sanctification* by Melvin E. Dieter, Anthony A. Hoekema, Stanley M. Horton, J. Robertson McQuilkin, and John F. Walvoord. Counterpoint series. Grand Rapids: Zondervan, 1996.

Hamilton Jr, James M. *God's Indwelling Presence: The Holy Spirit in the Old and New Testaments.* Nashville: B&H Academic, 2006.

Jeffery, Steve, Michael Ovey, and Andrew Sach. *Pierced for Our Transgressions.* Wheaton, IL: Crossway, 2007.

Johnson, S. Lewis. "Romans 5:12—An Exercise in Exegesis and Theology." In *New Dimensions in New Testament Study,* edited by Richard N. Longenecker and Merrill C. Tenney. Grand Rapids: Zondervan, 1974.

Lewis, Clive Staples. *Surprised by Joy.* Boston, MA: Houghton Mifflin Harcourt, 1966.

Mahaney, C. J. "Cultivate Humility." In *Dear Timothy: Letters on Pastoral Ministry,* edited by Thomas K. Ascol. Cape Coral, FL: Founders Press, 2004.

Morris, Leon L. "Propitiation." In *New Bible Dictionary,* edited by D. R. W. Wood with I. Howard Marshall, A. R. Millard, J. I. Packer, and Donald J. Wiseman. 3rd ed. Downers Grove, IL: InterVarsity Press, 1996; Logos Bible Software, 3.x.

Motyer, J. Alec. *The Prophecy of Isaiah: An Introduction & Commentary.* Downers Grove, IL: InterVarsity Press, 1993.

Murray, Andrew. *Abide in Christ.* Fort Washington, PA: Christian Literature Crusade, 1972.

Naselli, Andrew David. *Let Go and Let God? A Survey and Analysis of Keswick Theology.* Bellingham, WA: Logos Bible Software, 2010.

Owen, John, Kelly M. Kapic, and Justin Taylor. *Overcoming Sin and Temptation.* Wheaton, IL: Crossway, 2006.

Packer, J. I. *Keep In Step with the Spirit.* Grand Rapids: Revell, 1984.

Piper, John. *The Pleasures of God.* Portland: Multnomah, 2000.

Reymond, Robert L. *A New Systematic Theology of the Christian Faith*. 2nd ed. Nashville: Thomas Nelson, 1998.

Spurgeon, C. H. *An All-Round Ministry: Addresses to Ministers and Students*. Bellingham, WA: Logos Research Systems, Inc., 2009.

Tenney, Merrill C. "John." In *The Expositor's Bible Commentary, Volume 9: John and Acts*, edited by Frank E. Gaebelein. Grand Rapids: Zondervan, 1981.

Van Til, Cornelius. *Defense of the Faith*. Phillipsburg, NJ: P&R Publishing, 1967.

Waltke, Bruce K., with Charles Yu. *An Old Testament Theology*. Grand Rapids: Zondervan, 2007.

Warfield, Benjamin B. "Trinity." In *The International Standard Bible Encyclopedia*, edited by James Orr. Grand Rapids: Eerdmans, 1939.

Watson, Thomas. *Body of Divinity*. 1890. Reprint, Grand Rapids: Baker, 1979.

Wells, David F. *The Courage to Be Protestant: Truth-Lovers, Marketers, and Emergents in the Postmodern World*. Grand Rapids: Eerdmans, 2008.

Young, Edward J. *The Book of Isaiah: Volume 1, Chapters 1–18*. Grand Rapids: Eerdmans, 1965.

Select Scripture Index

About the Author

Dan Phillips earned his MDiv in Old Testament at Talbot Theological Seminary in 1983. His thesis was titled "The Sovereignty of Yahweh in the Book of Proverbs: An Exercise in Theological Exegesis." (The typist half-seriously complained that half of the thesis was in the footnotes.)

Since then Dan has served as pastor in four churches, and has taught classes both at Talbot and in other seminaries and institutions. He has preached, and presented seminars on Proverbs and on the sovereignty of God, written biblically related newspaper columns and tracts, and hosted a radio talk show. Presently he works as a professional in the IT industry, and continues to preach and teach.

Dan is most broadly known for his writing in the team blog *Pyromaniacs*, with Phil Johnson and Frank Turk (http://teampyro .blogspot.com), and at his own blog, Biblical Christianity (http:// bibchr.blogspot.com).

Dan lives in Sacramento with his amazing wife, Valerie. They have four children and around five cats.